CAMPO

Still entertaining

DAVID CAMPESE

Published in Australia by
FLICK PASS PRODUCTIONS
121 Macpherson St, Bronte, NSW, 2024

ISBN 9751130 0 3

Designed by Anna Warren, Warren Ventures Pty Ltd
Printed in Australia by McPherson's Printing Group

Contents

Acknowledgements

After 15 seasons of international rugby and more than a decade in the business world, there are so many people who have played important roles in my life to this point. Many of them will be mentioned in this book, others will not, but not because they have been forgotten or overlooked. It is simply a task beyond me to list each and every one of them. Especially those who have not directly come into contact with me but have followed my career, from the grandstands when I was playing or through my newspaper columns now in the *Daily Telegraph*. Without the appreciation and (usually) the support of the fans, sport would be a lonely place, even in a team environment.

Hopefully this book will offer you an insight into my world, from the final few years of my playing career, on to my post-rugby life, my views of the modern game and the people who make it tick. Love me or loathe me, I do have opinions. I hope you find the ones contained on these pages to be both considered and thought-provoking.

From Queanbeyan to London to Milan and to Cape Town. These are just some of the cities I would never have dreamt of visiting. Rugby has been a fantastic adventure and to the sport most of all I am truly indebted.

Over the years I have also had a stream of sponsors. They include Qantas (Steve Loader), adidas (Jim Tanzey), Tag Heuer and Canterbury. As a World Cup 2003 ambassador for Coca-Cola, it has also been a terrific honour to be associated with one of the world's leading corporate names.

But my major thanks go to Telstra Corporation, and its chairman Bob Mansfield, for their faith and encouragement by backing this book, a project I was desperately keen to see through in this, a World Cup year. The game's global showpiece holds a special place in my heart after our 1991 triumph. And to bring my thoughts on the game to print has only been possible through the generosity and support of Telstra. To Bob Mansfield and to Ted Pretty, a Telstra executive, I say a wholehearted thank you.

To Paul Newton, the artist whose portrait of me graces the front cover of the book, I also offer my heartfelt thanks. The portrait was painted for the 2000 sporting portrait prize held as part of that year's Archibald Prize Exhibition at the Art Gallery of NSW. Paul's work of this former footballer was a finalist in the competition and a similar version of the portrait has been acquired by the National Portrait Gallery in Canberra to form part of their permanent collection. The portrait on the front cover also won first prize in the Portrait Society of America's 2002 International Portrait Competition, held in Philadelphia. It is currently hanging in an art gallery in New York.

To Robert Tuckwell and Associates, for permission to use the photographs from my AM medal presentation, I offer my thanks. Also to News Ltd for the action pics in the photo sections. And to Mike McClellan whose flattering tune 'I Saw Campo Play' appears on the back cover.

To the Australian Rugby Union, I know there have been times when my comments have caused you grief. But I still thank you for the past honour of being an ARU ambassador. To Randwick Rugby Club, where I got to play some of the rugby of my dreams, I wish them all success in the future.

There are so many other people who have helped me along the way. The list includes John Kananghinis, Alan Crouch, Andre

Sekulic, Phil Salter, Jeff Sayle, Peter Trunkfield, Tony O'Reilly and Dennis Hanlon. Their friendship and advice over the years has been greatly appreciated.

To my parents and the rest of my family – thanks for putting up with all the flak you've had to wear because of me. Hopefully their lives are a little more peaceful these days. Then again, with my nephew Terry on his way to the top in rugby league, there might soon be another Campese in the spotlight.

To my friend Peter Jenkins, for his help on this project, it is appreciated (even if I have been on the golf course when he's been slaving over a laptop with an out of control cursor).

And finally to my beautiful wife Lara, for bringing new meaning to my life. When I can go home to her, and to the dogs, Demi and Tyson, what more could any man want?

Buona Futura Sempre

DAVID CAMPESE August, 2003

Foreword

David Campese and the great game of rugby union have been intertwined for more than 20 years. His impact on the sport has been profound. As one of the greatest players of his generation, his dazzling skills have produced some of the game's most memorable moments – an individual with special genius, inventive, free-spirited and capable of turning a game at any time.

David Campese's retirement as a player in 1996 has scarcely diminished that impact. His forthright comments on the game and the important issues that confront it, and on the authorities, coaches, players and himself have continued beyond his stellar career. Inspiring to some, infuriating to others, but always entertaining, they are the comments of a man who knows no other way than to say what he thinks.

Not everyone may agree with Campo, but that hasn't prevented him from expressing his views at any time he has the opportunity to do so.

This outspokenness, borne of a genuine passion for and intimate knowledge of the game, along with his self-belief in his place in rugby history, is much in evidence throughout this book. This is the continuing story of a true maverick, still saying and doing his own thing.

I can only claim to have more recently had the opportunity to get to know David Campese personally. My appreciation of his incomparable talent has been as one of millions of avid rugby fans around the world, privileged to witness his individual artistry from the sidelines – the elegance, the swagger, the sheer presence. And yet I think a key part of his influence, then and now, has been the impact he has had not just on regular fans, but on non-rugby followers (yes, there may be one or two out there). He has taken the sport to a wider audience – and that can only be a good thing, particularly in Australia where competition from other football codes is so intense.

That audience is set once again to witness the most marvellous sporting extravaganza of the year – the 2003 Rugby World Cup. Telstra is especially pleased to be sponsoring this year's Cup, as well as providing the state-of-the-art telecommunications services that are integral to the successful hosting of such an event. This will be a spectacle of drama, excitement, brilliant individual performances, team heroics, exhilaration and despair – played out on a world stage very familiar to David Campese, always the entertainer.

David Campese once wrote: 'I could have asked for no more from any sport.' Equally, the sport could have asked for no more from him as he mesmerised us with his magic. And yet, while he no longer dons the number 11, he remains a compelling contributor to the game today.

This book is an important part of that ongoing contribution. I trust you enjoy it every bit as much as I did.

Bob Mansfield

CHAIRMAN, TELSTRA CORPORATION

MAXIMUS AND HIS MASK

When I hung up my boots at age 36, the game had already given me more than I could ever have imagined.

The black Mercedes was parked at the kerbside across the road from my shop. If it stayed there much longer, I thought to myself, the darkened windscreen would soon be lightened by having a ticket slapped under the wipers. It was an autumn day in Sydney, the historic Rocks area was already humming with tourists and the telephone rang the second I pushed open the glass front door and stepped off George Street. It was 10am. Another day of making coffee, selling sports gear, dealing in memorabilia and chewing the fat with friends and customers who dropped by 'Campo's' was about to begin. As soon as I answered that bloody phone.

'Where the hell have you been?'

The voice on the other end was unmistakeable but the question left me a little confused.

'What are you talking about?'

'I've been sitting in the car for ages waiting for you to show up.'

With that the phone went dead and Russell Crowe emerged from the back of the black Mercedes. He headed for the shop to make the exchange we had arranged some months before.

The first time I met the Oscar winning actor he was staying at the Park Hyatt Hotel in Sydney while preparing himself for his role in Gladiator. He had his personal trainer from Queensland with him and most mornings they would walk by the shop on their way to the gym. He stopped in for coffee on a few occasions and we got talking about memorabilia. He is, as most people probably realise, a sports fanatic. Rugby league, rugby union, cricket . . . he has a knowledge and love of all of them and a keen sense too of how they should be played. So we sat and chatted and he eventually asked if he could buy one of my Test jumpers. I still have quite a few of them at home, neatly folded in a wardrobe drawer. Many have been given away, some for charity auctions. But the prospect of actually selling off a Wallaby jersey did not sit that easily with me. Instead, we agreed to make a deal. If Russell gave me a piece of movie memorabilia from one of his films, I would give him a Test jumper. The swap was agreed to with a handshake.

A few weeks later he was off overseas to shoot the movie that won him an Academy Award and, when we next made contact, the trade was organised over the phone. One of my jumpers for a vase off the Gladiator set. It sounded good to me.

Yet when he crossed the road that morning, dodged the footpath coffee tables and walked on into the shop, what he carried was far more recognisable, more valuable too, than any vase. He had in his hands the Gladiator mask. There were two masks made for the movie. Russell has one and I am honoured to say I now possess the other. Feeling a little humble, I wanted to make the exchange worth his while. So I gave him in return two of the jerseys I most treasured from my playing days. The first was the Wallaby No.11 worn in the semi-final of the 1991 World Cup. It was the match where I managed to score a first half try and set up another for Tim Horan with a pass over my shoulder. We won the game and the following week carried off the Webb Ellis trophy. The other jersey was the one given to me by Jonah

Lomu after our first ever Test against each other, at the Sydney Football Stadium in 1995. I had come off the bench for the second half, replacing Damian Smith. I had both the jumpers framed and sent to him. Russell was rapt. So was I. The mask was a beautiful find.

It is amazing how sport can change your life. I was a kid from Queanbeyan who started playing rugby union for the pure joy that it gave me. There were never any dreams, at least not in the early days, of playing for Australia and travelling the world, of meeting the rich and famous, of retiring and counting as my good friends some of the most powerful people in the business community, both here and overseas. When I hung up my boots at age 36, the game had already given me more than I could ever have imagined. Almost everything I have now, I owe to rugby. And, most important of all, it helped bring me together with my wife. How else would this son of a wine-making Italian immigrant have found his way to South Africa, and to a Durban gymnasium, to meet the woman he would marry? It has been an incredible journey. One that had me living in Italy part-time for a decade. I loved it there. The pasta, the wine, the language, the people. One of the groomsmen at my wedding in January, 2003, was Vittorio Minari, the little man from Padova who was so instrumental in my annual trips to Italia. The country is in my blood. My dad was born in the north, near Padua where I played my 100th Test in 1996. It was not the only way that Italy played a big role in my rugby career. Many used to scorn the standard of play there, referred to it as Spaghetti Rugby. They never seemed to understand that Italy in the amateur days of this code allowed players as fortunate as myself the chance to taste a new culture and to see a part of the world we might not otherwise have been lucky enough to visit. Let people insinuate it was all about money and outside the International Rugby Board regulations. As I will explain later in the book, I was a rugby professional not a professional rugby player. Confused? Then you'll have to read on.

There are times, I am sure, when every sportsman, regardless of his pursuit, becomes bored or disinterested with what he is doing. Whether it's the training time or the weather conditions, whether it's an injury and a stint on the sidelines. No-one can constantly spend their career in the positive mindset that you do need to be successful. There are the occasional down times and, when you start to reach the end of your career, it allows that dirty retirement word to enter your consciousness. Let me advise those sportsmen still active enough to chase their dreams. Squeeze every last minute out of your playing career because, as the old adage goes, you are a long time retired. You miss it when you give it away. Especially the highest levels of a game. You miss that unbelievable competitive nature that the best in their sports require. You miss the testing of your skills, your fitness and your all-round ability. You miss even the pain of tired muscles that represented a hard day's work. It was a challenge and an adrenalin rush all rolled into one. But above all it was enjoyment. For years when asked what rugby meant to me, I always gave a standard reply. But every time I said these words, I meant them. It was as if I had never delivered them before. Rugby is my life, I would explain. There was nothing else sharing centre stage at the time. I was never going to be an academic. I was never going to split the atom. But I did know how to play rugby, even if sometimes instinct took over and I would play without having to think. My legs would carry me somewhere before even I had time to register what they were doing. To give all that up was painful. Married now, there are other things in my life. There is wife Lara, and thriving businesses, from the coffee shop in the Rocks to various sports stores and a management company. Hospitality events and speaking engagements, usually overseas, keep me close to rugby, as do my writings for the *Daily Telegraph* newspaper in Sydney and my radio commitments with 2GB and the Macquarie Network. The diary is always full. But I can tell you now, if I had my time over I would swap it all to be on the rise again as a teenager, to be making my first tour of New Zealand, to have a 15-season career with the Wallabies all laid out ahead of me. When I hear current players whinge about the amount of money they are getting, or the size of their World Cup bonus payments, it is enough to turn my stomach. Yes, the game has been good to me. It has made me who I am, it has opened doors and brought recognition to the name Campese. But they were by-products of playing this game as well as I possibly could, not sticking out my hand and demanding a pay rise at every opportunity. The traditions of rugby and the spirit of the game should always be respected. Sometimes I think the modern-day pros forget about what has gone before them. Sure, I was not a student of the Wallabies or any other team for that matter when I first came into the international ranks. I caused an outcry in New Zealand in 1982 when I went there and knew nothing about their wing legend Stu Wilson. They informed me none too subtly he was the guy I'd be marking in the Tests. But as my career continued, I knew enough about the Wallaby ethos to know it commands and deserves respect. Anyone wearing the gold jumper is only in it for a period of time. We all have to hand it on to the next generation. I only hope that ever-so-amateur ideal is never lost the further we move into the pay-for-play era.

There is another thing about retirement. No-one really prepares you for life after rugby. They try, I know. I had a lot of wonderful friends who throughout my career helped me make the right business decisions to ensure when I did leave the game I would do so in a position to succeed on the 'dark side'. People like my long-term business partner Daryl MacGraw and former coach turned top-rating breakfast radio host Alan Jones were a constant source of guidance. But there was, when I initially retired, a feeling of emptiness on occasions. You would miss even the Saturday afternoon club games, standing around afterwards and signing autographs for kids. The tours overseas, that for so long had been part of my winters and springs, were no longer on the program, unless I was making a whistlestop trip to the UK to speak at functions. There was also the lost thrill of winning. Nothing could beat it.

I had put everything into rugby from the ages of 19 to 36, so it is little wonder I fell off the retirement bandwagon, albeit for one game in 2001. I was almost 40 years of age when the invitation to play in a tribute game to the Cuttitta brothers, Massimo and Marcelo, arrived. It was to be a Barbarians style match against Italy A to raise money for an Italian player who had been left a paraplegic after an accident. I was asked to play for an Invitation XV and readily accepted.

The game was played in Sardinia, and I had been out of the game at international level in the 15-a-side game since 1996. Lining up against the Italian A side that day made me realise how robotic and static the game had become by 2001. Our Invitation team had one training session together of about an hour. We had an Italian halfback, a Romanian fullback, a French winger, a Kiwi and a South African in the centres and I played at five-eighth. After 20 minutes, against a team coached by the then Italian Test coach Brad Johnstone, we were leading 20-nil. During that one hour training session I referred to, all we did as a backline was trial a few simple calls, practice the odd cut out pass, a loop and a midfield switch. Basic stuff, all of it, but good enough to have the Italian A side in defensive meltdown. On attack they took the ball up one out, one after the other. In the end we won something like 50-20. Our side contained mostly ex-players. It just goes to show you. While some players and coaches in the modern era would have you believe they are re-inventing the wheel with the styles of rugby they are trying to introduce, the truth is not so dramatic. Rather than building a new wheel they are taking us back to the stone age to when the first one emerged.

I am thankful I played in an era when the attitudes and styles of game were not so negative. Rugby these days is so much about not making mistakes. Risk-taking is not encouraged. Well, that was the case until mid-2003, when the All Blacks opened the Tri-Nations series with two blitzkrieg performances against South Africa and Australia. They played rugby that you could not help but marvel at, regardless from which country you came. They were entertainers, showmen, talented footballers who seemed to revel in the freedom they were given by coach John Mitchell, whose own transformation was quite stunning. An old forward from the Waikato region in New Zealand, he did not appear to be the most free-spirited thinker about modern-day rugby. But when gifted the talent he was able to showcase, you would be a fool to ignore the matchwinning potential. And Mitchell is nobody's fool.

But now I am on the other side of the fence permanently, I have to make do with watching rugby and commentating on it, which can at times be more dangerous than getting caught at the bottom of a ruck. As a player who copped plenty of criticism, I know how much it hurts. I also know, as an ex-Wallaby, I'm entitled to have an opinion on the game. I never called for those who had a crack at me to shut their mouths. Nor will I be told to shut mine. When you think about it though, the media speculation and comment international rugby players have to put up with is a fly speck on the Opera House compared to what worldwide names like Russell Crowe have to endure during their careers. Admittedly, Russell makes more from one movie than the entire Wallabies side would make in something like four years. But in some respects, that money comes at a substantial price. I remember heading down to Melbourne for the Australian formula one grand prix and, while I was there, I received an invitation to attend the premiere of *A Beautiful Mind*. My mate Steve Loader from Qantas was with me as we attended a post-film function. There we were on the rooftop of this theatre when I spotted Russell in a small, roped off area by himself. People were clearly in awe of him and many perhaps too scared to approach him. Others would go up and have a chat — but only over the rope. It was a security measure of course. He is such a big name. But he is also great company and a talented and funny bloke. Yet here he was, like some museum exhibit. That same night I got the chance to meet his mum and dad. The first thing his father said to me was: 'You're the bastard that's got my mask'. I hope Russell gave him one of the jerseys to make up for handing me his Gladiator face plate.

Just in that 20 to 30 minutes I came to understand in a very small way what people like Russell Crowe have to deal with in terms of a fishbowl existence when they are out in public. In sport, we don't have to worry about that sort of adulation. The only time I can ever recall being mobbed is after the 1988 Barbarians game at Cardiff Arms Park when it took me a couple of hours to walk the short distance to the team hotel because well-wishers and autograph hunters were stopping me at every step. One writer tagged me the Pied Piper because of the kids that tagged along for the entire duration. But they were people who had been to the rugby that day. They had, in some way, lived the experience with you.

Clearly, the profile of Hollywood's finest is up there on another planet somewhere. They have to be cautious and guarded. There have been times when Russell has called in to the shop wearing a hat pulled down over his eyes and dark glasses. No-one knew who he was. It was a different story in November 2002 when I was across in the UK during the Wallabies end-of-season tour. Russell had been in Ireland for Richard Harris' funeral and we caught up later, when he got to London, for dinner and drinks at the Dorchester Hotel. It was on the Tuesday before the Wallabies played and lost to England at Twickenham. He was a charming host, relaxed in the company of six people, with no-one standing around and staring. I guess at the Dorchester that would simply not be the thing to do. We spoke that night about rugby and he does have a terrific knowledge of the game. Not surprisingly for someone who was born in New Zealand, went to a GPS school in Sydney and then completed his education in the Shaky Isles. He might love the South Sydney rugby league club but his bloodlines scream rugby to me.

But what of this game that so dominated my life, before retirement, business and marriage? It really struck me how much things had changed with that Barbarians game in Sardinia and the tour to Australia that same year by the British and Irish Lions. I was speaking to a Welshman, Scott Gibbs, a tough centre against whom I'd played. He was called out to join the Lions when they suffered a rash of injuries early in their trip. Before the first Test at the Gabba in Brisbane, I was chatting to him and the former Welsh skipper Ieuan Evans. For those with a thirst for trivia, it was Evans who scored the try in the third Lions Test of 1989 when my pass infield to fullback Greg Martin hit the deck near our goalline. What Gibbs was saying was a real eye opener. Even he suggested it was scary, compared to how the game had once been played. In a nutshell, he said the English players on the tour did nothing but eat and sleep. Apart from training, they would sleep every couple of hours, only getting up to graze their way through several meals then head back to bed. Even to Gibbs, who was still playing, it was a different culture altogether. But had the English coach Clive Woodward already started to grab a jump on the rest of the rugby-playing world back then? He had assembled a team with only one focus – performance. Even with the Lions, they were there to do a job, not to go sightseeing or enjoy themselves. Sad in a way, even though England arrived at World Cup 2003 as one of the tournament favourites. It is disappointing because some of those players will never realise what they missed. Rugby tours are a unique experience, one to savour for years and decades into the future. I remember during 2003 how the 1953 Wallabies held their 50-year reunion. Even after all that time they all still got on famously. That is camaraderie.

From another perspective, that Gabba Test, won by the Lions, really showed Australia how big rugby was becoming in this country. The Brisbane ground was covered on all sides by red as British and Irish tour group travellers, and heaven knows how many UK expatriates, filled the grandstands. They brought to life a tour that will go down as one of the most successful ever undertaken here. There have been plenty of memorable ones, including the All Blacks tours of 1984 and 1992, and the South African visit of 1993 – their first visit to these shores since 1971. But the 2001 Lions brought an increased profile to a sport that had really taken off here after the game went professional and was further kicked along by the World Cup success in 1999.

I sat in the stands the night of that first Test, along with former England captain Will Carling and former rugby league international Benny Elias. They were part of a corporate venture that had brought a number of people to Australia from England to watch the series. And it was amazing to witness how some of the Poms reacted to the win. They were simply beside themselves. But it was probably not too surprising, really. After all, England had never been able to beat Australia on home soil. The Poms eventually corrected that historical anomaly in 2003 at Telstra Dome in Melbourne. But two years earlier, English supporters were just as happy to cling to a victory by a side representing not only the red rose, but Wales, Scotland and Ireland as well. The crowd also enjoyed and thrilled to the style of rugby played by the tourists. The speed of Jason Robinson and the midfield explosiveness of Brian O'Driscoll. Perhaps Australian coach in waiting, Eddie Jones, learned a lesson that day. When he came into the Wallabies job just a month later, he promised a new style based on attacking other teams wide. Midway through the Tri-Nations series of 2003, we were still waiting to see it happen.

In the second Lions Test, Australia squared the ledger in Melbourne so the two sides headed to Sydney for the decider. I suspected it would be a busy week for the shop, especially when we were selling the official Lions jerseys. But what happened next absolutely floored me. We ended up staying open from one Sunday to the next, and not closing at night until 10. It was simply insane as people flooded in for autographs, photos, jerseys, videos and any sort of memorabilia. And it demonstrated just how far rugby had travelled. Not only in Australia but on a worldwide basis. By the Wednesday of that week leading up to the Lions finale, we had to order a further 35 boxes of t-shirts and jerseys, just to keep pace with the in-store demand. As soon as new stock came in it left by the same door. It was our busiest week ever, bigger and more profitable than either week during the Sydney Olympics. The Lions tour was massive and the World Cup will be as well. Two years ago they wanted Lions jumpers, Wallaby jerseys, ACT Brumbies kit. Whatever they could lay their hands on they bought. And I ended up signing about 95 percent of all purchases. The RSI twitching has only just stopped.

I am sure this time there will be a demand for various other playing strips. I just hope the tourist numbers reach expectations. The World Cup organisers were forced to scale back their initial figures from some 70,000 to 55,000. I just hope they do come in those numbers because it promises to be a tournament of high drama. If they do, I am sure the shop at the Rocks will be open long hours again, and seven days a week. But I can guarantee there will be no black Mercedes across the road. As I pointed out to Russell, he had been illegally parked.

CAPE TOWN CATASTROPHE

Should Horan be selected for the World Cup?
I answered the question — honestly. I said no.

My mother Joan was clearly worried. You could see the concern in her eyes. So she came right out and asked me. 'Are you on steroids?'

It was 1995, the year of the third World Cup; the season the Wallabies would head to South Africa to defend their crown; the winter the game would change forever.

To a certain extent, rugby had already changed. Money was in the air — just how much we would soon find out — and there was a growing emphasis, on the pitch, towards power.

Bob Dwyer was the coach, as he had been four years earlier, and for this campaign he was heavily influenced by the need for weight training and fitness work. The fitness stuff, no problem. The weights? I think, looking back, it was counter-productive. Yes, I increased my strength immeasurably, and that helped me in contact situations. I could put more weight into a tackle, and when opposition defenders tried to bring me to ground, I could offer more resistance. But what separated me from other players during my career — the ability to be elusive — had come under question. I still had the footwork, but not the pace. My flexibility had also suffered. On reflection, I know that now. I would have fought and argued against accepting the fact at the time. But deep down, in your subconscious, you do know, and it shows in your game. It did in mine. I started to back myself less, kick the ball more. I was not as confident taking on a defence. It just wasn't happening for me as that year went on. I think the way I liked to play the game, I just wasn't meant to be the big and strong type. Mat Rogers in the current side is a bit the same, I think. I would hate to see them build him up too much, in terms of weight and muscle. He is such a supple, athletic player, with the pure ability to beat defenders on the inside and outside, they would be playing with fire to change his physical make-up. Critics might scoff and say that is an over-reaction, that the reason I started slowing down was because age had descended on me. I was, at the time, 32. But I tend to think it was not the advancing years, rather the the expanding chest, biceps, thighs and bum which began to pull me back. Put it this way. In 1991, when we won the World Cup, I was 82 kilograms. Lean and fast. In 1995, I had bulked up to 92 kilograms, adding 12 percent of my original body weight to the frame I wanted to take to a third World Cup campaign. I felt great at the time. Quite enjoyed having the extra weight and size. Others found it disconcerting, but their anxieties were completely misplaced. They thought I had turned to drugs for the new look. Nothing ever did or ever would tempt me to take drugs of the performance-enhancing or recreational kind. So there no problems on that front. But I do think my game suffered a bit as a result of the added muscle. My mum Joan was the first to quiz me on the steroids suspicion, followed by my long-time Italian mate Vittorio Minari, the man who initially organised for me to play in that wonderful country and where I spent the best part of 10 off-seasons enjoying the life of a rugby traveller.

Australia's all-time leading points scorer Michael Lynagh was another who found Italian off-seasons to his liking. 'Noddy' married an Italian girl and, in 1994-95, wanted to head back to Italy for another run with the Treviso club. It was not, many thought, in the best interests of World Cup preparation. But the Australian Rugby Union gave Lynagh the go ahead to spend the summer and autumn in Europe. It was a strange decision by the administration. Our assistant coach Bob Templeton had wanted to spend the same off-season with the Harlequins club in England. His request was refused. But here was the Australian captain given the green light to do the same. To be fair to Noddy, if I had also wanted to go, I could have. The ARU would not have stood in my way. But I wanted to be in the best physical condition possible going into the World Cup and, to me, that meant staying at home and using the off-season to fully prepare. The World Cup of that year, significantly, was held over a May-June time period, not the regular October-November timeslot it has since been given. So, having spent a decade splitting my time between my two favourite countries — six months at home and six months in Italy — I took the decision to give Europe a miss. I felt by playing and training with the guys back in Australia on a more regular basis, it would help build better combinations. I wanted to be part of the 'team', despite the fact some people viewed me as an out and out individual who struggled with that 'all for one' concept. Strangely enough, not too many openly criticised the Lynagh decision. But he was required to return to Australia to attend our summer training camps at Coolum, on the Queensland Sunshine Coast. I guess, given the amateur era in which we played, administrators were not entitled to prevent the game's stars from pursuing opportunities elsewhere. After all, we were not under contract like the modern-day players. But I still find it hard to reconcile that the Wallabies captain, and I know he had an Italian wife, would opt to spend that particular off-season out of the country.

It was not, of course, the first time Lynagh and I had agreed to disagree. We never swapped harsh words but we were never good mates either. I remember in 1991 having to apologise to Noddy when we arrived in London for what would be our triumphant World Cup campaign. In my autobiography *On A Wing And A Prayer* I had, what I thought, offered faint criticism of the Test five-eighth. It followed the 1990 Sydney Test against France. I had played in the curtain-raiser that day after a shoulder injury I had, ironically, sustained in Italy, encouraged the selectors to leave me out of the Test side. It was the first time in my Test career I had been dropped from the Wallabies team. In those days, if you came back from overseas with any sort of fitness query you had to play locally to convince the selectors you were right. I had not played on Australian soil since returning and it was felt I should have come home earlier. Despite my protests that I was right to play, I was left out of the team. Paul Carozza from Queensland was given my spot and there was no appearance for me against France in the opening Test of the season. Instead, I watched the game from the grandstand. I saw the massive fight break out early, saw Abdel Benazzi, the massive French forward, sent off in his Test debut after just 13 minutes, and saw Lynagh kick the ball, in my opinion, too much. I thought the Australians should have attacked more with the ball in hand. France were down to 14 men and I would have presumed the best way to sink them would be to run their seven-man pack around the ground. Australia won the Test 21-9 but I made the observation about Lynagh's tactics in my book, which came out the following year. So, we turn up to London for the 1991 World Cup and skipper Nick Farr-Jones pulls me aside at the first training session. He tells me Michael wasn't happy with what I'd written in the book about that game and that I should go across and apologise to him. In the interests of the team, critics please note, I did just that. Nick pointed out we couldn't have strained relations in the squad, not if we wanted to win the tournament. I agreed and walked over to Noddy, offering my apologies for upsetting him. I seem to have a habit of doing that because there was a similar incident four years later. Only this time it involved not Lynagh but another Queensland favourite son, inside centre Tim Horan.

Earlier that year I had been to a BMW coaching clinic at a school with prop Ewen McKenzie. They held a question and answer forum after the session and someone asked me if Tim Horan should be selected for the World Cup squad. Tim had suffered one of the worst knee injuries imaginable the previous year, in a Super 10 match in South Africa. The damage was so bad there were real fears he would never play again. Initially, they even thought he might struggle to walk without some sort of limp. So we are talking serious injury here. To his credit, Horan worked incredibly hard to rehabilitate himself. He spent a lot of time in Sydney with legendary physiotherapist Greg Craig, a man who can work miracles as I can attest to through my years with NSW and the Wallabies. Craigy would tell horror stories of how Horan would bury his head in a pillow to muffle his own screams as Craig, in the painful early months, had to work some flexibility into the surgically overhauled joint. I don't know if I could have put myself through that sort of torture. Horan was immensely strong mentally, we all knew that from the way he played the game. The work he put in to beat this injury only confirmed how special he was in the steel-trap mind department.

But the question still had to be answered: should Horan be selected for the World Cup? People don't ask what you think of Horan. They just want to get to the bottom line. So I answered the question — honestly. I said no. As I pointed out, there was no way he could be at his best for the tournament. Apart from simply getting over the injury, he would not accrue sufficient game time before the World Cup to have him ready for the step up to international rugby. I also wondered whether Horan would ever again be the great player he was before his knee exploded that day in South Africa.

Little did I know there was a journalist in the audience as I was delivering my answer. I sure knew about it later. The next day there were headlines in the newspapers. There I was, telling the selectors not to pick Tim Horan in the World Cup squad, that he would never be the same again. I did not mean for those comments to be aired so dramatically or as widely as they were, but it was too late to take my words back by then. I did try to limit the danger. I didn't hide from Horan. In fact, it was quite the opposite. I telephoned him to apologise for the way it was all presented. I also spoke to Paul McLean, the former Wallaby five-eighth and fullback who was then an Australian selector. I told him what was said and explained how it came about. He told me not to worry, because he would be giving it to me big-time in the paper the following day. That was fine, I could cop that.

If I upset people's feelings, I will ring and apologise. At the same time, I'm prepared to be honest when people ask me questions. Others have criticised me in their books. That's fine, too. But one thing that does bear consideration now, long after the wounds have healed, is this: How did Tim Horan play at the 1995 World Cup, when we fell in the quarter-finals to England? I know David Campese had an ordinary tournament. But so did plenty of other Wallabies. Interestingly, Horan spent the next two seasons, 1996 and 1997, playing at five-eighth, outside centre and wing in the Test side, apart from appearances in his specialist inside centre role. There were few people saying then that Horan was the same No.12 he had been earlier in his career. And you know why? Because knee injuries of the magnitude he suffered take a long time to get over. In Horan's case, it could have been the death knell to his career. But he he did keep fighting, he did keep working on regaining his confidence in contact, and re-establishing his trademark acceleration and, by 1998 he was back, unchallenged, as the best inside centre in Australia. The year after that he was the player of the tournament at the 1999 World Cup. That was one incredible achievement when you consider what he had to endure. I will, therefore, put my hand in the air and admit I was wrong in 1995 when I wondered whether he would ever return to the player we once knew and admired. I think history has shown the other comments to be not too far wide of the mark.

Still, the 1995 World Cup year had not opened too well for yours truly. I had been in the headlines for criticising Lynagh and another icon in Horan, and I was looking more like a bodybuilder than a footballer. But things were only going to get worse. I would have the occasional run-in with coach Bob Dwyer and money raised its head even before the game went professional. More about all that a bit later but I mention it here, in passing, because I think it contributed to our downfall at the tournament. Our focus was not what it had been in 1991. The feeling was different, so too the morale. Perhaps because we were all a bit older and it was pretty much the same faces as four years earlier. Maybe we had lost a bit of freshness, that wonderful enthusiasm of youth, and the hunger of a team that in 1991 so wanted to claim the game's ultimate prize for the first time. There were also the injuries. Horan had just come back, front-rowers McKenzie and Phil Kearns were carrying niggling problems, as were several other players. All the warning signs were there, and we never saw them.

The Australian Rugby Union had invested a lot of money in the World Cup defence. There was even a song written about our campaign. Run Wallaby Run, sung by Doug Parkinson, proved about as successful as we would be on the fields of South Africa. Or one field in particular. Newlands Stadium is set in a leafy Cape Town suburb of the same name, almost at the foot of Table Mountain. It was where we had beaten the Springboks in their return from sporting isolation in 1992. They had been cocky enough to take on the All Blacks and Wallabies on successive weekends and somehow thought they would win both, despite not having played Test rugby since 1984. They came close to toppling New Zealand at Ellis Park in Johannesburg. But in Cape Town, where the Australian forwards were superb on a wet and difficult track, we blew them away with a record scoreline of 26–3. That game had happy memories for personal reasons. I had scored my 50th Test try, after brilliant work from Horan. He had set off on a run from deep inside our half, kicked ahead and tackled the big South African centre Danie Gerber when he retrieved the ball from his own quarter. Horan then jumped to his feet, stripped the Springbok legend of possession and fired me a pass. I had no-one to beat. Bringing up a half-century had never been so easy.

Three years later we were back, and confident we would open the tournament with a victory over the Springboks in this, their first World Cup. They were given little hope of beating us, despite whipping Western Samoa 60–8 in their only pre-tournament Test of the season. We went into the match on May 25 after two big wins over Argentina a few weeks earlier. Leading up to the first game, Dwyer had planned an intensive and gruelling training regime. We were getting belted at training as Bob ripped the work into us. By comparison, the Springboks were apparently training very old-school, and quite poorly. Media reports suggested they were looking slow and ponderous and were committing the simplest of errors in their sessions. So much for training form being a guide to what will happen on match day.

It was a Springbok ambush. They came out and blew us away and, in doing so, trumpeted their challenge to the rest of the rugby world. They played very physically, and we had no answers. Not withstanding how they muscled up, we did not play anywhere near as well as we could. A lot of things just didn't work on the day. Combinations were breaking down and we carried, by my count, four injured blokes in the pack. Horan had been left out of the side, not considered ready for his first Test since 1993. Jason Little played inside centre with a young Daniel Herbert beside him. George Gregan was at halfback having broken into the side the previous year and making his name with that unforgettable tackle on Jeff Wilson in the Bledisloe Cup match at the Sydney Football Stadium. Matt Pini had been preferred to another young guy, Matt Burke, at fullback and, in the forwards, we had five survivors from our 1991 final win over England. But, this time, it just didn't seem like the Wallabies of old. Maybe we weren't prepared as tactically as we could have been. We were not underdone for fitness, though, so no criticism can be levelled at Dwyer in that regard. And if I'm going to be honest about who played well and who did not, then I most definitely fell into the latter category.

I was not anywhere near my best and missed a crucial tackle on my opposite winger Pieter Hendriks, allowing him to score. We had been ahead 13-9 at the time, with Lynagh scoring the opening try of the tournament in the 32nd minute of the match. Five minutes later the Springboks had snatched the lead from us when Hendriks beat me on the outside, raised his fist in triumph, and scored in the left corner. We never led again. They stretched their advantage to 27-13 in a dominant second half showing before Phil Kearns scored in the final minutes to make the scoreboard look a little more respectable. But we were gutted by the loss. We were shocked that we had been beaten as we had, even though we were below our best. It was only later that we realised the Boks had been targeting this one game for months. While we had gone about our build-up with the big picture in mind, they had launched their assault on the title knowing their entire campaign might hinge on beating us at Newlands. The reason for it were the draw repercussions awaiting the loser. As we discovered, our path now involved a likely quarter-final with England and a semi-final against the All Blacks. The Boks had a less dangerous run-in – a quarter-final showdown with Western Samoa, a side they had already beaten by 52 points that season, and a semi-final against the French.

In the 2002 biography of Chester Williams, to which I wrote the Foreword, the Hendriks try is highlighted because the South African winger was almost certainly playing only because Chester had been withdrawn from the squad through injury. Ironically, Chester spent that afternoon, as an employee of the Western Province Rugby Union, looking after the needs of our reserves on the bench. This was, remember, the days of amateurism. Here's a snippet from Williams' book:

'The man who had replaced Chester in the Springboks team, Pieter Hendriks, provided the turning point in the match against the defending world champions. The Transvaal winger straightened the line, sized up Campese and took him on, one on one. Few players in world rugby had done this. Hendriks won the contest hands down and scored arguably the most memorable try of South Africa's World Cup campaign. The Springboks won handsomely and Hendriks was one of the stars.'

After the game I remember our 1991 skipper Nick Farr-Jones, who was in South Africa for the tournament, going up to Gregan. Nick told George he was going for a drink that night and if Gregan wanted to join him, he would be only too happy to have a chat about a few things. George, after all, was in only his second season of Test rugby. Nick had seen 10 seasons at the top. George, to the best of my knowledge, did not take up the offer. Somewhat surprising, I thought, given Nick's standing in the game. Anything he passed on would at least be worth sifting, to see if one gold nugget might emerge. The remaining two pool matches went as expected. We beat Canada 27-11 in Port Elizabeth, with Joe Roff making his Test debut on the opposite wing, and Tim Horan returning to inside centre for his 34th Test. Roff picked up one try in that game and another two in the following match against Romania in Stellenbosch as the Wallabies won 42-3. I did not play in the final pool match but was back for the quarter-final against the Poms at Newlands. We had finished second in our pool to the Boks, and had to take the low road.

But before the knockout stages got underway, all eight remaining teams had to assemble in Johannesburg. It seemed pretty stupid to me and an unnecessary waste of time, making players board planes and fly to the city. We had played our last pool game in Stellenbosch. It is only a half hour drive from Cape Town. But the schedule demanded we fly to Johannesburg and back to Cape Town again. Crazy stuff. I mention Johannesburg because there was an incident there which further underpinned a suspicion we might be on the wane, that our focus was not fine-tuned to the state required. We were to go to training and had a team meeting planned beforehand, as per usual. But at the designated time, there were four players and a member of the coaching staff still absent. The meeting had to be delayed, not by much, but it did start late. On the eve of World Cup quarter-finals it was completely unsatisfactory. As it turns out, the five-man party had been out shopping. The bargains, it seemed, were too good to miss.

In training for the England game there was also — little did we know at the time — a spy watching our every move. England captain Will Carling told me about it later. This bloke was part of their set-up but was unknown outside the England camp. He would take up a position, sometimes out of our sight, and watch our training sessions, reporting back soon after to the England management. Strangely enough, on the day, they did seem to have answers to everything we tried. I'm not saying the spy brought us down, but he certainly didn't help.

There was another interesting sideline to that game as well. When you think about the frequency with which the Wallabies play other leading nations these days, it is quite bemusing to look back to 1995 and realise that the Newlands quarter final was the first time we had met the Poms on the field since the 1991 World Cup decider. In that respect, it was pretty tough to gauge what we were up against. There is a big difference between watching a team on video and confronting them out in the middle. The match itself saw the English pounce on a couple of our mistakes. Damian Smith on the other wing scored a spectacular try for us with a high-flying take from a Michael Lynagh bomb. And basically it could have gone either way. A fairly obvious observation I suppose when the scores were level heading into injury time. Coach Dwyer was convinced we were headed for extra time and had left his seat in the grandstand to make his way towards the touchline. That was when Rob Andrew struck. The English five-eighth launched a massive dropped goal from some 40m and we were sunk. But the realisation hit me a couple of weeks later, after South Africa had beaten New Zealand in the final, ironically with another drop kick, this one in extra time, that we would not have been good enough to defend the title even if we had edged past the Poms. Maybe we were getting old. It was basically the same players and the same coach who had been there done that in 1991. And we were playing pretty much the same style of rugby. I could see a dangerous comparison looming there in the countdown to the 2003 World Cup. The Wallabies had won the title in 1999 but were still carrying a few too many players from the previous campaign, and had not shifted their game plan that much from when Rod Macqueen was at the helm.

But back to 1995 and after the loss to the Poms we went back to the hotel and it was not the world's greatest feeling — being there in a Cape Town hotel that was also housing our conquerors. Just another of those quirks from the amateur era; staying in the same hotel as your opposition. But the enormity of the defeat had me moping around the place for a second and, to me, far more lasting reason. I was thinking, again, about retirement.

The morning after the Newlands game I went to see Bob Dwyer because I wasn't sure about my rugby future. Hanging up the boots was high on my priorities. It's always the case that when you get down, like I was after losing to England, you dwell on the negatives of life. So I had a chat to Bob and said I was unsure what to do. He told me to have a good think: 'And if you want to retire, retire.' The Wallaby squad was scheduled to head home a short time later, two weeks before we had planned. But I was one of several players who decided to stay on a bit in South Africa.

I was in Johannesburg in the lead-up to the final and bumped into our team manager Peter Falk, who was with a tour group. I didn't even have to raise the subject. As a friend he advised me to give the game away. He suggested it might be best if I retire because he'd heard I was not going to be picked for Australia again. Even though I had been swaying between retirement and playing on, seemingly every five minutes, his words hit me with a silent force that left my ears ringing. I knew my efforts at the World Cup were unlikely to be on any career highlights tape. But to hear you are set for the chop can be quite frightening. I guess the easy option would have been to opt out then. To get in before the selectors and announce my retirement. As every sportsman likes to say — leaving on my own terms. But there was something about what Falk had told me that stirred my competitive juices. Perhaps the fact it hurt so much to hear the selectors were planning my demise made me realise how much I really would miss playing at the highest level. So if I was even the slightest bit unsure, and clearly I was, then I should tough it out and see if I could prove the wise men wrong. I made the decision there in Johannesburg. Despite Falk's forecast of doom, I was going to see if I could force my way into the side to play the All Blacks. Having made my choice, I actually enjoyed my last few days in Johannesburg and then headed home to one of the biggest challenges of my career.

The interstate series was played the month after the World Cup. The equation was simple. I had to play so well the selectors would have no option other than to select me. Pick me to mark Jonah Lomu. I had spoken to Dwyer again, looking for advice on where I needed to improve my game. He told me straight to stop kicking the ball. Another sobering barb. But when I thought about it, I could hardly disagree with Bob. I was kicking too much. In the World Cup match against South Africa, I kicked the ball three or four times when I could have run. Maybe I was worried my speed was going, and that was affecting my confidence, especially to counter attack. So I took on board the Dwyer advice and headed up to Queensland for the interstate match. I was marking Damian Smith, who always wanted to knock my head off. Dwyer was looking for big strong guys and Smith fitted the bill. In our head-to-head battle, I made a few mistakes, Smith did nothing. I tried to get involved but nothing was working, and I knew the mistakes would cost me a Test position.

Bob Dwyer had been my first Test coach, way back in 1982. He took a gamble and picked me as a teenager. We had, over the years, experienced a lot together through our association with the Wallabies. But that seemed to count for nothing when Bob dropped me for that first Bledisloe Cup Test against the All Blacks in Auckland, 1995. It was not the axing that hurt most, but the fact that Bob did not take the time to let me know after he'd made the decision. After the Queensland game, we were flying back to Sydney. Bob was on the same flight as the NSW team. The Test side apparently had been selected and, for me, it was the longest one-hour flight of all time. I had no idea whether I was in or out of the side, and Bob made no attempt to tell me during the trip. But when we arrived in Sydney, the doors open and there's a photographer, snapping away, taking shots of me. I felt sick in the stomach. I knew straight away. The word must be out that I'm not in the Test side. I knew because if I had been retained, the newspapers would not have bothered sending out a bloke to photograph me.

I sought out Bob straight away, walked up to him and said: 'I'm not in the side, am I?'

I told him about the photographer incident. Bob didn't say anything straight away but while we were collecting our bags, he wandered up and confirmed I would not be going to Auckland. I was devastated. I went home and that word retirement resurfaced briefly. I called Paul McLean, an Australian selector, and asked him what I needed to do to be considered again. He told me to get involved when I played club rugby for Randwick that weekend against Eastwood. I did, from fullback, on the same afternoon the All Blacks beat Australia at Eden Park with Joe Roff and Damian Smith on the wings. But what caught my attention later was an injury out of the Test. Not to either winger but to fullback Matthew Burke. They would need a stand-in, at least until they knew if Burke would recover. I presumed the name Campese might be somewhere there in the mix. I should have known better. The selectors plucked an untried guy from ACT. His name was Rod Kafer and he'd come out of the blue to get the call-up. Unfortunately for Kafer, he did not last long. At his first training session with the team, he fell awkwardly and broke his leg. As much as I wanted to be part of the set-up, you would not wish such a freakish and heartbreaking setback on anyone. As the news spread about Kafer's injury, my good mate Mark Ella rang me the same afternoon. 'Interesting to see what they'll do now,' he laughed.

I found out the following morning. The telephone call came from Rod Macqueen, another of the Australian selectors. Macqueen had coached me in the 1991-92 NSW side. He enjoyed enormous success in his first season but I was never a fan of his playing style. It was too rigid, almost devoid of flair, even though we did smash the Welsh side of 1991 with a record-breaking score. He was more into no-mistake footballers than risk-takers. I can't say we ever really saw eye to eye. He did, of course, have significant success with the Wallabies after taking them over in 1997. His Wallaby teams roped in Bledisloe Cup series, a Tri-Nations trophy triumph, a series win over the British and Irish Lions and, the crowning glory, the 1999 World Cup.

In 1995, that was all ahead of him. So too was an appointment as the ACT Brumbies coach the following year for the first Super 12 season. Macqueen phoned to tell me they needed a player to attend training. If Burke proved his fitness that player would not be required. If Burke was out, the shadow player would be on the bench against the All Blacks for the Test at the Sydney Football Stadium. 'We've thought about it,' Macqueen told me. 'And we think you're the best man for the job.' I did my best not to laugh. It must have killed them to have to call me back. They had made it plain enough they wanted me gone and here they were having to give me another shot at the Test side. I was delighted. Over the moon. I was prepared to take any opportunity offered. But Macqueen had further instructions for me. 'The team has a great spirit,' he said. 'They're playing well, so just go to training and shut up. Say nothing, just train.' It was like a teacher dressing down a pupil. Here I was, out of the Test side for one game, and they're making out as if I was some new intruder who had to mind his manners.

I headed to training, walked on to the field and shook hands with Dwyer. 'Good to have you back,' he smiled.

I got through the session without saying a word and Burke ran without incident. But, for some reason, I was meant to play that weekend against the All Blacks. Another training injury, this time with centre Daniel Herbert pulling a hamstring, led to my selection on the bench. It was the first time in 14 seasons of international rugby that I'd been a Test reserve. I had absolutely no idea what to do, or how to prepare. I was asking other people for advice right through that week. As I said, it was fate that I would get a run that day.

Jonah Lomu was on fire for the All Blacks, up against Damian Smith. But Smithy got one back on the big bloke when he made a fantastic run through several All Blacks to score just before halftime. But he had also sustained an injury and at the break our team doctor John Best approached me in the sheds. He'd just examined Smith and said simply: 'Out you go'.

I was walking down the tunnel, taking my tracksuit off, when Bob Dwyer took me aside and said 'just don't give Lomu any room'.

The first thing that crossed my mind was: 'If the other 14 out there can't stop him, what am I supposed to do?'

As chance would have it, Jonah got the ball in the opening stages of the second half and ran straight at me. Imagine standing on the railway tracks as a freight train approaches. That's how I felt. I think I shut my eyes, but I tackled him. Later in the half he pushed me aside to score a try, but I could at least claim to have cut him down once.

It had been a changing of the guard in 1995. The Wallabies were no longer kings of the game. Our style of play had become outdated. The All Blacks were again showing the way, even though they had been beaten in the World Cup final by South Africa, and Jonah Lomu was the man. After that meeting in Sydney, we caught up in the changing rooms and swapped jerseys. He gave me his No.11 and I gave him my No.16. But it was a funny time as the amateur era drew to a close. Unless my memory is failing these days, I think back to that post-match chat with Jonah and I don't recall there being any other Wallabies in that All Blacks room. Probably a fitting and disappointing note on which to end that season. We had lost the World Cup, lost the Bledisloe Cup. We were back in the pack. It was so far removed from the joys of the previous World Cup four years earlier. And off the field we were about to witness the greatest change of all.

SHOW ME THE MONEY

So was I a professional player? No, I was a rugby professional. There is a subtle difference.

If money is the root of all evil, then rugby union will soon be finished as the Game They Play In Heaven. Too many have been 'tainted' by the folding stuff since the amateurism dam broke in 1995 and sent the code into a play for pay format once reserved for those mungoes of rugby league. Money had been floating around the game previously, on an unofficial level of course. There were blind eyes turned everywhere. But this was the real deal, and it was amazing to be a part of the whole transformation. The entry of Rupert Murdoch on the rugby union scene, directly and indirectly, started the whole ball rolling.

He bankrolled a Super League concept, a breakaway rugby league competition, sparking a bit of panic in the rugby union ranks. Because there was a mad scramble for players in the rugby league war between Super League and the Australian Rugby League – they needed personnel to fill their separate competitions – it was quite clear rugby union players would make an appealing option to flesh out those numbers. Rugby union bosses in Australia and New Zealand sensed the danger and got their heads together with South African powerbrokers. They needed to come up with a plan to keep rugby union players in the 15-man game and the only solution, an inevitable one, was to take the game professional. There was one major problem, though. How would they pay for such an historic and monumental shift in the game's ethos. It would cost multi-millions.

Ironically, the one man who could provide the funds was the

same Rupert Murdoch who had launched Super League. In a nutshell, it was agreed two new competitions would be set up — the Super 12 provincial championship and the Tri-Nations Test series — and the broadcasting rights for all major matches in the three countries would be sold to Murdoch. And so it panned out, with Murdoch paying a staggering $US550 million.

But rugby union administrators were not the only ones to have concerns about the threat Super League might pose to the then amateur code. A group of rugby-loving businessmen felt equally aggrieved and put in motion their own proposal to take the game professional. The World Rugby Corporation, which pushed the game to the edge of a precipice in July and August of 1995, was born. Without going into the absolute fine points, the WRC mob, led by a Sydney lawyer Geoff Levy and former Wallaby prop and Australian team manager Ross Turnbull, designed a blueprint where rugby would have a global season. There would be regional teams set up all over the world, they would play each other in their respective areas and gradually expand the ring of competition until northern hemisphere sides were playing southern hemisphere sides at the pointy end of the pyramid in a showdown for the world provincial title. A similar system, if less grandiose, would apply to the international game. Effectively, there would be a World Cup staged every year. And a real attraction for players is that everyone would be paid, and paid handsomely.

But before we get to the fight between WRC and the administration for control of the game, it is worth going way back in 1995, to those early days of squad camps in Coolum. You will then understand why the Rebel v Establishment donnybrook was so divisive and why players were sympathetic to a breakaway movement. Essentially, they were tired of being mobile banks for the respective unions. Alan Jones first coined the phrase and it was right on the money, so to speak. The game had become more and more demanding on players' time and they wanted to be recompensed. The Australian Rugby Union did its best. Former ARU official Dick McGruther drew up contracts worth up to $80,000 for players. He got away with it claiming the payments were not for playing the game but for making time to promote the sponsors' products and to fulfill other off-field commitments. A smart man. But it was never going to be enough in the long run. I could tell that from those meetings in Coolum.

The ARU had set up a company for the Wallabies through which they could fund raise and, obviously, make a bit of extra cash. At the last camp in Coolum though, where we gathered to prepare for the May-June World Cup, there was this focus on company activities. There were a couple of players on the board, Phil Kearns and Rod McCall, and coach Bob Dwyer. It did not seem right to me, not when we had a World Cup defence coming up in a few months. So when the ARU chairman Leo Williams addressed the squad during the camp and asked for any questions, I jumped in. 'A lot has been spoken at this camp about goal setting and focus,' I started. 'Why don't the people on the board, for the next few months, give it away and focus on the things that we need to concentrate on to win the World Cup?' Money, I suggested, could be a distraction.

How does it feel to be a pariah? Let me tell you, because I could feel a few sets of eyes burning holes in me. Campo had opened his mouth again. But it was interesting that the following day — I had to return to Sydney for the opening of my first sports shop in St Ives — there was a vote held about the company and the board members staying in place. After assuring everyone it would not divert their attention from the importance of what lay ahead on the field, the players voted to keep them going. But there would be one change on the board. Bob was to be replaced by Ewen McKenzie. There had been nothing like this during the 1991 World Cup preparation where everyone just wanted to get to the UK and Ireland and get our hands on the Webb Ellis trophy. Making money never even entered our heads before that campaign. But did the sweet smell of cash have a role to play in our World Cup downfall? Not directly. It was just part of a whole raft of things, in my opinion anyway, that helped slowly but gradually derail us along the way.

As you can see, the injection of money to the game had started before Super League, which triggered WRC and finally kicked the rugby union establishment into action. I suppose, when you consider the long history of the game, professionalism did hit quickly. Revolutions usually do. But it seemed to drag on at the time. WRC did approach, either directly or through intermediaries, a number of Australian players during the World Cup, just to brief them that there was another alternative out there for the following season. I was not one of those players. I was made aware of the WRC proposal when I stayed on in South Africa after Australia was eliminated from the World Cup in the quarter finals. I met a South African lawyer who was involved in the whole thing and had a chat with him about the concept and what they wanted to do with the game, where they wanted to take it.

I was immediately impressed with the scheme. The idea of playing a mini World Cup every year would, I felt, be great for the game. So too the chance for players to be reasonably paid and for the game to be run as a professional business, not like some private boys' club. There was a different, vibrant feeling about WRC and you could sense things were going to erupt.

I was asked to set up a meeting between this same lawyer and England captain Will Carling during the last week of the tournament. The Poms were to play France in the third place playoff match in Pretoria. So I travelled up to Pretoria, spoke to Will, told him a little about the concept and said these blokes were keen to have a chat with him. I left soon after and the meeting, at some later juncture, went ahead. When I got back to Australia, we had an interstate series and a Bledisloe Cup series to play but we also had this WRC issue mushrooming behind the scenes. There would eventually be teleconference hook-ups between Australian, New Zealand and South African players so we could all pledge loyalty to the WRC cause. There were suspicions all round about what each country might do, and the conferences were designed to give everyone a feeling that, in the southern hemisphere at least, we were the Three Musketeers of the game. One for all and all for one.

Not that the establishment were sitting idly by, watching their power base crumble at pace. They were mounting a resistance, fuelled by the massive broadcasting rights deal Murdoch had signed with the Australian, South African and New Zealand rugby unions on the eve of the World Cup final in late May. That deal alone was tantamount to a declaration of professionalism, as it was intended to be. But while the three superpowers were now flush with money, they could not come out and say they were about to take the game into a new era. And, suddenly, they found their players were in danger of heading elsewhere.

The battle divided people in the rugby community. It was like a civil war. There was one ex-Wallaby, firmly in the establishment camp, who was known to be ringing around telling players: 'Don't you dare sign to go across.' Young guys in particular were starting to get terribly confused. The older players not so much.

They knew what they wanted, and many were leaning towards WRC. At one stage, I was named in a newspaper as one of the WRC organisers. I managed to get a retraction. But that just highlighted how crazy the whole thing became. Players were being offered more money than they could ever have dreamed of making. You had WRC, with some seed money from media magnate Kerry Packer, lined up against the establishment, who would have unbelievable sums coming in from Rupert Murdoch, providing they could deliver the players. This, for the players, was heaven come to earth.

I remember at a training session for NSW, one of Australia's best-known officials Phil Harry turned up and addressed the players, telling us how we had to stay with the establishment because they'd always done the right thing by the players and they had the best interests of the game at heart. I felt like telling him: 'What crap.' But I think I'd had enough of putting my foot in my mouth that year. What was clearly obvious is that the Australian Rugby Union realised it was losing control and could be sunk by a concept that I for one thought the game needed at the time.

As I have mentioned before, we had not played England between the 1991 World Cup final and the 1995 quarter-final. That was a simply ridiculous situation. The players wanted to play against each other, the fans wanted to see it, but the International Rugby Board could not get its act together on tours and schedules. Any idea that would have us playing quality Tests against quality opposition on a far more regular basis was always going to be appealing to players. There was also a frustration element tossed into the wash as well. Players had been waiting so long for a fair deal from the IRB that when someone else came along with a plump carrot, it was not difficult to win their support. And keep it. The southern hemisphere unions were trying to make inroads for their stars. But the IRB, at that stage, did not look like making any significant changes. The players were fed up.

I liked the idea of teams in the United States, where the South Africans were going to have a franchise. And right through the ranks, with players to be placed in various conferences all over the world, there would be reasonable money for all. It was going to be a revolutionary way of playing rugby in the 21st Century. There would have been exposure for rugby in countries where even today the game still struggles for profile. I don't know the ins and outs of how much money was really there or whether the scheme could have taken off, let alone flown for an extended period. But speak to players from that time and they'll tell you – as far as they were concerned, and clearly as far as the ARU was concerned – the WRC juggernaut was a fair dinkum threat to what was then a crusty establishment.

The fighting got dirty late in the piece and it soured a few relationships. Even players fell out with each other which was a real shame. I still believe WRC was a good concept and I support that with a conversation I had with an ARU official during the whole dispute. I asked him what he thought of the WRC proposal. He told me he thought it was 10 years before its time. But the dismissive tone of his voice left no doubt he was not paying the plan a compliment. Strange, though, isn't it? You would think if something was so futuristic it would be worth encouraging. And when you get it down to basics, the Super 12 and Tri-Nations tournaments did not look too far removed from some of the conference competitions WRC was spruiking. I signed up for WRC along with about 95 percent of Australia's players. But I was one of the last to sign, putting pen to paper at a Sydney law firm. Where it all fell apart for WRC was the defection of the World Cup winning Springboks back to the South African Rugby Football Union. Their captain Francois Pienaar had kept all their signed WRC contracts and was essentially their leader in these off-field dealings as well. But there was always a sense that the Boks did not have their hearts in the concept quite like the Wallabies and All Blacks. So we had these teleconferences. I went to one where other Wallabies were also in attendance. Other countries wanted to be re-assured about the Wallabies. There were rumours circulating that we had not signed. We were there to verify our support for the proposal.

But Pienaar might as well explain in his own words how everything eventually unravelled. This extract is from Edward Griffiths' book, The Captains, published in South Africa.

'After six nervous weeks of rumour and intrigue,' writes Griffiths, 'officials from News Corp made their move, through (South African rugby supremo) Louis Luyt, and offered to match whatever the Springboks had been offered by WRC. The squad met in Midrand and overwhelmingly voted to sign with SARFU, having apparently secured the best of both worlds: they had negotiated massive contracts and would keep playing within familiar structures.'

Pienaar is quoted in The Captains saying: 'We had found ourselves in a position where two groups wanted our services. We considered their respective offers and reached our decision. It was as simple as that . . . and perhaps the Australians and New Zealanders should have thought why the Murdoch organisation decided to break WRC by matching our contracts rather than theirs. It might have been because we were organised and disciplined as one unit with one voice.'

Whatever the reason, the South Africans signed with SARFU and, without the World Cup champions, WRC was dead in the water. But the attempted takeover had served a worthwhile purpose. It had basically forced the establishment to go professional. The days of amateurism, and of shamateurism, were finally over. In hindsight, if the IRB had been more relaxed about rewarding players for their time and effort after the 1991 World Cup, when the game's profile really took off, then the dramas of 1995 would never have occurred. It took WRC to make the IRB administrators realise – Australian officials already knew it – that rugby needed to step into the world of professional sport.

With WRC no longer an option, players drifted back to the establishment unions. But times had changed. Everything had changed. Relationships between players and players, and players and officials, needed mending. Not that the relationship between the administration and the players could ever be the same again. Not now that the players would be employees of the Australian Rugby Union. To a certain degree, WRC also made players more aware of their power. Certainly of their importance to the national unions. It is little wonder then that a dispute between the Rugby Union Players Association and the ARU headed to court mid-2003. Once again, the real culprit was the IRB. They had drawn up a World Cup participation agreement dismissed by RUPA as archaic and draconian. The players wanted a complete revision of the document, pointing out it did not comply with the ARU standard player contracts under which they had been employed. Push turned to shove to a bit of verbal, to a day in court in July. The Supreme Court hearing lasted just 90 minutes before the peace pipe was smoked. Players got major concessions on the participation agreement and a cash sweetener from the ARU to ensure they would not be disadvantaged by any other unresolved issue in the document. Just another example of player power. And it all came about because of WRC. Because of professionalism. The game, for the players, has come a long way when you consider the 1991 World Cup winning Wallabies received only a decanter from the ARU for our title success. And the rewards were not presented until 1993. Professionalism has certainly made an impact.

Which brings me to my own rugby career, namely my off-seasons in Italy. People always quiz me about my off handed comment, meant as a joke during an awards night, that I was rugby's first millionaire. It was, as I say, meant to be a funny. As if I would shout to the world the details of my finances. So was I a professional player? No, I was a rugby professional. There is a subtle difference. My job in Italy was to promote rugby. To promote and to coach the game. Any income was to be derived away from the playing field. Not that I worked for peanuts. But that is how the system operated. Whatever money I earned from my Italian adventures, though, pales into comparison with what it meant to me to go over there for six months of every year. I loved the culture, I loved the people and, most importantly, it gave me the chance to play the game year-round. That, for me, was the major attraction. But, all good things must come to an end.

REACHING THE CENTURY

As soon as I returned to the rooms, I took off my boots and gave them to coach Greg Smith.

Some people might call me hard to please. At the end of 1995, I had spent 14 seasons in the Wallaby side, played a record 92 Tests for Australia, and was running the risk of another axing if I tried to continue into the professional era. The closing days of amateurism, so it seemed to others, was the perfect time for me to make my exit from the game. I was not so convinced, and would not be pushed. In the end, my decision to play on was taken with one overriding goal in mind. I wanted to end my Test career on a high note. Not with an appearance off the bench in a Bledisloe Cup loss to the All Blacks. Rather than having that serve as the final chapter to my days as an international, I wanted to re-write the ending. Clearly, the prospect of playing 100 Tests had enormous appeal too. No Australian had ever managed to do it, only one overseas player — Frenchman Philippe Sella — had ever reached the landmark. And to the end of 2003, only one other player — England's Jason Leonard — had joined one of the game's most exclusive clubs. But, to be perfectly honest, the initial aim was just to get back in the starting side. That would have been achievement enough for me. I could have then walked away happy. As it turned out, 1996 was a season of opportunity beyond my expectations.

Bob Dwyer had lost the job as Australian coach and Greg Smith, my previous NSW coach, had moved into the role. It gave me some early hope of forcing my way back. I don't know for sure that Bob had written me off as a Test player. But judging by those closing months of the 1995 season, it would not have been too promising for me, I suspect, had he held on to the Wallaby post. From my perspective, a new coach meant it was time for me to set new aspirations. I convinced myself of the need to go out on a high. After putting so much of my life into the Wallaby jumper, not to mention the passion and pride that went with it, I was determined not to be remembered for being dropped at the tail end of my career. Importantly, I still believed I could do it. The self-belief outweighed the self-doubts. I knew I still had it in me. Rugby was still enjoyable, I was still clinging to it and, with these massive changes in the game sparked by professionalism, it was exciting to be part of the code's new world.

There was early encouragement from Greg Smith too, which meant a lot to me. He said to go out and play as if I was 19-years-old again — to think back and remember how carefree I had played the game when still a teenager and representing the Wallabies for the first time in 1982. Everyone knew I was coming towards the end but Smith said I should treat every game as if I was at the start of my rugby days. It was sound advice because I had become more conservative in the last couple of seasons. When you get a bit slower, you tend not to take so many risks, knowing you don't have the speed to get yourself out of any tricky situations. I had been in that limit-your-mistakes mindset and, to a certain extent, was compromising my own ideals. Throughout my career I had been known for pushing the envelope. It was that sense of adventure that allowed me to score 64 Test tries, rather than 34. After speaking to Smith, I promised myself I would bring an element of unpredictability back to my game.

Professionalism was upon us and the entire rugby landscape looked different. The former Super 10 competition involving teams from Australia, South Africa and New Zealand, was now a Super 12. Significantly, there was a new Australian team born out of the expansion. The ACT Brumbies were set up as a third Australian provincial franchise and signed a lot of fringe players from both NSW and Queensland. Guys like Brett Robinson and Troy Coker headed down from Brisbane while Owen Finegan, John Langford and David Knox made the short journey from Sydney. Long-serving Test prop Ewen McKenzie also departed the Waratahs to link up with the man who coached us at NSW in 1991-92, Rod Macqueen.

Players were signed to provincial contracts and the Australian Rugby Union had also shelled out big bucks to centrally contract some 40 players. It was the result of the WRC v Establishment war. The ARU were forced to pull out the cheque book to keep control of the game. I received a contract, it was worth $100,000. On my side of the deal, there was a lot of promotional work to be done. It was a sort of playing/ambassadorial arrangement with some bonuses there if I did make the Test side. Other players were signed to around $300,000 a season. But I wasn't going to bitch about any differences in pay. I would have done anything then to play for Australia again. Money was not the issue. But not to have been picked for Australia again would have killed me.

After Greg Smith was appointed as Wallabies coach, NSW were forced to find a new man and settled on the former Australian Schoolboys and Gordon coach Chris Hawkins. He introduced a new word to the rugby vocabulary — 'rotation'. It was about giving all players a chance to show their wares. There were 11 rounds of the Super 12 competition plus finals so it was, in effect, a mini-season on its own. We opened the tournament in South Africa, playing the Western Stormers in Cape Town. We won the match and prepared to head north, up to altitude for a clash with Northern Transvaal. I had played against the Stormers but was rotated out of the team for the match in Pretoria. Chris told me he wanted to give another player a chance. This was professionalism, the new era, and I would just have to go with the flow. I went to training that day determined to put everything into it and in no way showing how upset I was at missing out on the Northern Transvaal game. I figured I needed to play consistently, and consistently well, to force a spot back in the Wallabies team.

Word got around early that the Australian selectors were choosing a 'best of' Australian side every week from the Super 12 matches played by NSW, Queensland and the Brumbies. As the tournament progressed, I tried to be objective about my form and figured the season had gone reasonably well, despite being an early victim of rotation. But the Northern Transvaal game would be the only Super 12 match I would not start. As I mentioned earlier, I had to re-invent my game to be truly effective again, and Hawkins was happy to give me a roving commission. It meant I could bob up anywhere in the backline if I could sense an opportunity. It worked well. I would come into five-eighth on occasions to have the defence second guessing. While my pace might not have been quite where it had been in previous years, the footwork was still there. I could still beat a man one on one.

Fortunately, when the international season rolled around, the Australian selectors had been satisfied with my efforts. Greg Smith and his panel believed I still had something to give to the team and that was enormously satisfying for me. Sure, to play 100 Tests was an ultimate goal, but if I had only made the side once in 1996, I would have been happy. I just wanted to go out the right way — putting form on the board at provincial level and being considered good enough to warrant a wing spot in the starting side. That happened when my name was read out for the opening Test of the season against Wales. The match was played at Ballymore in

Brisbane. I was on one wing and NSW teammate Alistair Murdoch was on the other for what would be his second and final Test in Wallaby colours. We won 56-25 with Alistair scoring a try and a young Joe Roff also grabbing one, from the outside centre position. Pat Howard was the five-eighth and three players made their debuts in the pack — flanker Owen Finegan, hooker Marco Caputo and prop Richard Harry. There were 10 changes to the side that had been beaten in the last Test of 1995 by the All Blacks. When I looked at that statistic, I took even more pride from my selection. Eleven months earlier I had been virtually washed up, and reliant on injury just to get a start on the reserves bench. Almost a year on, I was back in a revamped run-on side.

There was a definite changing of the guard at the time. In the backline for that first Test, Tim Horan and I were the only real faces of experience. It was my 93rd Test and Horan's 39th. Next on the caps list was Matthew Burke at fullback with 12. The rookie factor was emphasised even further a fortnight later when we played Wales in the second Test. George Gregan was dropped as halfback as Sam Payne made his debut at the scrumbase. Another to play his first Test in a 42-3 hammering of the Welsh was a young speedster from Queensland, Ben Tune. He was still in his teens, like I had been in 1982, and he looked something special. He was exceptionally quick and had very good footwork. You could see from the start he was destined to be with the Wallabies for a long time to come. A third player to debut that day, off the bench as a fullback replacement, was Stephen Larkham.

It's strange to look back now and see how many of that successful 1999 World Cup team actually got their start under Greg Smith. For all the criticism he endured, compared to the praise heaped on Macqueen, Greg did give Owen Finegan, Richard Harry, Ben Tune, Stephen Larkham, David Giffin and

Andrew Blades their starts in Test football in 1996. He also blooded Matt Cockbain and Toutai Kefu in 1997, before being squeezed into a resignation that allowed Macqueen to take on the job. Not one player in the starting team for the 1999 World Cup final against France had actually been 'discovered' by Macqueen. But it should not be forgotten he was the mastermind behind a positional switch for Stephen Larkham — moving the Brumbies ace from fullback to five-eighth — which made such a crucial difference to the Wallabies' success.

Back to 1996, though, and the pressure was on from the outset of the international season. Greg Smith had this infuriating approach of refusing to tell people whether they were in or out of the side. He would keep his cards close to his chest, rarely give any hints, and leave players to read in the papers or watch on television if they would be on board for the next Test. A good example came after the Test with Canada which followed the two-game series against Wales. We crushed the Canadians 74-9 and I scored my first Test try in almost 14 months. The last time I had crossed the line was May 6, 1995, three weeks before the World Cup had opened. I grabbed two against Argentina in Sydney that day, only to go scoreless for my next six Tests. Again, I digress. After the Canadian Test the Wallabies were heading to New Zealand for the first ever Tri-Nations showdown between the two countries. NSW prop Andrew Heath had made his debut in the Canada win and was thinking he was on his way to the Shaky Isles in what would be the biggest moment of his career. But watching the television the night the team was announced, Heath was left heartbroken. His name was not on the list of squad members. No warning from the team management. No phone call to prepare him for the disappointment. And Heath came from the same Sydney club, Eastern Suburbs, as the Australian coach. It was just the Greg Smith way. It was bizarre and players found it not only disconcerting but quite stressful as well. I think behind all the mystery, that was the idea. To keep players guessing, to keep them on their toes, to not allow them to sink into that comfort zone where they consider themselves Test selection certainties week after week. Under Greg Smith, no one had that luxury. It actually makes for an interesting comparison with someone like Rod Macqueen. Smith favoured the caged animal approach. Don't tame the beasts. Just feed them when they need feeding. He was hoping, against hope in the end, that the atmosphere of uncertainty and edginess would be turned into positive, adrenalin-packed performance. Macqueen went the opposite way. He was a stickler for selection consistency, believing players would be at their best if they felt secure in the side. In the long run, I suppose it depends on the individual player as to how he reacts to those two environments. In hindsight, you would have to say the players who wore the Wallabies jumper from 1996-1999 blossomed more under the Macqueen approach.

I never played under Macqueen at the Australian level but I did find the selection quirks of Greg Smith — and he became a very good friend of mine — rather draining. You had to sit there each week unsure whether you were going to be part of the side. Clearly, Greg was trying to find his best combinations, and was prepared to undergo extensive on-field research to get the answers. But all that chopping and changing did have an effect on overall results. Combinations were never quite what they should have been and, in the background, you could hear players starting to question what was happening. That is always a bad sign because once a seed of discontent is planted, it usually grows. By the end of 1997, the player opposition to Smith was bordering on rebellion.

But the Smith coaching reign must always be put in perspective. He was diagnosed with a brain tumour not long after leaving the job. It had clearly affected his thinking for some time. On his final trip with the Wallabies, to South Africa in 1997 for a Tri-Nations Test against the South Africans in Pretoria, he became a virtual recluse. A lot of good people were extremely worried about him. Greg hardly came out of his room. He would sit there, in almost darkness. He ate nothing but toasted sandwiches and the perception was he was buckling under the pressure. The perception was wrong. Greg Smith was a very sick man. It is a tragedy to think his last Test in charge of the side was a record-breaking thumping from the Boks. It was 61-22 and the Wallabies that day were appalling. They played as if they didn't care, and there can be no greater insult paid to somebody wearing a Wallaby jersey.

Care factor is something I had in bucketloads in 1996. I was nervously awaiting the announcement of that first Test team to play Wales. I had been in Queanbeyan to see mum and dad and was driving home listening to the radio. But the naming of the side had been delayed. The team was to be announced late afternoon. Damn. More stress. When finally it did come out I had this overwhelming feeling of relief. If I hadn't been selected, retirement would have been forced upon me. That was the reality I faced. So I was breathing a little easier that night. I wasn't ready to go just yet.

The onset of professionalism had changed a lot in the game. Everything you ate was monitored, your strength and skinfold measurements were constantly under review. It was no longer about outright ability. The physical preparation was taking hold. Under Greg Smith, there was also this new cut-throat selection policy. He went a horses for courses path on occasions, selecting various players for various oppositions. He also had trust in a few of his former NSW players and elevated them to the Test side, only to discover there are some major differences between provincial and international rugby. A few of the new faces were unable to make the jump and did not last into the Macqueen era. There was a high turnover of players but Greg was trying to find the best combinations.

He also desperately wanted to beat the All Blacks. It was an obsession for him. He had tasted success against New Zealand as the Sydney coach in 1992. When the All Blacks toured here that year they travelled out to Penrith and got beaten. It was a major achievement for Greg as a coach but a victory he was never able to emulate in two seasons at the Wallabies helm. But the desire was there every week we lined up. In earlier games in 1996, against Wales and Canada, the focus of the year was still to beat New Zealand. Everything was aimed at downing the Kiwis. When we did get around to playing them for the first time that season, it was a complete disaster. The All Blacks belted us 43–6, a record defeat for the Wallabies.

It was also the first Test as skipper for John Eales against a major powerhouse. He made up for it, and then some, over the next few years. But for Greg Smith that Wellington defeat was the first of five in succession he would suffer at the hands of New Zealand. Not that he lacked any desire to avenge the pummelling. If anything, it made him even more determined to work out a way of beating them. And we should have delivered next time around, at Suncorp Stadium in Brisbane. We were in front until the death when their centre Frank Bunce scored in the corner. Our hopes of victory had been stolen away and Greg Smith was as gutted, perhaps more so, than any of the Wallaby players.

Between those two All Black losses, however, was a sensational win over the Springboks. There had been some changes made from the Wellington disaster. A new halves combination of George Gregan and Pat Howard replaced Sam Payne and Scott Bowen. Daniel Manu had come in for Owen Finegan in the backrow and Andrew Heath for Richard Harry at prop. It was a backs to the wall effort and one we hoped would signal the start of a new era for Australian rugby. If we had knocked off the All Blacks in Brisbane a week later, things would have been looking good. But we fell in the final seconds and compounded the feeling of lost opportunity by going down 25-19 to the Boks in Bloemfontein in our final Tri-Nations Test. South African five-eighth Joel Stransky, whose dropped goal in extra time had won the World Cup for the Springboks the previous year, kicked us off the park. They led 16-3 at halftime and, while we threw everything at them in the second half, we just came up short. Ben Tune scored a try, Burke kicked a few goals and fulltime arrived too quickly. The end result for the series was one win from four games. We really should have done so much better. We could easily have won three of those Tests, with the first loss to the All Blacks our only comprehensive defeat.

The Bloemfontein Test left me on 99 Test appearances. I had played all seven for the year to that point, despite the changes going on elsewhere. Along with Matthew Burke at fullback, I was the only constant selection in the backline.

Returning home, I played club rugby with Randwick, played in a winning grand final side as we kicked Warringah butt, and waited for the Wallabies squad to be selected for the tour to Italy, the UK and Ireland. My name was there and suddenly, having twice decided over the past 18 months not to take the retirement option, I felt justified for staying on. This would be my swansong trip for Australia and the perfect ending I could hardly have dreamed of when dumped from the team to play the All Blacks in July the previous year.

It was even more amazing to think my 100th Test would be against Italy, the country of my father's birth and my home for six months of every year for the best part of a decade while I enjoyed the life associated with never-ending rugby seasons.

The Test against Italy was staged in Padova, where I had played for three years from 1984 to 1986. It is a town in the north of the country and is, in fact, quite near to my dad's birthplace. He was born and raised in Vicenza, some 20 minutes away by car. The Campese family still has roots there and the Test, for me, was like a long-running family reunion. In the build-up to the game, I had uncles and aunts and cousins come to visit me in the team hotel. My father's brothers and sisters came along to the game, there was more than 20 family in the end and, on a personal note, it really made for a memorable night. It was the first time most of them had ever seen me play. Unfortunately, they were not treated to vintage performances, by myself or the rest of the Wallabies. The Italians stuck it to us and, in some respects, we were lucky to get away with a 40-18 scoreline. Tim Horan, who had started the season at inside centre, played that night on the wing, and scored one of our four tries.

After the game, in typically Italian fashion, the celebrations were underway. I was not too fussed about attending the official match function when my parents and their families and friends of their families were there to be entertained. It was a real sense of achievement to join Philippe Sella as the only Test centurion and extremely satisfying to have family and friends around me when I reached the milestone. It was a great honour and one I treasured given the mentally draining circumstances of the previous 18 months.

But from the high of reaching my century, the floor collapsed. This sacking thing was becoming a little too frequent for my liking. After the Italian Test, Greg Smith dropped me from the side to play Scotland at Murrayfield. Tim Horan and Joe Roff were named on the wings. But the urge to ride out the tour, content in the knowledge I had reached 100 Tests and had those never to be forgotten memories in Italy to tide me over, was again not enough. I realised there were just two weeks left of my Wallabies career and I was determined — for one last time — to win back a spot in the side.

There was a midweek match against Munster in Ireland after I had missed out on selection for the Scottish Test. I turned in one of my better performances for quite some time, scoring two tries, setting up another and perhaps defending like I'd never defended before. While I missed the Ireland Test in Dublin as well, I was back for the last Test on tour against Wales. John Eales was missing through injury and Tim Horan had taken over the captaincy. He had also returned to inside centre, opening up the opportunity for me to grab the other wing spot. Horan was paired in the centres that day with Jason Little. They were the third midfield partnership used in four Tests. And, in the second-row, David Giffin made his Test debut.

Knowing this would bring down the curtain on my Test career, I was determined to go out with a good performance. But it was not the easiest of Test matches. We were travelling comfortably at halftime, 18-6 in front, but when Gareth Thomas intercepted a George Gregan pass during the second half and raced away to score, the Welsh were on a roll. We were dominating territorially but not capitalising and when Jonathan Davies, an old mate of mine, banged over a couple of penalties to go with the Thomas try, the Welsh hit the front 19-18. Matt Burke landed a penalty goal to give us a two-point advantage and then a penalty try in the dying stages finally killed off the Welsh resistance. We had shown plenty of spirit in the end to get across the line. And I was relieved, I can tell you. A loss to Wales was not the way I saw the farewell tour ending. We copped plenty of flak from the media after our win. It was nothing new for that tour. We copped it from all quarters the whole way. Yet that 1996 Wallabies side, under the much-maligned Greg Smith, went through an entire European tour undefeated. It is something those of us who were there still hold dear.

So my last Test had been played. And at that wonderful rugby cathedral of Cardiff Arms Park. It is difficult to convey just what it meant to come through that last period of my international career and have everything fall into place as if some magical hand was putting together the jigsaw. I had fought back after being dumped for the All Blacks. I had managed to force my way back into the side in 1996, and keep my spot for eight games running. I had reached my Test century in Italy of all places, not far from where my dad was born, and my last Test, number 101, was played at possibly the greatest ground in the world. Certainly the venue I have fondest memories of after the standing ovation the crowd there gave me in 1988. It was during the Barbarians match, and my attacking game was about as finely-tuned as it had ever been. I had made a couple of really good runs and, after setting up one try and scoring another, the crowd got to their feet and clapped me back to halfway. I'll never forget it.

There was also a Barbarians match to be played to conclude that tour of 1996. This would be my final appearance in the Australian jumper and I was fortunate enough to score a try in the game. Hooker Michael Foley slipped me a pass and I went across in the tackle of South African five-eighth Joel Stransky. In the week before the match, I had been invited to play for the Barbarians and would, if I could, have accepted the offer. Only a select few have ever been chosen to play for the Barbarians against their own country and I thought 'what a way to go out'. But team management were not keen on the idea and that was the end of it. I bowed to their wishes and, in the final wash-up, it did not really bother me too much. I was satisfied with what I had achieved in 1996. The Barbarians game was not a maker or breaker in terms of my international career.

There were certainly no ill feelings from me towards Greg Smith over his edict that I play in the Wallaby gold rather than the black and white stripes of the Barbarians. I hope I proved that to him after the game. It was fun playing in the match and an honour to be accorded a lap of honour at the end of it. I'm not an overly emotional person, so there were no tears in the eye or anything like that. But I did want to make one gesture, in the privacy of the dressing room later, to mark the occasion. As soon as I returned to the rooms, I took off my boots and gave them to Greg Smith. It was, in my own way, a show of thanks. Greg had backed my talent in 1996 when so many others had given up on me. And, after that game, we became better mates than we had ever been when I was playing the game.

His coaching record, I feel, is unfairly judged at times. He was trying to build a new team after the disasters of the 1995 World Cup. Sure, he chopped and changed his personnel, but he set in train the Test careers of several players who would be crucial to the next World Cup campaign, a triumphant one, in 1999. It must also be taken into account that Greg, especially in his final year, was a very sick man. He was a good man, a good Australian and, after his passing in 2002, he is still greatly missed.

THE MALAYSIAN CAMPAIGN

It was quite humbling to have the Master Blaster tell you he had always wanted to meet you.

When eventually I retired from the game, the decision came to me in a flash. In a flash of lightning, if the truth be known. I was at the offices of David Campese Management. It was a Tuesday night, in the middle of the 1999 winter, and I was packing up to leave work, ready to make the drive across town for another Randwick club training session. I was 36, approaching 37, years of age and, as I looked out of the window at the rain pelting down, I thought about the trek to Granville Park, the ground they call 'Death Valley', to play Parramatta that weekend. There was just no appeal to it anymore. The fire had all but burned out. I knew I would miss the game. You can't be married to a sport for as long as I was without having severe withdrawal symptoms. But I also realised it was time to move on.

At that moment, I made my decision to quit. Just like that. I picked up the telephone, called Jeff Sayle, the club coach at Randwick and a great friend of mine, and told him I wouldn't be coming to training that night. He wanted to know if I was 'crook'. I told him no, I had decided to retire. To be honest, I hadn't really thought much about hanging up the boots in the weeks leading up to that point. There had been quite a few reflective times down through the years when I considered giving the game away. I remember in 1991, after the World Cup, thinking I might retire from rugby and become a golf resort ambassador in Italy. There was a small window of opportunity there. Fortunately, I didn't scramble through it and came to my senses when Wallabies coach Bob Dwyer urged a few of us to stay on after the Twickenham triumph so we could tackle the next great challenge — the Springboks in South Africa in 1992. That was the first time leaving the game had entered my mind. Almost eight years later I was finally ready to do it. I had been ambling along in club footy that season, running around at Randwick under coach John Maxwell, a guy I had played international Sevens with back in the early 1980's. But when the rain was tumbling down that night, my enthusiasm just could not be re-ignited. When that happens you really have no choice.

There was also a sense that my time had passed. The attitude of the new age players bothered me a little. Most of them playing at club level, and I'm not referring specifically to Randwick here, appeared to be in it not for the team, but in how they could benefit and launch themselves to the next level. I am not making a judgment call in saying that, it is merely an observation. This is the age of professionalism and money. Players want Super 12 contracts. Simply pulling on a club jumper, for most of them, does not seem to be enough. Perhaps Bob Dwyer could set them straight. As he used to say, worry about doing things right and keeping the team pattern. The scoreboard will look after itself. It is the same in terms of selection. You cannot sacrifice the best interests of the team to further your own individual ambitions. Play selfishly and you risk bringing everyone down, including yourself.

Aggression levels too had increased significantly. And I don't just mean the type of hard-nosed approach fostered by improved fitness and power conditioning. I found young guys willing to deliver cheap shots to established players, as if it was a way of earning their wings. Or perhaps impressing someone. I won't go into details, but I copped a few and it annoyed me enormously. You are out there to play the game, not to indulge in some vulgar macho points-scoring.

The game plans had been revised as well. Even at Randwick, where the running rugby ethos had been bred into generations of players, that high-risk had been pulled back. The good old days had definitely gone, so I might as well go with them. I think it's a crying shame for the game at club level to see that sort of thing happening. It's also a disappointment to me to see the way some young players and their parents carry on. Money spawns new attitudes, and a new breed of opportunists. One of the worst is the overbearing parent. Some of them actually ring clubs when little Johnny finishes his schooling and want to know how much the club is prepared to pay if their 'superstar' son comes down to play. What they should be doing is picking the right club for little Johnny so he can develop into the best footballer he can be. That is ultimately how he will benefit, both from a rugby perspective and financially. These quick grabs for cash do no-one any good. Being paid to play does not carry with it a cast-iron guarantee that you will be tagged a good player. That has to be earned out in the middle, not by your bank account. Some of the new kids on the block, and their parents, should take the tip.

While I had played my last Test in 1996, against Wales in Cardiff, there was still plenty of representative rugby ahead of me. In 1997, I played for NSW under the new Waratahs coach Matt Williams. This was a guy who lasted three years then got shoved aside when the Waratahs failed to make the Super 12 semi-finals – the ultimate yardstick for any provincial coach. Still, Williams managed to carve out a name for himself as an astute tactician, winning praise for his coaching success at the Irish province

Leinster. He was promoted to coach the Irish A team and did such a good job there he was recruited by Scotland. He will now coach their national team when Ian McGeechan stands down after the World Cup. Not bad for the bloke in the baseball cap who girls always thought looked like a young Robert Redford. Couldn't see it myself, but there you go.

The 1997 season also involved Sevens representation and a trip to the World Cup in Hong Kong. I thought it disgraceful that the Australian Rugby Union would not send its best team. But the blame cannot be laid at their feet alone. The egotist coaches at Super 12 level did not want to jeopardise their Super 12 prospects by releasing any of their star players. So we took a team minus the top players in Australia. The ARU had the view that Australia should target winning a Super 12 title, via the Brumbies, Waratahs or Reds, rather than pooling the best of their resources for a tilt at the World Cup Sevens crown. Just another example of the professional age. It was the Super 12 competition that helped pay the bills through broadcasting rights. It was also the nursery for our Test players, although I would argue against such a narrow vision of the game. Sevens can be a great stepping stone, not only to Super 12 but also to Test football. How many people during 2003, in the countdown to the World Cup, were bemoaning the lack of attacking skill in the Wallabies backline? There were claims we had lost our flair and footwork. Give all those guys a full season of Sevens in the International Rugby Board series, and see how rapidly their footwork improves and how much attacking brilliance they bring back to the 15-a-side game. My views on this are nothing new. But when the Australian team was winning everything in sight, no-one stopped to listen. I challenge anyone these days to argue against my assertions. Sevens should be seen as a great opportunity to blood young guys into international rugby, or to hone the skills of established players making the way back from injury or needing some remedial work on their attacking techniques.

Which ever you look at it, Sevens rugby has been the poor cousin in Australia for too many years. Even in 1998, when assembling a squad to go to the Kuala Lumpur Commonwealth Games, the best players were declared unavailable. I can tell you, without any question, that several topline Test players did want the opportunity to savour the Games experience. But it was not to be. The 1997 Sevens coach, Jeff Miller, had moved on at the end of that season to become an assistant to Rod Macqueen at the Wallabies. Macqueen had succeeded Greg Smith as Test coach for the end of season tour to Argentina and the UK.

Replacing Miller at the helm of the Australian Sevens team was Mark Ella. A great choice too. Here was a guy who knew precisely how the modified form of the game should be played. He was a wizard at it himself in the early 1980's, when Australia struck its only rich vein of Sevens success.

The 1998 season certainly started in bizarre fashion. I was still part of the Waratahs squad when we headed out of Sydney for a pre-season camp at a luxurious resort a couple of hours north in the Hunter Valley. Matt Williams was still the NSW coach and he spoke to me about changing my contribution to the team. He wanted me to become an impact player. Essentially, it meant coming off the bench at a crucial time in the second half with the aim of sparking the Waratahs attack. I do wonder about the modern twist on tactics. Is an impact player just a complimentary term for someone you don't think can last 80 minutes. Surely anyone coming off the bench in the final 20 minutes of a game should make an 'impact', given they have fresh legs to use against tiring opponents. It was like the Chris Hawkins 'rotational' policy in the first Super 12 season of 1996. You weren't dropped by Hawkins, you were rotated out of the side. But the explanation never eased the pain on the guy who was shown the door.

All these new-fangled buzzwords leave me cold. But in 1998, when we embarked on our pre-season camp, we actually spent a good deal of time sitting around trying to come up with a trigger word for the season. If we were in trouble during a match or just in need of a kick start, someone would simply shout this word and it would re-focus us on the job at hand. No, I'm not joking. This was a priority. So, what word did we come up with . . . I'm still trying to remember. That's how much impact it made on me. No wonder I was being rotated out of the side to be a stormtrooper off the bench. This, I swear, is modern rugby.

When Williams spoke to me about my role change within the squad, the Australian Rugby Union came along and sought my signature on a twofold basis. They wanted me to act as an ARU ambassador for the code, which meant travelling around trying to raise the game's profile throughout Australia. They also wanted me to take a more active role in the Sevens. And I like the sound of that. It was terrific being back in the Australian jumper and visiting almost as many different countries in one season as I visited in my entire Test career. We played Uruguay, Argentina, France, Hong Kong, Fiji, and made a trip to Israel to play in the Holy Sevens. It was a sensational experience for me, let alone the young guys brought into the team, like speedster Brendan Williams and fellow flyer, Ricky Nalatu from Queensland. These whirlwind visits were all part of the IRB World Series Sevens circuit and, for us, it was all valuable tournament experience leading into the Commonwealth Games in Malaysia. Having Mark there as coach was also a major plus. He was so technically aware when it came to Sevens and we always knew what each other was thinking when it came to tactics. I might have been getting older and slower, but the brain still worked pretty well, and to have Mark there was great. I felt as though we were, as we always had been, on the same wavelength.

While the Sevens became my real goal for the year, I was still involved in a limited capacity with the Waratahs. I remember coming off the bench against the Canterbury Crusaders in Christchurch, in a game where All Blacks halfback Justin Marshall snapped his Achilles tendon. I spoke to Matt Williams later and suggested if he wanted to use me as an impact player, then there was little point bringing me into the game on the wing. Basically, I suggested he use me somewhere else, with fullback or five-eighth the obvious alternatives. I could see no point in being injected into the game, to use your attacking skills, and then to be given the ball on just one occasion. Surely that defeats the whole purpose. My only other appearance for the Waratahs that season was again as a replacement against the South African franchise the Northern Bulls. The match was played outside Pretoria and from the outset it was a game to forget. Our team bus broke down and, for me, there was worse to follow on the field. I was sent out there in my impact role and made a bit of a run. But in offloading the ball I threw an intercept pass. I turned to see the Bulls scoring at the other end of the field. I certainly made an impact in that one. I don't know who was more upset later, me or Tiaan Strauss, the former Springboks skipper who had moved to Australia and was playing for the Waratahs, later for Australia. He loved nothing better, once he had made the move from one side of the world to the other, to grind South African teams into the dirt. Especially if it happened to be their own soil.

After my failed venture into impact play my concentration

returned to the Sevens and the ultimate campaign in Malaysia. Not that Mark Ella or myself had any illusions about the job ahead of us. Once again the ARU was not as supportive as we had hoped they might be of the Commonwealth Games program. Surely, at that level, it was worth sending our best possible team. If it meant taking a batch of Test stars and finding no room for me, I would have been happy with that. Disappointed but respectful that Australia was doing all in its power to win the first Sevens gold medal up for grabs at a Commonwealth Games. As I mentioned, we had been to numerous parts of the globe in the lead-up and, at the Paris Sevens, won the title. This was cause for celebration, given the last time Australia had won a Sevens tournament was back in 1988 in Hong Kong. I happened to be part of that side too.

It was refreshing to play with these young guys ten years later and restore Australia, albeit briefly, to the top of the Sevens tree. They were so enthusiastic, so determined to do well. They were an absolute credit to themselves and the country and it was criminal that they hardly received any accolades at home for what they achieved. The Paris Sevens win had been one of my most enjoyable experiences in years.

When the Commonwealth Games rolled around, we did not have much in the way of top-shelf talent. Jimmy Williams from the ACT Brumbies would make his debut for the Wallabies the following June against Ireland in Brisbane. Marc Stcherbina rose to Australia A level before taking a bait to go overseas. But there were no current Test players in the side, only a collection of young and talented players who became a tight knit team. There was also a certain self-belief there even though, in my heart of hearts, I knew we did not have the big guns to match the All Blacks artillery lining up for New Zealand. Where the ARU decided not to strip Super 12 teams of their best talent, the New Zealand Rugby Union made an unashamed bid to win Commonwealth gold. The great Jonah Lomu was included in their side, along with the electrifying Fijian-born flyer Joeli Vidiri, who happens to be a cousin of the latest All Blacks wing sensation Joe Rokocoko. Test fullback Christian Cullen was also in their side. It was a red hot Kiwi combination. The Fijians too were at full strength. They had the irrepressible Waisale Serevi, one of the truly great Sevens players of all time, leading their challenge. The Canterbury Crusaders winger Marika Vunibaka was another standout in the white jumper.

Even now when I speak at rugby functions, I will ask people to name three players from our 1998 Commonwealth Games Sevens team. Very few have ever managed to do it. There was Jim Williams and Marc Stcherbina and the flyers Brendan Williams, Ricky Nalatu and Matt Dowling. There was Tyron Mandrusiak from Queensland, hard-working forward Cameron Pither from NSW and Richard Graham, who has since gone on to skipper the national Sevens side. I was honoured to take on the captaincy in 1998 and when most of our guys, with the odd exception, were club players rather than internationals or established Super 12 stars, it was a case of trying to be mother hen to the brood.

To look back then and realise we won a medal is, I think, an astonishing achievement. We finished on top of our pool and beat England comfortably in the quarter finals. We had to play Fiji in the semi-finals and they had had the wood on us for some time. It proved again to be the case in our showdown to decide which country would go into the final. The Fijians though were outclassed in the decider by a star-studded New Zealand side while we collected the bronze medal after toppling Samoa in the third place playoff match. It had been an exciting ride, for me as well as the young blokes. We had been to Singapore before the Games, to get acclimatised to the heat. And when we arrived in Kuala Lumpur, the buzz about the athletes' village had to be experienced to be believed. We were like kids in a lolly shop. Everywhere you looked there were wall to wall sports stars. I can only imagine how much more overwhelming an Olympic athletes' village would be, if this was only the best of the Commonwealth. Our guys were elated to be there. It was the Games when cricket and netball had also been included as team sports, and I don't know how well that went down with some of our prominent individual sportspeople.

Perhaps they were not in favour of high-profile team sports being included in the program. Whether they felt those sports, like rugby and cricket, had their own major championships and should not be trying to muscle in on their Games experience, or whether they did not take kindly to the publicity the team sports generated, I'm not sure. What I do know is, we didn't get much in the way of a welcome from several Australians within the village. I must say I found the swimmers quite aloof and cool. Mind you, I was 36. Most of them were probably still in their teens. The words generation gap do spring to mind. But it was still off-putting, even intimidating to walk into Matt Dunn's room at the complex and have all these eyes staring at you as if to say 'what the hell are you doing here?' Dunney is on our books at Campese Management. He is a fine swimmer and a terrific guy. I am sure he would defend his swimming mates to the hilt. More than likely he would accuse me of misreading them to the extreme. As they say on Jerry Springer: 'whatever'. I know how they made me feel. I find that sort of attitude disappointing.

But it was not about to dampen my spirits. I headed down for breakfast one morning and got the chance to meet Sir Vivian

Richards, the great West Indian batsman. I have always followed cricket with interest and Viv had been one of my favourites. It was an absolute buzz to be introduced to him and to have him recognise me. That would have been, no doubt, the result of the time he had spent in England during his career. But still, it was quite humbling to have the Master Blaster tell you he had always wanted to meet you.

Meal times were like feeding sessions at the zoo. You would just stand and gawp. Curtly Ambrose was over there, towering over a couple of tiny gymnasts. The 100 metre sprinters would strut by, their finely muscled frames smaller than what I expected. It was just a fabulous experience.

We even got the chance one day for a game of impromptu cricket with Steve Waugh's team. Just a hit around out the back of the accommodation block. Us against them. I remember hitting one four, but will not name the bowler concerned. Given my ordinary cricket history, I don't want to kill off his career. The South African cricketers were a nice bunch as well. I met and chatted with Shaun Pollock. But one guy I should have sought out was Dale Benkenstein. He would, five years later, become my brother-in-law. Not that I knew him at the time. Small world isn't it?

The South Africans won the cricket gold medal, downing Australia in the final. In the rugby it was New Zealand who walked away as champions. Not that we walked away too down in the mouth. After taking out the bronze medal we were as happy as Larry. The next day, with smiles across the dials, we said hello to any Australian we passed in the village. There was one female swimmer who walked by and did not even respond to our calls of greeting. I sent the guys back to their rooms to apply the deodorant. For mine, her reaction, or lack of it, is not the Australian way. Still, what can you do?

All in all, it was an eye-opening experience, to attend a Commonwealth Games as a competitor. Even to study how other sports operate at that level was quite intriguing. The athletes involved in team sports appeared, to a great extent, to be the more friendly and outgoing. Maybe it was because the pressure to perform fell on the shoulders of them and their mates. The expectation of individuals could not be so easily diluted. There was the thrill of the opening ceremony. The guys were laughing that the only way to get their photos in the paper would be to stand next to me. They ribbed me about being the old man of the team, but the spirit in that side was great. It was a pleasure to call those guys my teammates.

In the end, my last game of Sevens for Australia, like my last game for NSW, was as a replacement. Going into the bronze medal game, I urged Mark Ella to select the young kids. Give them a chance to really enjoy themselves in a packed stadium on a glorious sunny KL afternoon. While spending most of the tournament in the playmaking role, I did not run out against Samoa until the last couple of minutes. And the rookies had done their job well. All that was left was for Brendan Williams to score a try, me to kick the goal, and for us to pick up our bronze medals.

An extra motivation to win that match against Samoa had been provided by Steve Loader, a close mate of mine and a Qantas executive. He promised to fly the rugby boys back in business class if we finished in the medals. What more enticement did they need?

Four years later, at the Manchester Commonwealth Games, the Australian team missed out on a podium finish. And if the Australian Rugby Union intends to send teams to major events such as that, then they should be prepared to send their best side.

It is the only fair thing to do, for both the players and the credibility of the game. If we fielded our number one side, including Test players, all the time, of course we would be in the top two or three Sevens teams in the world. I believe Sevens should be retained as a Commonwealth Games sport, because the format lends itself to a brief competition. Using Kuala Lumpur as a guide, it is also hugely popular. We had a full stadium in Malaysia, which is hardly a hot bed of rugby union. But the Sevens game has developed a growing following in Asia. That is not surprising. In the 15-man game, power and strength are necessary assets. A lot of Asian countries would struggle to match the likes of Australia, New Zealand and South Africa, not only on a skills level, but physically. At least in Sevens, the size factor is, to a great extent, removed from the equation. So Sevens should be given a permanent and respectable position within our game. It is from there that rugby union can launch a bid for more profile and to attract more players in minor nations, particularly through Asia and Africa.

In Australia, we have work to do as well. In 1998 we knew we would struggle when it came to playing against New Zealand and Fiji. We had a great management team with Mark Ella as coach and Dick McGruther as one of the most efficient managers I think I've ever come into contact with in an Australian team environment. But to be a force in the future we must select our best side. In 1983, when I debuted with the Australian Sevens team at Hong Kong, the team included Mark and Glen Ella, Brendan Moon, Peter Lucas and Gary Pearse, with John Maxwell as captain coach. Now they were the days.

COACHING DISCARD

I always felt Macqueen was a restrictive sort of coach. He was not a risk-taker, not one for adventure or thrills.

The first question came out of the blue.

'How do you get on with Rod Macqueen?'

Former Test flanker Jeff Miller was looking at me across a desk at Australian Rugby Union headquarters in North Sydney. It was late 1998 and I was pitching for a job. The Australian Sevens coaching position had been widely advertised. The former five-eighth great Mark Ella had decided to give the role away after taking the Australian team to a bronze medal at the Commonwealth Games in Kuala Lumpur. I had captained the side, at the age of 35, and while aging legs were not going to carry me through further playing campaigns at that level, the prospect of contributing in a hands-on way, through coaching, really appealed. Sevens is a form of the game with which I have always felt an affinity and, without banging my drum too loudly, I believe I have an understanding of its nuances that few people in this country could match. So I applied for the coaching role vacated by Ella.

Some time later I was invited to HQ for an interview. I presumed, in my naivety, the process would take this course — they ask for my Sevens credentials, for my plans for the team, for my tactical insights, for the coaching philosophies and training regimes I would want to introduce. Basically, I thought they would want to know what I knew about Sevens and how I thought I could improve the Australian team. But when question number one was tossed on the table, it might as well have been a rattle snake.

'How do you get on with Rod Macqueen?'

Miller was the head of the ARU's High Performance Unit. A man who held some serious weight in the ARU, probably second in command under managing director John O'Neill. Miller, a former Test teammate who now, in my eyes, had the power to hire and fire. He was a mini-kingmaker.

So how do you answer a question like that? Do I get on with the national coach, a man who had come into the job the previous year, replacing Greg Smith, and who would stay on as Wallaby boss until 2001 and the Lions series in Australia? Everyone who read my newspaper columns knew I had reservations about Macqueen's coaching style. He had coached me at NSW for a couple of seasons, including the World Cup year of 1991 when the Waratahs went through the year undefeated. We belted Wales in Sydney on a record breaking afternoon, that was probably the highlight, but I always felt Macqueen was a restrictive sort of coach. He was not a risk-taker, not one for adventure or thrills. You only have to look back at the teams he selected. A bloke by the name of Jim Allen was his five-eighth for quite a while at NSW. Lovely bloke Jim. Good footballer too. But his forte was carrying the ball forward and back to the pack. He was a crash-ball midfielder moved to No.10. It was what Macqueen wanted. A team that could hold on to possession. He did not want to risk surrendering possession by taking gambles in the backline, and Allen fitted the mould for him perfectly. We broke out of course against Wales, running in try after try. But let's be honest. That Welsh team, which ended up imploding when players fought amongst themselves at the after-Test dinner in Brisbane, was an awful advertisement for the once great rugby nation. They had no idea on the field. They could not tackle, were clueless in attack and had fallen apart up front. At the World Cup later the same year, John Eales and Rod McCall embarrassed them even further, winning the lineouts something like 28-3. Unheard of these days, with jumpers lifted at the lineout. But more than a decade ago, athletes like Eales could assert their dominance in such a manner. So while the Welsh result for NSW was great, you have to acknowledge the opposition was an absolute rabble.

It appeared to me as though nothing much had changed in Macqueen's thinking when he was elevated to the Wallabies coaching job in late 1997. Another former NSW coach, Greg Smith, had resigned from the Australian post. It was quite clear he was going to be shafted, after failing to beat the All Blacks for two years and suffering a record hammering at the hands of the Springboks in Pretoria in the final match of the Tri-Nations series. The pressure was weighing heavily on Greg and so too, in a hidden and insidious way, was the brain tumour that would only be discovered several months down the track. Greg had changed considerably, his moods and his behaviour had become erratic. He was not the bloke I had remembered. And we all realised why when he collapsed one night and doctors revealed the life-threatening growth on his brain. Greg returned to coaching after initial surgery to remove the tumour, getting jobs in Fiji and the UK, before he required a further operation. Tragically, in 2002, Greg Smith passed away. He is still missed by his many friends in the game.

When Smith stood down from the Wallaby job, Macqueen was installed as his successor. It was a fait accompli. Macqueen was the flavour of the time after stitching together the rejects from NSW and Queensland, mixing in a few very talented ACT players and forming a powerful new provincial force with the ACT Brumbies. They finished fifth in the first year of Super 12, in 1996, and made the semi-finals the following season. Macqueen was on the rise. I do admit his statistics were exceptional. He had done a great job with the Brumbies, who were written off as no-hopers before the Super 12 tournament began, and had set several players on the road to Test selection. At the same time, I was not a fan of his footballing tactics. I always felt he was too conservative, and I was not afraid to voice my views. I had no personal grievance with Rod. I was told, however, he did not take kindly to any Campese criticism. I didn't have a problem with that, it's his prerogative. But I was surprised, when interviewed by Miller at the ARU, to hear that first question.

'How do you get on with Rod Macqueen?'

You start to think 'what's all this about, what does this have to do with coaching sevens?' It floored me, caught me completely by surprise. I couldn't even tell you now how I worded my initial response. What I did tell Miller was how I viewed Sevens as an opportunity to blood some young guys, improve their skills and their tactical awareness, before they go up into the higher levels of the game. You have to remember of course that the days of Wallaby stars playing in the modified form of the game had long since passed. Sevens as an important part of the calendar was undermined once the game went professional and the Super 12 and Tri-Nations series came on the scene. There was no window for the Sevens and the franchises did not want to release them for the traditionally big tournaments like Hong Kong. As a result, Sevens was seen more as a feeder program. A chance to bring on and view young talent. I also thought it would be a good avenue through which to bring back injured Wallabies. It was not as physical as fifteen-a-side, but it was quick and skill-based and would bring the top stars back to their best a lot faster. In my humble opinion. You think about players like Ben Tune, who had knee problems and other injuries that kept him sidelined for a long time. To get his confidence back quickly, he could have been loaned to the Sevens side. Then, instead of struggling to get involved at say Super 12 level, he's actually getting a lot of ball, sharpening his skills and creating opportunities for some of the young kids around him. Then when he goes back to fifteen-a-side rugby, he finds it a lot easier to blend in. I think that view was taken on board. But I knew it was never going to happen because, unfortunately, the top coaches, and here I mean the Super 12 and national bosses, just don't look on Sevens as a priority. The ARU administration are a bit the same. I don't think they are that concerned at the results returned each season by the Australian Sevens side and I wanted to turn that around.

I told Jeff Miller I wanted to start a culture of improving skills and tactics so Australia could take a pre-eminent role on the Sevens stage. And that was it. I felt I'd put forward a pretty good case. But I never got the gig. Perhaps the problem, for me, were my views on Macqueen's coaching style. If we didn't have a good relationship, maybe it was not in the ARU's best interests to have me under the same umbrella. Please excuse me for feeling cynical, but I get the impression if you want to be involved you can't rock the boat, otherwise they don't want to know you. The official line back was that I lacked the experience to take on the job.

I probably did not have the required coaching certificates either. Playing the game for 20 years is clearly not enough. Playing in 101 Test matches obviously does not compare to a Level I, II or III coaching certificate. And, remember, we're talking about an application to coach Sevens here. We're not talking rocket science. So I defend my knowledge on Sevens rugby with a few statistics. I played at the Hong Kong tournament 11 times. We won in 1983, 1984 and 1988 – the last time we took out the title there.

I love Sevens rugby. To a great extent it's about individual skill. It really tells you how good you are as an individual because of the one on one confrontations. In fifteen-a-side you don't often get that chance too much anymore. If the guys inside you don't ensure you get the ball in space, you've got to try and create it yourself. But invariably you have more players in front of you than you'd like and even the greatest Houdini escape artists will find it difficult to breach defences under those circumstances. In sevens it's easier to create the space — that's an obvious statement I know because there are eight less players from each team on the field. But it still requires individual flair to make a real difference. Sevens is also about hard work. Seven minutes a half is a long time when you're constantly on the move and covering so much more territory than you would ever cover in the full-blown version of the game.

To be perfectly honest, I would rather watch a game of Sevens, played well, than an average Test match. It's exciting. It's quick. It's full of action and ad lib rugby. It has spirit and flair. People look at this great game of rugby differently. Some love the contest of a scrum, perfectly directed throws to a lineout, and the heads-down aggression of a driving maul. Each to their own, and that is why rugby union is so superior a sport to games like rugby league and AFL, where there is so much sameness to the product. But, in my eyes, there is nothing more inspiring than creative, brilliant, backline play. And you all too rarely find great rugby Test matches these days where there's a lot of creativity from the guys wearing numbers nine to 15 on their backs. There has been too much emphasis on continuity in recent seasons. People talk about playing ball in hand. But that does not necessarily mean they are involving the outside backs. Ball in hand simply refers to not kicking the footy. Teams can continually shift the ball just one pass wide and bring the first receiver back to the forwards and they're playing a ball in hand game. It can be on a par with watching paint dry for entertainment value, but the coaches boast a ball in hand philosophy. Fourteen phases of punching the ball up ad nauseam is not my idea of a sporting spectacle. It's simply a paler version of rugby league. It is not what rugby is all about for me. Rugby is about throwing the ball around, forwards doing the hard slog to get it, and backs using it to entertain. I know I'll be branded old-fashioned. I know the new, sensitive modern-age forwards like to think they have the ability to play in the backline. You see enough of them out there these days. But the truth of the matter is, any self-respecting centre or winger, when in possession, should be able to stand up a second-rower or front-rower. They should also encourage the tight five glory seekers to keep the backline free of clutter. How many times have you seen a prop or second-rower standing in midfield and dropping a ball, or throwing a lousy pass? Even more pointedly, when did you see one put on a sidestep, draw in defenders and put his winger away for a try? I can't recall one off hand, so what the hell are they doing out there? Let them play decoys, but keep their hands off the ball.

While forwards want to play like backs and backs like forwards in this modern age, the fifteen-a-side game is still too structured for my liking. And the players rarely have any thinking to do for themselves. How can they when they have a head coach, an assistant coach, a backs coach, a forwards coach, a defence coach and so it goes? Would I like to be involved in such a set-up?

I would have to say no, which is why I have only ever applied for the Sevens job.

At the fifteen-a-side level it's just too hard for anyone with their own strong opinions. As a backs coach you are still tied to the thoughts and beliefs of the head coach. He is the one who wants the structure of the game put in place. The backline coach is not there to put his own stamp on proceedings. He's there to polish as a foreman, making sure the workers – the players – get the job done the way the CEO – the coach – wants it. In Sevens, there is structure but there's also freedom. Players can express themselves a lot easier. That's why I think, played properly, it can be a better game. Fifteen-a-side is so predictable. You can see what players are going to do before they do it. A lot of the time, they are running into brick walls, setting a target for their forwards so another phase can be set in motion. I was always taught to run between players, not at them. These days, the opposite applies. You run at a rival, take him out of the defensive line, and recycle the ball. Someone else does the same and eventually you hope to take enough defenders out to create an opportunity. You need patience to do it, but this was the basic philosophy of so many coaches for a long time. What it does, however, is blunt creativity of players. They lose what should be their ultimate focus, to beat their opponent with skill, to search for ways of going around or over the top of their opposite number. It's sad we do not make that the number one priority for our backs. We're more impressed with how much they weigh, with how much they can lift in the gym, with how hard they can hit in defence. We might as well be playing rugby league.

I would jump at the opportunity to work the other side of players' brains. The creative side. I would welcome the chance to have one-on-one sessions with players, see what they think in certain situations, give them options, have them thinking more laterally, and encouraging them to show more flair. A lot of the time, it is all about confidence. And practice. People used to say I had a lot of natural ability. I tend to disagree. I might have had natural ability, yes. But I worked on improving it day after day. I didn't just go out in a game and pick up the ball one-handed off the ground without having done it a thousand times at training. I would practice all those little individual skills. Chipping and regathering, scooping up a rolling ball at full pace. I would do those things in my own time, outside of regular training sessions. And that was in the amateur era. It is why, perhaps, I am so intolerant when modern day players show a shortfall in the skills area. They are professional footballers, it is all they do. Sure, they train hard. But don't tell me they cannot find spare time in their days to fine tune the particular skills applicable to their own positions. Instead of spending time on the golf course, why would they not be making themselves even better than they are? No halfback at the top level should have anything but a bullet pass. No backline player should be incapable of throwing a spiral pass to either side. They should be able to step off both feet, kick with both feet. And how many can? Not enough, that's for sure, and it's an indictment on the professional age.

There are no ambitions, on my behalf, to become any sort of head coach. But I would enjoy helping out with backlines, even on a consultancy basis. I was very frustrated when I missed the Australian Sevens coaching job. Watching the modern game, watching the way that these players play, I don't think there's that much difference from when I was around — except that the players aren't given the freedom to actually create things on the oval anymore. It's a very structured game and, just watching, you see simple things that you could put into the game and the players would react to easily. It would only involve them taking on more responsibility than they have now. I had the same idea for the Sevens. I would have taught the guys how to play, and without trying to play like every other team. Even in Sevens now there's not a lot of depth, there's no creating spaces, they're not telling the guys the angles to run. They just seem to play a game where you take it up and get the ball back, and take defenders out of play until you have the numbers to score. It's like playing fifteen-a-side in sevens, which is not the way to play.

Despite the reluctance of the Australian Rugby Union to blood me into the elite coaching ranks here, after turning down my Sevens application in 1998, I have had the chance to help out overseas and on a lesser basis in Australia. I went to Singapore for a month in 1997 and assisted Justin Sampson, a former player with Northern Suburbs in Sydney. He was coaching the Singapore team. They won the second tier Asian championship that year for the first time. From my perspective, it was a lot of fun. It was all about instilling the basic backline skills in these guys.

All I worked on was teaching them to run straight, to catch and pass the ball efficiently. They were so far behind in terms of raw knowledge. The poor guys couldn't do so much as simple loop moves or switches. They seemed to pick it up fairly quickly but when they got into games they tended to fall back on all their old habits. But that was to be expected. They hadn't been ingrained with the basics from the age of eight, like so many players are in this country. So, obviously, it was a lot harder for them.

There would be people out there, who think they know me, that would assume trying to teach battling players the ground level skills would be hugely annoying for me and drive me to impatience. But I enjoyed it immensely. The good thing was, at the time, I could actually train with them. Show them in person so to speak. If the No.10 could not grasp what I was saying, I would move into the five-eighth position and show them in slow motion. It was a hands-on method of showing them how to do something. But I wouldn't say 'you have to do it this way'. What I would say is: 'Look, pick a way to do this. If you think you're too flat, stand back. If you think you're too deep, try and find a position where you are comfortable'. I'd try to show them the options. I was still fit enough to be part of the team and train with them and not just stand there and tell them. I really enjoyed that. I think they did too. It can be frustrating when a coach simply tells you do something and you're not quite sure what they're talking about. Getting in there and demonstrating made it easier on both parties.

There have been opportunities in Australia to help out at a lower level too. Interestingly enough, I did a lot of coaching for the ARU when I was a roving ambassador for them, helping out with the various states during the Bundaberg series. I went to country towns, down to Victoria to coach their first team and their under 19s. When I turned up, I think 90 percent of them were Kiwis. The approach I took with them was again a concentration on the basic skills. Catch-pass, what do in three-on-two and two-on-one situations, how to beat your man. I also tried to have them thinking about the game. Instead of me telling them what went wrong in a certain situation, I would ask them what happened. 'Why did that pass go to ground? Why did you not successfully draw in that defender?' I put the onus back on them to tell me. If you come across and say 'mate you don't do it that way this is how you should do it', after a while they say 'who do you think you are?', or they do it your way because they've been instructed, not because they understand. The idea was to take a back seat and let them tell me what the problems were and, after about 15–20 minutes of that, they relaxed a lot more, they talked and they learned a lot about backline play. That was about three years ago and I've always enjoyed my association with the so-called minor states. I remember a few years back going to the ARU and saying: 'Now you've got this Australian Rugby Shield competition starting, why don't you send me to Western Australia a month before the championship, let me help the backs, and then go to South Australia and so on?'

They thought it was a great idea at the time. But I never got to spend the time I needed in each place. I was in South Australia, for instance, for one session. There is not a lot you can do in that short space of time so I decided it was no good trying to change things. Instead, I said to the guys: 'What are you bad at? Tell me what you need help with.' They explained a few areas they needed improving in and we worked some drills. You need to spend a week with each team to really improve their basic skills and give them an understanding of what you're trying to achieve. There can be frustrating moments as well. I was in another state, I won't say which one, helping out with an under 16 rep team. These guys had terrible basic skills, so I figured the coach should be in on the training session as well because he clearly needed to brush up his knowledge. But every time I looked around, the coach wasn't watching. He was over with his mates talking. I was trying to coach the kids the basics of throwing and catching a pass, the positioning of the hands, all those sorts of things. And the coach didn't care. I felt like throwing a pass at his head.

He is not the only one to make me wonder. I was in Western Australia on another occasion doing a few drills with a team and the coach of the side was there, with a Wallaby tracksuit on. He had finished a level three coaching course, had a certificate to coach at the highest level. Yet the skills drills he had been using on his team were, to put it bluntly, being performed poorly and he did nothing about it. These guys were throwing passes above or behind their teammates. I made a few alterations, the players improved out of sight, and he just stood and watched. Strange that. I did not have the experience, or the necessary certificates, to be considered for a high-powered coaching job by the ARU. But this bloke had the credentials. Makes you wonder, doesn't it?

A lot of the stuff I try to pass on are the drills and secrets I picked up from various coaches during my own playing career. Over the years, you sift through them all, work out what's good, what's not, and what is worth handing down to the next generation. It is not about re-inventing the wheel. The basics of rugby, regardless of what professional era players and coaches might want to tell you to justify their pay packets, have not changed.

I've seen some of the drills these professional teams use now. It's all witches' hats and rubber bands on legs so players improve their leg drive. To me, it's over-complicating things, especially when some of the players at the highest levels of the game do not have a flawless grounding in the basics of catching and passing the football. It's fine to get technical, to blind people with science. But if you can't perform the very skills that drive this game, then you will not succeed, whether you have exceptional leg strength or not. So many drills these days also have no ball involved. No wonder some blokes look so uncomfortable when they actually see one headed their way in a game. Does all this new age stuff really help? Or has it come about because the coaches have got so much time on their hands, they have to come up with something different, whether or not it will make their players better footballers. I heard the great Welsh halfback Gareth Edwards talk recently. He's regarded by some as the greatest player the game has seen and he said: 'If all we (old-timers) played in this era, if we were to train every day, I still don't think I would be any better a player'.

Sure, he'd be fitter, and stronger, and faster. But would he be a better, more-skilled footballer? He thinks not. And I tend to agree. Mark Ella once said: 'You try and get from one end of the field to the other as easily as possible. Don't make it hard or complicated'. I think that sort of advice is pretty sound too. If I was a coach now I'd be very skill-orientated. I know they have to have explosive power to compete, because all sides have developed physically. But the skills would be a priority.

This will not sit well with a lot of people, but I would also I would encourage players to find a pursuit away from the game. Get a job of some description, if they can. I would also cut back on team training sessions to four days a week. There is no point them being there every hour of every day, getting stale and thinking about nothing but the little oval ball. More importantly, we would train at night. Ninety-five percent of games these days are played under floodlights. So why do teams train during the day? It is totally beyond me. Players could do weights sessions in the mornings, as players did in the old amateur days. Then they would have the day to work or study before coming back to train at night. They would get the break they need to stay fresh, they would be training under match conditions. Tell me how it would not work.

I was with New South Wales when we first went professional in 1996. You'd walk out to the training paddock and guys didn't want to be there. They were bored because all there was was training in the morning, sessions at lunchtime, training in the afternoon. It's like any job. If you're there nine hours a day, you can get bored. And I think half the guys these days do get bored. This professionalism of training every day of the week, no drinking after games because they have a recovery session the next morning. The fun is going out of the game and the players will be the long-term losers.

But it is these sorts of opinions that have put me offside, I'm sure. No Super 12 sides in Australia have ever called, asking me to come down and help out. But that doesn't surprise me, and I'm not the only one seemingly on the outer. This country has produced a lot of great rugby players, but how many of them have been encouraged to get involved. One that springs to mind immediately is Mark Ella. Perhaps our greatest ever player, a five-eighth genius who understood everything about the position, about backline play, about which attacking lines to run. Has anyone been on the telephone to him requesting his presence at training? Or, should I say, has any Australian union made contact with him. Overseas interests have not let the opportunity slip by to get a player of Mark Ella's stature involved. The Japanese Rugby Union signed him up for the World Cup. He was working with them earlier in the year too, when the Australia A team visited the Orient. How does this happen? How can he not be wanted in his own country? Is it that some coaches here, past and present, do not want others coming in and stealing their thunder? Are they insecure about their own positions and want only to be surrounded by those they do not perceive to be a possible threat? This is obviously in the realms of conspiracy theory, but I can't find another way to explain away the waste of talent in Australia. There are people, good people, willing to help and those in power do not want to know.

In my case, the strong opinions I have always expressed do not help my cause. I get under people's skin. But I've always said if you're passionate about the game, you should have views and you should express them. I haven't played since 1996 and journalists still ring me to ask what I think. They know I'll tell them straight. Maybe they don't hear that too often elsewhere. There was a ridiculous situation in the 2003 Super 12 series where NSW coach Bob Dwyer did not want to speak to me, and did not want his players having anything to do with me. I had been asked by Fox Sports to provide expert commentary on a match and they were wondering if I could do some sideline interviews. Only weeks before, I had called for Dwyer to be removed as Waratahs coach at the end of the season. I felt the team had plateaued under his coaching and it was time to bring in new blood, with new ideas and a new outlook. More about that later but Bob, clearly, did not appreciate my view. If NSW, under their new coach Ewen McKenzie, an old teammate of mine at Randwick, NSW and Australia, happened to call and ask if I would like to come down and help with the Waratahs backline, I would only be too pleased. But I won't go holding my breath. It would be Guinness Book of Records stuff before the telephone rang. Besides, professional coaches and their offsiders these days are well paid. How can they justify the pay packets and still call in further assistance, even on a one-off basis? It wouldn't look too good, I guess. People might think they're dud coaches.

There is also the belief out there that I talk a lot but don't understand the modern game. I remember at the start of the 1999 World Cup, Wallabies hooker Phil Kearns tore into me over a column I wrote suggesting the Australians needed to go back to some simple old-style moves to break up defences, rather than playing crash ball all the time. Kearns, a hooker mind you, took a shot at me saying I just don't get it, that the simple moves no longer worked in the new age of rugby. He spoke as if I was some relic of the past. I had, in fact, been retired only three years. Among the 'simple' moves I suggested were old chestnuts like the loop, where the five-eighth doubles around the inside centre, takes a return pass and shoots between the opposing midfielders. Strangely enough, soon after Kearns made it clear he thought I was living in the past, Tonga produced a loop in their World Cup pool match against New Zealand. Lo and behold, the islanders scored under the sticks. Phil should have kept his comments to his personal expertise – scrums and lineout throws.

This whole concept of the game being unrecognisable from what it was only a few years ago is a bit of a myth. Yes, in some respects it has changed considerably, but the basics have stayed the same. Tactics and the rules and the pace of the game have been altered. The fitness of players has increased enormously. But the area that has not come along in leaps and bounds is the skill base of players. That and adventurous thinking from coaches. They are all so scared of failing these days they just don't want their players to take risks on the field. There is too much percentage-based football being played. And it all comes back to a fear of failure. It is a pity most coaches have failed to embrace the old adage that Who Dares Wins.

I must admit, I think New Zealand are getting it right, even if it is through private enterprise. There is an Academy set up in the Shaky Isles now where players and coaches can attend to be taught by some experts in their respective field. Murray Mexted has been part of the set-up and, when I saw him in 2002, he explained to me all about the Academy. I told him I'd love to help, especially when there was nothing doing on the coaching front for me in Australia. So I went along with a brief to teach counter attacking. There were these 19-year-old and 20-year-old kids there, who had come from all over the world. There were plenty

Maximus and the mask...Russell Crowe hands over the treasured memorabilia from *Gladiator*.

Before an appearance on the *Question of Sport* TV show in London with presenter and former Scotland soccer international Ally McCoist and Britain's Olympic 400m bronze medallist Katharine Merry.

Left: The Campese kids taking a ride in Singapore on our way to Italy for a holiday in the mid-1960s. From left: sister Lisa, brother Mario and myself. *Right*: At home in Queanbeyan with Lisa (seated), Mario and kid sister Corrina.

Who said rugby was all I cared about…receiving a cricket trophy at a Queanbeyan Blues awards night. I was nine.

Former Welsh skipper Ieuan Evans must be telling former England captain Will Carling how he scored that try for the Lions in 1989.

Queanbeyan Rugby Club's Wallaby quartet...from left: Peter Ryan, David Campese, Ricky Stuart, David Grimmond.

At a gathering of sports stars in Milan…the guy on my right is the Dutch soccer international Ruud Gullit.

On tour to the Melrose Sevens in Scotland with the Randwick team in the early 1990s.

At full stretch…launching a kick downfield during my last appearance against the All Blacks in Brisbane in 1996.

As I was saying...meeting rugby-loving actor Peter O'Toole.

Drawing the curtain...I was given the honour of opening renovations at the Queanbeyan rugby club a few years ago. I'm with club boss Murray Maxwell.

Family affair…sister Lisa, brother Mario and myself with our grandfather, Pa-Pa Campese.

of coaches there as well hoping to learn something. One was from the staff of the Sale club in England. They came in for tuition, to learn from some of the so-called best in the business. The former All Blacks second-row great Andy Haden was there, so was Grant Fox, the ex-Test five-eighth. Grant and I took this bunch of players for handling drills. They were elite youngsters coming through the ranks. But as the degree of difficulty was raised, they struggled with the drills. I wondered why they had not been schooled in this way already.

There is one aspect of coaching, however, that would drive me insane. All these video sessions and management meetings. The modern-day coach can keep it as far as I'm concerned. Consulting is what appeals to me. I've done it in Singapore, I've helped out in New Zealand, I've had offers to coach in both the UK and South Africa. It would be nice to play a part in my own country as well. But if that is not going to happen, I will consider heading offshore. I have already discussed the prospect with my wife. It was late in 2002, only a couple of months before I married Lara and I told her then: 'If the right opportunity comes up, we'll go'. There was a half chance to go to England but I just couldn't take the jump at that time. Another stumbling block, I guess, is the absence from my portfolio of those magical coaching certificates. You've got to have those coaching certificates. Perhaps I should relent and go and sit the exams. But I just think what I have to offer is not necessarily going to be found in a textbook. There is also this fundamental belief I hold that one of the major concerns for the modern game is the approach and tactics adopted by coaches. For mine, most of them are in need of coaching, whether or not they have their prized certificates.

There is also the option of heading overseas to help out one of the lesser countries, especially in the field of Sevens. There have been a number of feelers made to me. Again, it's all about finding the right opportunity. I don't want to be a fulltime coach. It would be too much. Those blokes just don't have a life. You would have to have something else, another interest, to keep your mind active, otherwise you'd be a robot. And you don't get too much lateral thinking or creativity from a robot.

MEN OF INFLUENCE

I could have been a boring wing, sitting at the end of the line, doing nothing, acting brain dead. But it would have driven me mad.

There were several coaches who had a major influence on my development as a player, and many of their lessons were about life rather than what to do on a rugby paddock. There was Peter Morton who coached down at the Queanbeyan Whites where I started my career. He was a black belt in karate and a guy who believed clean living was the key to fitness. Peter encouraged me to make the most of the talent that I had, to not dilute it in any way by drinking heavily or eating poorly. He taught me well. I have always been very health conscious, more so in my playing days than now.

When I made the ACT under 21 side, a guy named Brother Bob Wallace was the coach. Again, he was not an overly regimented coach. He did not tell you what to do on which part of the field. He encouraged you to use your skills and helped fine tune those skills. The key elements I really picked up on from the start were what to look for when you get the ball and how to prepare yourself to counter attack. In basic terms, it involved looking for possible weak links in the approaching defence. It was not terribly high tech stuff, but that early grounding in those basics set me on the right road. When I came into the Australian side, obviously it was very different. Coaching then was more specific on individual skills. But there was also an enormous input from the players around me. I was young, I wanted to learn, and the guys who taught me so much were the Ellas. After a game they would say 'this is what you should be trying to look for, this is the angle you'll be trying to run'. Being around those guys, they just taught you everything. You didn't need a coach really. The coach will give you the tactics, but the players are the ones who have to go out there and play. Once you set foot outside the dressing room door, you have to cut the apron strings. There is nothing a coach can do you for then.

The Ellas had a huge influence on me and on my psyche. Probably in ways they didn't even realise. If we're going to be completely honest here, I was probably a harder trainer than those guys, but the way they played the game smacked of that 'go for it' attitude. They never seemed to suffer from a lack of fitness as they embraced the running rugby philosophy more than anyone before them or since. They knew to score points, to dominate your opponent and to enjoy the game, you have to take risks. That rubbed off on this kid from Queanbeyan. I saw these blokes playing the game the way I want to play it and it gave me the confidence and courage to back my instincts. And without those two assets — courage and confidence — you can never reach your potential. Players who go into their shells, players who take the negative options all the time, how many of them have become greats of the game? Think of the great Wallabies through history. You have names like Ken Catchpole, an extraordinary halfback who played kilograms above his weight. He seemed to be constantly playing behind retreating packs, but he never let that stifle his attack. He was always sniping, always challenging a defence with his pace and elusiveness. He could defend like a demon too. Mark Ella is another. Is he remembered for his left-footed kicking or his defence? No. He is revered as perhaps the most gifted footballer this country has ever produced.

You see what I mean? As Australians we love the bloke who 'has a go'. We like to see people putting themselves on the line, prepared to walk that tightrope. But going back to the point I was making before. The Ellas gave me the confidence to play that way. And without confidence, taking risks would be akin to footballing suicide. You become hesitant when lacking self-belief and, like curiosity killed the cat, indecision can quickly ruin a footballer.

As Mark Ella once told me: 'If you want to be a risk-taker, you've got to be good at it'. You have to sell the whole package. You have to let people know you have the confidence in your own ability to put one over them. If you back up that air of superiority, the battle is half won right there. They start to worry about what you're doing, or going to do, and lose focus on their own game. As much as I tried to keep mind games out of my own performance, I just went out there and did my own thing, subconsciously I guess you're always looking for an edge over a rival.

The Ellas certainly intimidated an opposition simply with their presence, especially at club level with Randwick. Yet the secret to their success was nothing mystical. It was a well-honed, well-disciplined, very basic asset they boasted. They had a wonderful, intuitive communication with each other. It looked unbelievable when they were in full flight together. But they simply knew what each other would do, where they would run, where to be in support. They had played together since they were kids. The combination was so familiar it was second nature for them. So for me, at NSW and Wallabies level, whenever I played with the Ellas, I tried to be on the same wavelength as them. Once you locked in, the game became easy. They could create, you could finish. They were wonderful teachers. A real inspiration in my rugby education.

But because of that I find it so frustrating now to see a coach like Glen Ella in charge of an Australian backline that has struggled at times in recent seasons to score tries. There are obviously other factors at play here. You can't just hang a coach without looking at why things might be breaking down. For one, have head coaches allowed him to mould the backline the way he would want to? Is the backline given the attacking rein he might offer them if he was setting the team's tactics? And has he had the necessary talent at his disposal to turn the Wallabies into an attacking force? He was such a great player, such an innovator, it's hard to imagine he wanted to play the crash-it-up, no-risk style that Australian teams turned to after the mid-1990s. It is no secret Rod Macqueen saw the way to win a World Cup in 1999 was to hang on to the ball, to employ a style of play that did not involve taking too many risks, and to play it reasonably close to the forwards most of the time. It is on record that I was no fan of the Macqueen approach. But I certainly can't take away from him the success he managed to bring to the Wallabies. Look at the records. He won Bledisloe Cups, the Tri-Nations trophy, he guided the Wallabies to a series win over the Lions and, of course, he was at the helm when the Wallabies were presented, for the second time, the Webb Ellis trophy on November 6, 1999.

At the same time, the legacy he left Australian rugby was twofold. One, we were the premier rugby nation in the world. And that remains his crowning achievement. Two, he left his successor Eddie Jones with the difficult task of reinvigorating the Australian attack. By 2002 it was quite evident the game was shifting again. You had to have some joie de vivre about your game to be successful. The days of just hanging on to possession and waiting for an opposition to crack had passed. Defences were improving at such a rate that teams wanting to monopolise the ball simply found themselves running into brick walls time and time again. Eventually, they were the side under pressure as they failed to consistently reach the advantage line. But Macqueen, in the halcyon period he presided over, did have success and I hope in the column I wrote following that World Cup final victory in Cardiff paid proper respect to his efforts. Here's what I said:

'The most points by a side in a World Cup final, and a record winning margin to boot. Australian players are entitled to feel they could do no more in disposing of France. I don't think any of us will fool ourselves into believing it was a high-class affair. There were a few too many mistakes for that.'

But World Cup deciders have a habit of being rough around the edges. It comes with the territory. These are the biggest matches of your life, and the nerves can be almost overwhelming. One player who did not suffer today, at least with his goalkicking, was fullback Matthew Burke, who managed to pass the 500-point career mark with his haul of 25 points – another new milestone for the tournament.

The first half of the game never really developed and neither side held a clear ascendancy. But after the break the Wallabies came out and they took their opportunities. The French? I get the feeling the semi final win over the All Blacks took a lot out of them mentally. They played their final a week too early. Besides, they got plenty of good bounces of the ball against New Zealand and that never happens two weeks running. Today was when they needed them too, because they could find no way through the Wallaby defence.

The Australians have been superb in that area all year.

John Eales said defence won them the final. I would go even further and say defence was the real foundation stone of their whole tournament. They've worked very hard on tackling techniques, and power in defence, and obviously that wins matches in the modern era. Even an old running rugby romantic like me has to accept that situation.

Back in 1991, we had to defend for 20 minutes as England threw everything at us at Twickenham. And I think it was somewhat similar here for a brief period in the match. But breaking all the accepted practices of the game, the Australians don't mind if they sometimes get caught without possession. They seemed quite happy to let the French have the ball, knowing they had their measure.

Under those circumstances, the French quite quickly get frustrated, and all the ill discipline creeps in. We saw enough of that at Millennium Stadium to suggest they still have a long way to go to bring a professional maturity to their game.

But enough of the negatives. The Wallabies in defence were outstanding. They never gave the French much in the way of field position, and from inside your own territory it can be difficult to put pressure on the opposition. As for the Australian attack, we didn't see as much as would have hoped, but replacement Owen Finegan stood out when he finally joined the fray at the 52-minute mark.

Every time he has got a run in the World Cup he's brought a sense of urgency and enthusiasm to the pack. The Australian scrum deserves praise as well. I have a feeling Alec Evans, our old assistant coach from the 1984 Grand Slam side, has had a fair input into this side. To me, Alec is a hero behind the scenes. He's achieved so much in this game and he's still going.

As far as the Australian tactics are concerned, it was hardly a variation on the theme they have followed right through the World Cup. I still maintain the Wallabies have been the best team in the tournament. They made it hard for themselves early because they were struggling to find form. But what that tells me is that we haven't seen the best of this team yet. Stephen Larkham is still finding his feet to a certain extent at five-eighth. He's played extremely well but if you have a five-eighth that can run the ball a bit better, then the Australian backline will end up with far more opportunity. Joe Roff hardly touched the ball in the final and I find that disturbing. He had it all over his French counterpart for size. Why didn't he get more ball?

But improving those areas is something we can now look forward to as we push ahead to the 2003 tournament in Australia and New Zealand. In making those suggestions, I'm not in any way trying to demean the magnificent achievement of the Wallabies. It was a magnificent victory over France, scoring 35 points and never looking in doubt in the second half. Perhaps it is also the right time to pay credit to Australia's best two players, centre Tim Horan and number eight Toutai Kefu. I thought Kefu was exceptional despite missing two games through suspension, and he must have run Horan close for the player of the tournament award. He reminds me a lot of Willie Ofahengaue, with that same explosive acceleration not usually found in a forward of his size. Kefu is still young too, he could lead this Australian pack for some years to come.

The job now for the Wallabies, even though their playing schedule is finished for the season, is to maintain level heads and not let the pressure of being world champions get to them. In many ways, these guys set the standard, now they've got to continue it. But that's a small price to pay when you have the opportunity to win a World Cup. Congratulations to Rod Macqueen and his players. A great job from the lot of them. They are very deserving winners.'

But, as I hinted at in that column, the Wallabies had to move on and I don't think Macqueen did develop their play any further. They squeezed every last drop from the style he embraced, capping his time as coach with that series win over the Lions. Eddie Jones moved into the driver's seat for the overseas tour that followed and, to be perfectly honest, how much change had we seen in the Wallabies heading into the Tri-Nations campaign of 2003 – the final hitout before the World Cup? Earlier in the year I said the time for talk was over. Jones had to start delivering on his promise to make the Australian team an attacking tour de force. We had heard for so long – almost two years – how Jones wanted to transform the Wallabies, move away from their regimented style and patterns of play. As he himself admitted, what had succeeded for the Wallabies in the past was not going to win the 2003 World Cup.

But Jones' reluctance to sweep aside the Macqueen conservatism from the outset, despite promises to the contrary, confused me. In the same way the failure of the Australian backline to make sweet music with Glen Ella as their mentor had me scratching my head. Jones, like Ella, was a product of the Randwick club in Sydney. The kings of running rugby. Cyril Towers had brought the attacking philosophy to the club between the World Wars and it had been followed religiously ever since. Jones was a hooker for Randwick. A small but mobile player who represented NSW. A free-flowing game always suited his physique and indications were, after he had the ACT Brumbies playing such terrific football in Super 12, that he would take the Wallabies back to their running rugby roots. Midway through 2003 we were still waiting to see it.

Jones has marvelled at the speed and skill of rugby league's State of Origin series, the annual three-match interstate battle between NSW and Queensland. He has already claimed it is the sort of benchmark our game needs to reach. He is not alone in that assumption, judging by the purchase of international rugby league backs like Mat Rogers, Wendell Sailor and Lote Tuqiri. Andrew Walker from the ACT Brumbies had also been a league Test player before being signed a couple of years earlier. But Walker had played senior rugby before first heading to the 13-man code. Rogers, Sailor and Tuqiri had not. Still, if Jones believed the skill and pace of players like the three I have mentioned are capable of re-shaping the Wallabies for the future, why have they not been better used? Why have they seen only limited opportunities with the ball? If Jones went ahead with this transformation process, and returned the Wallabies to the days of swinging the ball to the end of the backline, then the recruits would no doubt provide a better return for the investment.

It's funny, you know, because I read late in 2002 how Jones considered rugby union almost a mirror image of rugby league except for the offside law, where it is essentially a one-metre divide between the teams in our game, compared to 10 metres back in the rival code. Jones even suggested adopting rugby league tactics. According to Bob Fulton — a rugby league legend both as a player and a coach — Jones could revolutionise the 15-man game with the ideas he planned to unveil at the World Cup. Jones had an attacking blueprint where the Wallabies spend a lot of time rolling their forwards down the middle of the park. On either side of the ruck or maul they would field a playmaker. Alongside each playmaker would be a centre and a backrower. Further towards the sidelines you would find the speedsters. This is not your traditional formation where the ball travels from halfback to five-eighth, to inside centre, to outside centre and on to the wing. The fullback might provide variation if he joins the line as an extra man. The Jones scheme involved the ball shooting to a first receiver who might be a five-eighth or a fullback. The ball might then be thrown to a centre and on to a flanker or No.8. Defenders would be drawn to the big men and the backs with the footwork would have the space created to go one-on-one with a rival. It turns current thinking on its head because a common approach in rugby union is for sides to attack to one side continually until they position themselves near a touchline. They will then swing the ball back in the opposite direction, taking it to the other extremity in the hope of utilising a massive open side.

Jones wants to foster a new approach where the forwards, when they can, work towards the middle of the field and leave the option with the backs to go left or right, with plenty of room either side. He admits it is an attempt at re-inventing the wheel. In rugby league, they have been employing similar attacking strategies for well over a decade, with the idea born from a necessity to break down defences that had become too well organised. Rugby union has only now reached the same point of evolution. Jones claimed new ideas were needed to breach the walls. Peter Jenkins in the Daily Telegraph, before the Wallabies tour to Argentina and Europe at the end of 2002, spoke to Fulton about the concept. Another high-profile rugby league coach, Wayne Bennett of the Brisbane Broncos, once said the first rugby union side that adopted a centre-a-side approach would put a significant gap between themselves and their opponents. Fulton agreed. 'If the Wallabies get it going properly, they could revolutionise backline play in rugby,' he said. 'At the moment, the way teams take the ball laterally from one side of the field to the other...it's very easy to defend against. But if you suddenly ask questions of the defence, and leave them guessing as to which side you're going, it makes it far more difficult for them. Their players even have to make basic decisions like which side they go to defend on. You'll be putting questions to them all the time. They won't know whether you'll keep the ruck or maul going, they won't know if you're going right or left.I'll tell you now. Whoever they play against when they start trying the strategy will really struggle to come to grips with it.'

Fulton outlined other benefits too. Like attacking from centre field to one side and leaving the defending team's winger in two minds as to whether he needs to stand flat to help shut down the offence or stand deep to cover the kick. If he moves forward, the kick in behind becomes a far more potent weapon. When a team is attacking to a wide openside, the defending winger has far more time to see how the play is developing and far more time to make his decision.

'It is also more difficult for a defending fullback,' he said. 'If he stands himself on one side, it's an invitation for the attacking side to go the other. But I've often wondered why in rugby union they haven't adopted things like the grubber kick across the face of the posts in the attacking quarter. The chances of the other side taking the ball cleanly are pretty limited if the kick is good. So you have a chance of scoring or regaining possession and, if they knock on, you get a scrum near centre field, where all their forwards are pulled in.'

I don't agree completely with Fulton that all these tactics would enhance rugby union backline play. I would certainly not be in favour of kicking the ball in the opposition quarter. It only highlights how different the two games remain. I think we have to be a little wary of embracing too much from the league code.

But the ideas Jones has conceived do involve shifting the ball. They do involve turning the Wallabies into a potent attacking weapon. But the theory and the practice have been a long time in gestation. The question needs to be asked why? The obvious answer is the Wallaby forwards have not, in Jones' time, been sufficiently dominant to ensure enough quality ball. But then Wallaby teams going back through the years survived and had flourishing, risk-taking backlines, on far less possession than what the modern-day Wallabies have feasted upon. Jones would counter that defences are far stronger these days and simply flinging the ball wide is useless. I don't know about that. Moving it from set pieces, that's scrums and lineouts, at any time gives a backline the chance to set up one-on-one battles, and that's the key to the whole game. If you can work it so you have just one defender in front of you, then the rest is up to the individual.

Perhaps that is where the real problem lies. Maybe this is part of the Macqueen legacy. Is the underlying issue here that Jones had doubts about the skill levels of his backs? Did he consider them, under pressure, to be short of what is required to excel at the highest echelons of the game? If that is the case, it's quite sad. These blokes are, after all, fulltime professionals. They do nothing but play rugby. There is no job they have to spend eight hours a day sweating over before making time for a training session. Rugby is their sole commitment. So how can skill levels be down? Their fitness is obviously higher than anything we were used to in those earliest days of professionalism, back in 1996, shortly before I played my last Test for the Wallabies. But the skills are no better now. In fact, they have deteriorated when you compare some of the guys now to the likes of the Ellas and Michael Hawker and other wonderful backline players of the past.

I mentioned that the Ellas were did not set the world on fire when it came to training. But they obviously worked hard enough on their skills to possess the silkiest hands in the game, capable of delivering the softest of passes or firing the ball wide on demand. When it came to playing rugby, I can say, hand on heart, I was always a keen trainer. If anyone quizzed the coaches I played under, I would say with some confidence that none of them would accuse me of being slack on the training paddock. I enjoyed it and never understood how some guys could shirk in their preparation. There were times when I would lose my temper with younger members of a touring squad because they might have been guilty of taking things easy. Back then, you had some players arrive as Wallabies, think they'd made it, they were at the top and there was nothing more to be done. Shortcuts get you nowhere, except on a downhill slide. People might have watched the way I play and thought I'm just as carefree or erratic when training. Others presumed most of my success came down to natural ability. On both scores, those observers would be wrong. Part of the reason I did have a carefree attitude on the field was that I knew I had done the work. If I tried something and it didn't come off, it would not be through lack of fitness or being under prepared. Most importantly, I never expected to make it as a player on natural ability alone. I always worked hard on the skills side of the game. I never really worked on the goosestep, that's just something that did happen in games. But I did try to hone and polish other little tricks of the trade. I did it in my own time, on my own, at a local park. I would head down there and kick and chase footballs, trying to scoop it off the ground with one hand, then the other. When it happened in a match, like it did against Western Samoa in 1994 at the Sydney Football Stadium, people thought it was natural flair, something out of the box. In reality, it was something I had practiced, alone, for hours. They are the sort of skills you are not going to find practiced in a team situation so you have to do it by yourself. They are also the sort of skills coaches should never try to destroy by making players conform to less risky methods. But how much of that sort of stuff do the modern-day Wallabies undertake, when they have all day to fine tune areas of their game in which they are not 100 percent proficient? Why does it appear the on-field team sessions, and the gym sessions, and the other commitments they are asked to perform, is considered enough? Surely they are not so worn out they cannot work on handling or passing drills. Without going into detail, how many Wallaby players have we seen trotted out in the so-called professional era who are incapable of passing a ball properly to one side or, more damningly, can't kick with both feet if they are playing in a position which demands this skill consistently. That is, at five-eighth or fullback. I'm afraid I find those sort of inadequacies completely unforgivable.

The coach who best seemed to understand this was Alan Jones, the man who changed the face of Australian rugby by leading us to a Grand Slam over England, Ireland, Wales and Scotland in 1984. It had never been done before and really put the Wallabies on the rugby union map. In many respects, Jones kickstarted a Wallaby era which, almost 20 years later, continues. There had been periods when previous Australian teams had blossomed. There was the Bledisloe Cup winning side of the late 1940's, a successful run during the mid-1960's and the mighty All Blacks were tamed in 1979-80. But the 1984 tour really put Australian rugby on the front foot and we have not backed off since.

Jones was a stickler for practising the basic skills of the game. He figured if you were well-armed in that area, you could handle any situation which might emerge on the field. They were also drills to be done with intensity. None of this namby-pamby stuff for Jones. You had to train at pace, as if in a game. There were times when all we ever seemed to do was basic skills. On the Grand Slam tour, you could spend two hours a day on the basic stuff. That's all. No fancy stuff. But when we played, we knew we had the armoury of skills that would allow us to put on the tries we did. If you look back on the highlights of that tour, where Mark Ella scored a try in every Test, you can see it was slick and precise. Put the video on, take a look. Some of those moves, the style of rugby, I think it would stand up today, regardless of all the talk you hear about well-manned defences. A lot of our moves back in 1984 came from scrums and lineouts. What is to stop modern day teams adopting the same attitude? We had Ella calling the shots and people like big Roger Gould steaming up from fullback. So Jones' idea was to give you the basics, the tools to work with, and from there you needed a sense of creativity to make the opportunities.

That is where, to a great degree, the beauty of Jones' coaching style was misrepresented. And I for one overlooked it at times. I had my fallouts with him during his time in charge, especially on the 1986 tour to New Zealand, when we won the Bledisloe Cup. But Jones had far more knowledge about this game than many people were prepared to credit him with, me included. He did not try to program players or turn them into robots. He tried to arm them with skills that would make them the best players they could be. The rest was up to them. By the same token, Alan knew how to give you a spray if he did not like what you did on the field. I can vouch for that. But at least I had the option of trying something. These days it seems to be about setting match plans in such fine detail there is no room for individual creativity. Players are told: 'This is what you will do on this part of the field'.

Hookers have a set game plan. Five-eighths have a set game plan. The whole game is broken down and sanitised to reduce the prospect of error or miscalculation. Do they think players are so dumb they are incapable of taking right options? Sometimes it seems to border on the ridiculous. It always amused me, for instance, when I heard coaches in the professional era tell a No.10 how he has to get in there and clean out at the breakdown. What sort of crap is that? As an opposition player, you could not think of anything better. If a playmaker goes in to clean out and help win quick possession for his side, who is going to create for the attacking team? As a defender, you would take the odds that the first receiver, whoever he might be, is simply going to crash up the ball. No prizes for picking that one.

But, in effect, those are the skills coaches are now implementing across the board. From numbers one to 15, players have to know how to do the dirty work at ruck and maul time, they have to know how to punch the ball up in case they are isolated. To my way of thinking, these general skills only serve to dilute the specifics each position, especially in the backline, requires. You get the impression coaches are trying to say, in terms of skill sets, you don't really have a number on your back these days. Call me old-fashioned but I don't know why you want your wide runners, especially your wingers and your fullbacks, spending so much of their time 'cleaning out' at the breakdown. They're supposed to be scoring tries. That's their role. If they have their heads down trying to ensure their team wins back the ball, how are they then going to inject themselves into the game when the pill comes out? That's why we have these ludicrous situations where the players at the end of the line as the ball moves wide can be props and hookers.

There will be those who say all teams play that way. That wingers do need to clean out in the modern game to prevent the risk of a turnover. I'm yet to be convinced that wingers need to get themselves involved at the breakdown unless absolutely necessary. Half the time they look as though they're doing it because it's expected. They are not always effective and, again, it makes you wonder why they are being told to take themselves out of the game by following what has become a worldwide trend. Not that sheep-like activity is uncommon in rugby. You tend to find what is successful for one team is quickly embraced by the next. If someone gets ahead of the pack, rivals are quick to mimic in a bid to close the gap. Take the Brumbies, for instance. They developed this multi-phase game, the same one the Wallabies used to win the 1999 World Cup. Overseas teams watched the videos and copied. That was the time for Australia to take their game in a new direction and have the rest on the run again. Unfortunately, it did not happen that way and others are now making the running.

It is the nature of the beast though, to pick up on successful trends and adapt them to your own situations. It happens in all walks of life, not just rugby, and not just sport. If you want to be the best you've got to follow the best and improve on what they have done. To my way of thinking, the next really successful team will be the one willing to take chances, to do the unpredictable, to nurture the flair that will break down these seemingly impregnable modern-day defences. Oh, for another Serge Blanco to emerge. Now there was a player with skill and grace and class and flair. He could create, he could finish, he could do anything on a rugby field. It's very hard in the modern game to find people like that and, at the risk of tarring all international coaches with the same brush, it's because really talented players are having the flair and the instincts coached out of them.

They are being told: 'This is the plan. If you don't stick to the plan you don't play.'

A great example is the Wallaby fullback Chris Latham. He is a great runner of the football. But in 2002 he was under a lot of pressure. He had been pigeon-holed as this player who supposedly made the big mistakes in big games. What people seemed to be overlooking was that Latham always got himself heavily involved. Of course he was going to make the occasional error. It happens when you want to get your hands on the ball all the time and put yourself up there in the firing line in attack. Other fullbacks would be well advised to take a leaf out of his book rather than acting like glorified backstops in the position. We didn't see the real Chris Lathan in 2002 because if he kept making mistakes he was going to be dropped. So he became far less adventurous. He handcuffed himself to ensure survival and that to me is such a shame. This game is about scoring tries and attacking an opposition and creating opportunities. It is not about negativity, hesitancy or fear.

How would I have coped in the modern era then? How would I have felt to be shackled, told to toe the company line and rein in my natural instincts? I guess it is easy to say this in hindsight, given I have had my time and spent 15 seasons in the No.11 Test jersey I treasured. But I wouldn't play under those conditions. I could have been just an ordinary boring wing, sitting out at the end of the line, doing nothing and acting brain dead. But it would have driven me mad. I'm sure there would have been opportunities to go elsewhere, like Italy, Japan, France or the UK, where you could at least enjoy your rugby and have the freedom to express yourself, albeit at club level. On second thoughts, scrub the UK. I have bashed on for so long about England and its boring rugby that I could never have considered playing there. Rory Underwood, the former England winger who did score plenty of tries but spent many afternoons watching the action like a lonely sentinel out on his wing, must have had the patience of a saint. I would have told the coach where to shove his jumper.

Fortunately, I never had to do that during my playing career.

At Test level, I had three coaches – Bob Dwyer, Alan Jones and Greg Smith – and none of them tried to dull my natural instincts. Sure, I had my moments with all of them, but I do owe them the recognition and thanks for what they allowed me to do on the rugby field.

These days I have a great relationship with one of those men. Alan Jones is a good friend and, approaching the 2003 World Cup, we were also business associates in a sense. Alan is Sydney's top-rating breakfast host on radio station 2GB and I have commentary duties with the same station. It is great to see Alan, even now, be so passionate about rugby union. He has a great mind for the game and enjoys talking about it when he finds time in what is an unbelievably hectic schedule. He was the driving force of 2GB's World Cup coverage and the weekly meetings were always entertaining, as well as informative. Our relationship is better than ever. I consider it an honour to call Alan a friend.

During my playing career, I always seemed to have a problem with coaches at some stage. It always started off well, and I seemed to get along great with all of them. But time can eventually put a strain on relationships. Rugby is no different. And it is amazing how it can affect your play if that player-coach bond comes under siege. You find yourself playing with less confidence. It is one of those behind-the-scenes factors the general public are sometimes oblivious to, yet it can have a major effect on performance.

In the case of Alan Jones, though, I have to say he has always been extremely supportive of me since he stopped coaching the Wallabies at the end of 1987. I asked him to launch my book in 1991, and he did not even hesitate before saying he'd be happy to help out. It is a side to Alan Jones that is often overlooked. He enjoys helping out people and, on many occasions, it is well away from the public glare. There are the offers of assistance we do hear about. Like when he helped out the Queensland side before they played NSW in 2003. Andrew Slack, his 1984 Grand Slam captain, was coaching the Reds. They were struggling for form and results at the time. Alan joined them in the lead-up, spoke to them, raised their levels of self-belief and out they came and beat NSW. Jonesy goes out of his way in cases like that, and never asks a cent for his services. Tell me how many people of his stature have that sort of attitude, especially in this professional era?

There has also been plenty made over the years about the rivalry between Alan and Bob Dwyer. But I can recall after the 1991 World Cup semi-final in Dublin, where we beat the All Blacks to qualify for the decider, I received a telephone call from Alan. At the end of it he asked me to pass on his congratulations to Bob and the rest of the squad.

There is also the Alan Jones whose good deeds I could fill the pages of this book outlining. He will hate me saying this but he has played the Good Samaritan to so many Australian sportspeople. Not just those in the football codes either. There have been so many acts of generosity that few people have ever heard about. But that's the way he wants it. He doesn't do it so he can soak up the publicity and resultant kudos. He does it because he likes to help. I, for one, can attest to that.

Another coach I must mention is Jeff Sayle from my days at Randwick. Sayley was a great coach in that he knew what talent he had at his disposal and he never tried to over-complicate things. He was very relaxed, allowed players to make their own decisions on the field and never bothered sending out messages with runners which now seems to be all the rage. The success of his teams is there for all to see. Jeff Sayle – one of the great personalities of the game, and a good mate.

RAIDING THE RIVAL CODE

The explanation that players swap codes for the 'challenge' is always camouflaging what most really think. They go for the money.

There is a real dilemma facing rugby union administrators these days. The game is professional and, as we've seen through the recruitment of high-profile rugby league players, an appealing alternative to footballers who once would never have considered taking up the code. What concerns me is how rugby union will look after its own, how it will nurture the talent it has coming through the ranks. I'm talking about the kids who have always played rugby union, worked their way through school and junior ranks and eventually into club football. But, from there, the pathway narrows dramatically.

There are only three professional provincial franchises in Australia — the NSW Waratahs, the Queensland Reds and the ACT Brumbies. They sign less than 40 players each on an annual basis. The mathematics are not too tough. Around 120 players on professional contracts. Compare that to the 13-man game where the National Rugby League has 15 teams. If they have around 30 players on their books, we're talking an overall pool of some 450 players, almost four times that of rugby union. The opportunities for young players in rugby union to reach the top is considerably more difficult. Even more so when rugby league players are signed to cross what was once the great sporting divide. Just take a look at the NSW Waratahs in 2003. They had Lote Tuqiri, Mat

Rogers, Ryan McGoldrick, Rocky Elsom and Milton Thaiday, who had all been signed over a two-year period from rugby league. A league international winger, Nathan Blacklock, was also contracted, only to leave and head back to his original NRL team, the St George Illawarra Dragons. There are six players, taking up some 15 percent of available positions in the Waratahs squad. How does that encourage young rugby union players to hang around and shoot for the top? As I mentioned earlier, it is a dilemma.

As a professional game, rugby union wants the best footballers it can recruit, from within or outside its ranks. That is the nature of playing sport for money. But there is a long-term danger in the current policy. Wallabies coach Eddie Jones has spoken about rugby league players reaching their competitive maturity before rugby union players. He believes league players in their mid to late teens are more developed physically and better able to cope with the progression to the higher ranks. Surely that tells us something about our own game. While the game has been professional since 1996, the emphasis has been on the top end of the pyramid. On paying and bringing up to speed, on a fulltime basis, players at Wallaby and Super 12 level. The grassroots has been, in my opinion, neglected. We need to bring on the juniors and schoolboys at a faster rate, give them more opportunity, provide them with fitness programs that will not leave them with a disadvantage when they have to move into the senior ranks. But it will take time. You cannot build fitness bases overnight. You cannot construct tournaments or identify talent in the blink of an eye and bring it through to its full potential. These building blocks take time to put in place, but I get the feeling rugby union in this country has been slow to move. Instead, there has been this desire to rush out and buy rugby league talent. It is a quick fix, one the ARU believes has been necessary, but one they need to carefully manage. If they continue to raid the rival code, they will only discourage their own or, worse still, give them the impression the way to succeed is to head off to rugby league, grab an opportunity there and hopefully be noticed and brought back to rugby union.

It is happening already. I know, because my nephew Terry Campese has taken that route. He just missed out on the Australian Schoolboys in 2002 and was placed in a shadow squad. But he never got the call-up. The Canberra Raiders rugby league team were interested enough to sound him out but, initially, he wanted to stay in rugby union. His priority was to stick with rugby in Queanbeyan, our family's home town, and win a spot with the ACT Brumbies. He was in a junior Brumbies development squad but when it came to offering contracts for 2003, there was nothing there for Terry. He can play in the midfield or out wide but the talent the Brumbies already had made it difficult for a young guy like him to force a spot. The Brumbies had some up and comers with Matt Giteau, already a Wallaby, and the impressive outside back Mark Gerrard moving down from NSW. So Terry's gateway to the big time was blocked. The Raiders kept showing interest and, when you're a young guy, it's nice to feel wanted as a footballer. He decided the opportunity to go to rugby league was worth taking, so he did.

Terry might take a few years to develop, although the Raiders have clearly been impressed. He has recently signed a new three-year deal with them. And the rugby league environment will help shape him into a better footballer than he would have been if he had stayed in rugby union and been stifled in terms of development by a lack of quality competition. This is the issue the administration needs to address. Ambitious players on their way through will not want to sit idle, without Super 12 contracts. They will look to rugby league and, to a lesser extent, overseas to further their careers. I say to a lesser extent for the overseas option because clubs in the UK, Ireland, France, Italy and Japan are generally after established players, not the untried guys. Rugby league then remains the major danger to our game, at least when it comes to keeping the talented youngsters underneath that top tier. And who can blame the teenage players with stars in their eyes? Is that not what professional sport is all about? Making and taking opportunities to allow you to become a well-paid athlete. The answers for rugby union, unfortunately, are not easily found. Clearly, it will help to have a fourth and possibly fifth Super 12 team. The ARU has already earmarked those goals as major priorities. But the decision to expand the southern hemisphere provincial tournament is out of their hands. It requires a consensus from the three competing unions — Australia, South Africa and New Zealand.

There also needs to be more grass roots development and I trust that will come once the ARU pockets the $50 million profit expected from the 2003 World Cup. The form that development takes requires careful consideration. Do we organise more intensive, elite competitions for our younger players? And that could cause problems in itself with the private school competitions so entrenched. Will the individual schools allow their players to be siphoned off into other competitions? In rugby league, each of the NRL clubs has junior representative teams through the various age groups. Players are acclimatised to tougher matches, and they play plenty of them throughout the course of a season. Our schoolboys play a shortened competition and in the exclusive Greater Public Schools tournament in Sydney, there has become a lopsided look to games in recent seasons. Schools without the top talent are being beaten by a century of points. That does no-one any good.

So while some people in rugby union continue to point to how far the game has come in a short period of time as a professional sport, there are hidden problems, like opening up the pathway for young players, that frequently get lost in the telling of the tale. This is why I have been outspoken at times about the recruitment of rugby league players for enormous sums of money. There is, I can see, a certain public relations aspect to their signing. Young rugby league players will see their idols go across to the once amateur code and perhaps be drawn there themselves. But what good is that if those young kids do not have the opportunity to progress, just like the young blokes we already have in rugby union?

I was fortunate, perhaps, to play when I did, because I was fast-tracked into the Australian side at the age of 19, straight out of the Australian under 21 team. Matt Giteau is the only modern-day player I can think of who has been able to do the same. He was taken away with the Wallabies on their end of season tour in 2002 without having played Super 12. He came out of the under 21 system and had played first grade football with the Canberra Vikings in the Brisbane club competition. But only one player being brought into the highest level without playing a Super 12 game, in almost a decade of professional football, shows two things. One, there is a reluctance to rush young players. Two, there is such a chasm between club football and Super 12. It could, in effect, be crucifying young players to elevate them, out of their depth. It would be like a prize fighter in the middleweight ranks stepping up to take on the world heavyweight champion. It would be irrelevant how skilled a boxer the little bloke would be, he simply would not have the size and strength to go the distance with the big hitting monster.

But closing that gap between club and Super 12 rugby is something that can be addressed. The ARU, in the past, has been treading too carefully with its paid personnel. They have not forced them to play club football on a regular basis and have even released players from their contracts so they can head off overseas when they should have been playing domestically. That has been nipped in the bud in the last couple of seasons. But there has to be a way found to have more representative players filtering back into the club ranks and playing more often at such an important level. Without those top players around, the emerging players in club football are robbed of the chance to learn more about the game from the players at the pointy end. And that is crucial to their development. You can only improve by playing with better quality players.

I remember back in 1996 playing with a young bloke by the name of Chris Latham. He had not taken up rugby union until his late teens but he was a quick learner. When I was alongside him in the Randwick side, I would try to pass on my experience and knowledge. I was 33 at the time and nearing the end. I felt it my duty to give him a hand. When he did something wrong, and when he excelled, I would tell him, trying to be as constructive as possible. He was learning on the job and it was obvious, even then, he had special talent as an attacking rugby player. His timing was exceptional and I have always felt that tells you a lot about a footballer. Knowing when to make your run, heading for the holes, and reading when a playmaker is going to give you the ball is the sort of sixth sense stuff that only the best players have in their make-up. It is why the top players can make something brilliant look so easy. They have put themselves into position to carry out the big play.

But getting back to the club scene, which is a hot topic of

mine, the competition in Sydney, and I would imagine the same applies in Brisbane, needs to have its standards lifted. The ARU also has a responsibility to promote it better. They are pumping in a fair bit of money, but we should be reading more about it, getting its profile back to where it once was, rather than allowing it to be lost in the backwash of Super 12 and international rugby. I still get the impression the Wallabies are so important to the ARU that they only consider the grass roots as an after thought. But in 1991 we won a World Cup with only two provinces, where the game in this country relied on a solid foundation of club rugby. Former Wallaby hooker Phil Kearns came out of second grade at Randwick to play for Australia. The first grade hooker, incidentally, was 2003 Wallaby coach Eddie Jones. But who could do that these days? Come out of a club reserve grade side straight into the Test side. I am not an ostrich. I do not have my head buried in the sand. I know the game has changed immeasurably since 1991. But it is too easy to simply dismiss club rugby as a weak third tier and expect our three professional provinces, and the Wallabies, to carry the game into the future alone. The numbers alone show how dangerous that would be, especially at the end of World Cup years when so many players, approaching the end of their careers, decide to either retire or seek greener pastures offshore.

During the 2003 season, visitors to my shop in Sydney would constantly ask me: 'Are there any players you would bring into the Wallabies team?' Realistically, you could only look to the existing Super 12 players, and most of them had been tried. One guy who should have been is Mark Gerrard, the ACT Brumbies winger. But it would be impossible to look at a club player because of that gap in standard. It would be doubly difficult for the selectors because when would they find time to see club games? These are quandaries the ARU has to work out, especially when it comes to developing young talent.

If you leave promising youngsters in a pool of mediocrity, eventually they will sink to the same level. There have to be further inquiries into an elite national competition. At least, that way, there is an intermediate competition, a buffer zone, between club football and Super 12. But, and I can't state this more emphatically, there has to be a way found to get Test players turning out in club jumpers more than they do at present. There would be some Wallabies who would be lucky to have played a handful of club games in recent seasons. It is not healthy, for the game, for the clubs, or for the young players who need exposure to the best in their code.

Even at Super 12 level the lack of opportunity issue can raise its head. A couple of aboriginal speedsters spring to mind. Willie Gordon had a terrific game for the ACT Brumbies against the British and Irish Lions in 2001. But it was a rare chance for him. Brendan Williams was another. He was contracted to the NSW Waratahs but dropped off the scene after having a few personal problems. Which is another story in itself. At the ACT Brumbies, Andrew Walker was looked after well. But his disappearing acts with the Wallabies led to him being left out of the selection equation. That was such a shame because Walker was another exceptionally gifted footballer. Here was a guy who could have, I believe, been turned into a quality Test five-eighth. He was played as a winger and fullback by the ACT Brumbies, but he had the vision to be a terrific playmaker and an alternative to Stephen Larkham at Wallaby level. Walker, however, went off the rails a couple of times. Like Williams, his culture is different to ours, and understanding these guys sometimes means cutting them slack. They are under different pressures away from the field, sometimes they struggle to be away from their families or to fit in to what can be an unfamiliar environment for them. They can react a little differently as a result but the last thing we want to do is cut these players loose.

In a far less demanding way, I had a bit of trouble assimilating when I first came into the representative ranks. I was the product of a government high school. There was no private school background for me. I was not selected for the Australian schoolboys so, in that respect, did not follow a popular pathway for future Wallabies. Funnily enough, I could have walked that road if I had elected to go back to school in the year 1980. At an end of season presentation night for the Queanbeyan Whites rugby union club in 1979, an Australian Schoolboys official approached me about my future. I had just turned 17, was fresh out of school, and had spent the winter months that year running around in the Whites' fourth grade side. It remains one of my most enjoyable seasons. Brother Bob Wallace was a leading figure in the schoolboys rugby movement and was a genuinely nice guy. He sat me down for a chat and, in a nutshell, wanted me to go back to school. Apparently he'd been impressed by what he'd heard about this kid running around in the lower grades with the Whites and suggested I could make the Australian Schoolboys team if I resumed my education. He was also fairly specific about which school I might attend. A place at one of Canberra's most notable rugby union nurseries, St Edmund's College, was offered. It was the school where Brother Bob was based. It was flattering to be approached but I turned him down flat.

We lived in the working class area of Queanbeyan, near Canberra, and mum and dad were the furthest thing you've ever seen from pushy parents. I had attended Queanbeyan High where rugby league was the dominant sport and where the kids were generally not from wealthy families. I played mostly rugby league at school. The Buckley Shield and University Shield were among the big competitions and, while we had a rugby union team for a couple of years, it was usually taken on in a light-hearted way by the rugby league players, including myself. There was very little training, we just turned up and played. Rugby league was the serious stuff in Queanbeyan. It had always been that way. It's a working class town and rugby league has always been seen as the working man's game. Rugby union was linked to tweed jackets, leather patches and private schools. The turning point for me was playing with the Queanbeyan Whites. I enjoyed it immensely and sort of fell into rugby union that way.

Initially I was a rugby league player and the story is now well told as to what turned me off the game. I was playing in a junior grand final, in the under 16 age group, for the Queanbeyan Blues club against Belconnen. I missed a tackle or two, got blamed for it and, as far as the memory goes, that was my last game in the 13-man code. I was never the greatest tackler in the world. I put my hand up to admit that. When I was a kid, and a fairly skinny kid at that, I was actually a bit scared about going into contact situations too hard. But the criticism as a 15-year-old hurt. I was sensitive then, was during my career, and to a certain extent still am when it comes to people taking a crack at me. Most of us are, I suppose. But I've always tried to hide any internal bleeding. Whether the criticism be warranted or not, I learned very early on in my career you simply have to wear it, that people will speak out, will voice their opinions, regardless of whether you think they are entitled to make those observations. I copped plenty of stick over the years. Perhaps some of the people who get their noses out of joint when I say something should go back and read what others once said about me. Then come back and tell me how hard done by they are when most of what I say is based on first-hand experience at the international level. Many of the critics who fired barbs at me had never set foot on a rugby paddock.

But getting back to that meeting with Brother Bob Wallace – it's hard to believe it was almost a quarter of a century ago – I elected to stick with what I was doing, not to go back to school, and two and a half years later I was touring New Zealand with the Wallabies. Could the same thing happen now? Who knows. But if I was arriving on the scene these days, I would certainly look at the rugby league option, just as Terry Campese has with the Raiders. As a young guy you would be inclined to say to yourself: 'Am I going to get a run in Super 12 and, if not, where can I go?' I'm fully aware not everyone can make it, but I just feel we're not giving enough young players the chance to strut their stuff. So why should they not go to rugby league, make a name, and then come back when rugby union is prepared to pay for them? NSW Waratahs flanker Rocky Elsom is a case in point. He was playing for the Canterbury Bulldogs, but not in the top grade, after being recruited from rugby union, where he played his schoolboys football. Waratahs officials took a look at a tape of him playing and thought he was worth a shot at Super 12. They gave him a training contract but, after forcing his way into the starting side, he was signed to a fulltime deal. Thank you very much. Could he have made the same impact if had been playing club rugby union? I wonder. It is tough these days to make a name for yourself at club level. The competition doesn't seem to get much in the way of acknowledgement anymore, the top representative players don't play on any sort of regular basis and the crowds are limited because you're not getting the stars.

There was an opportunity for me to go to rugby league very

early in my career. It was 1983, I had been in the Wallabies team less than a year after my debut on the tour to New Zealand the season before. Parramatta made the first serious approach and they were the gun side of the time. They had won the premiership two years running and would win again in 1983. They had some of the best backs of their generation. Players like Peter Sterling, Brett Kenny, Mick Cronin, Eric Grothe and Steve Ella. The club's chief executive Denis Fitzgerald contacted me. He made the initial approach. But I was happy in rugby union and the money, strange as it might seem, was not the issue for me. It did not even cross my mind to cross over. There were too many opportunities open to a young rugby union player in those days to travel the world and, after the first year of it, I was having too good a time to contemplate switching codes. There were other offers to come at a later date. There was the celebrated one from England club St Helens in 1988 while the Wallabies were touring England and Scotland. We were staying in a hotel in Surrey when the phone call came in the late afternoon. The north England accent was unmistakeable. As it turns out, the St Helens organisation had contacted the former Wallaby turned rugby league star Michael O'Connor as part of their research into whether they should make an approach to me. I presume, given they placed the call, what he had to say was positive. And so we cut to the chase. What were they offering me?

The reply caught me by surprise. It was a three-year deal worth 350,000 pounds. On today's exchange rate, some $A875,000. Almost $300,000 a year. This, remember, was 1988. Even in today's professional game, that figure would be highly competitive. Certainly enough to make you stop and think. I explained to the St Helens official I was involved in a tour and needed time to ponder their generous proposal. The phone went back on the hook and five minutes later I had made my decision. Moving to the north of England would not be on the agenda. As I wrote in *On A Wing And A Prayer*, some dozen years ago, my decision had everything to do with money. Yes, I liked the thought of raking in that much cash. But no, I was not prepared to forsake my lifestyle for the almighty dollar.

'It would have meant living in England throughout the northern hemisphere winter,' I explained at the time. 'I was not at all keen on that side of the equation. I didn't know exactly where St Helens was, but I knew enough to realise I would be in for a cold, grey winter, month after month of it, if I signed. When you are far from home, the one thing you want is to be happy with your surroundings. I somehow doubted that I would be deliriously happy to find myself in a flat in St Helens.

After their first approach, St Helens persisted. After the Wallaby tour had concluded at Cardiff, they kept on ringing me in Italy, where I had gone on to play. And when I finally got home to Australia, they rang me there, too. They offered to fly me over to London to watch the Cup final in which they were playing that year. I hedged and put them off, which was bad on my part because I had made my decision. I listened to them but had no real intention of going through with it. The saga drifted on until the night after the final Test match between Australia and the British Lions in Sydney on July 15, 1989. It was a disastrous match for me personally and afterwards I just went home. I was at the home of my friend Daryl MacGraw when St Helens caught up with me. They asked Daryl: 'Will he come?' Daryl promptly said no. Then, incredibly, and quite beyond my expectation, they immediately offered more money — another 10,000 pounds — but the answer remained the same. I suppose I was shocked that the interest from St Helens was still there after my performance that day. But perhaps they figured I would be an easy target after a game like that.'

Back in Australia, the Canterbury Bulldogs, the Canberra Raiders, Manly Warringah and the Gold Coast also talked to me at various times. The answer, though, was always the same. I was happy where I was, and with what I was doing. There was no real hunger or desire on my part to up and leave. It always interested me to hear some players, when they did go across, to say they did it for the challenge. Looking back now, as a long retired Wallaby, it does not bother me in the slightest that I didn't accept an offer to play rugby league. Sure, it would have been a challenge to see just how good I could have been in another game. I always think good footballers, as opposed to good 'athletes' can excel in either game. Russell Fairfax, who played for the Wallabies in the late 1960s and early 1970s before heading to rugby league, was a great example. So too Michael O'Connor, a talented international rugby union threequarter who made the switch in the early 1980s. They were class rugby players, be it league or union. And nothing beats class.

But is it really that much more a challenge than reaching and staying at the top in your first-choice sport? I somehow think the explanation that players swap codes for the 'challenge' is always camouflaging what most really think. They go for the money. Not that I would ever criticise anyone for making that decision. It just surprises me that not one footballer, in my recollection, has ever put hand on heart and said 'I want the cash'.

Am I being too cynical? I doubt it. Rugby league players coming across to rugby union now say the same thing. If that was the case, why did it take such large sums of money to convince them the challenge was worth taking. As I say, what is the stigma about admitting you want the money? This is professional sport.

Perhaps we are still naive in this country and want to think loyalty, to a team or to a game, is driven by love and not the stuff that pays mortgages and buys cars and an education for your children. Those idealistic days are long gone, in both codes. Rugby league players rarely spend their entire careers at one club and in rugby union, just take a look at how many players change their provincial allegiances. Two Wallaby second rowers, Dan Vickerman and Justin Harrison, left the ACT Brumbies at the end of 2003 to link up with the NSW Waratahs. They had been Brumbies through and through. But the reality of the situation is that Harrison wanted opportunity after spending most of the 2003 season on the bench, and Vickerman wanted to live in Sydney where his fiancee was attending university. Perfectly reasonable on both their parts. Yet the Brumbies expressed their outrage at Vickerman leaving, complaining how they had put so much time and effort into his development. It was a strange argument to make, given how many players the Brumbies have signed from both NSW and Queensland over the years. Supply and demand determines where players go these days. It is the way of professional sport. There are times, I think, when sporting bodies in Australia, rugby union bodies especially, lose sight of this. They want the game to be surrounded with cash but they don't always like the consequences.

RATING THE CONVERTS

In all honesty Wendell, the business is going pretty well. Not securing your signature was never going to make or bust us.

Our first meeting was pleasant enough. Wendell Sailor and I were invited to take part in the Jack Newton Celebrity Golf Classic at the Twin Waters resort on the Queensland Sunshine Coast. It was 2001 and the seeds of a code swap for Sailor had already been sown. My business partner, Daryl MacGraw, who runs Campese Management, had been speaking to Wendell about representing him in any negotiations he might want to undertake with the Australian Rugby Union.

Daryl had already put in a fair bit of work on Sailor's behalf, speaking to ARU heavyweights and would organise a meeting with High Performance Unit boss Jeff Miller. Miller, who would become the Queensland Rugby Union chief executive and is now the Reds coach, was the man in charge, at that time, of signing players to the ARU. So the idea was if Wendell changed codes, left the Brisbane Broncos and his career as perhaps the most high-profile player in Australian rugby league, that Campese Management, through Daryl, would look after his interests.

As a result, when I made the trip to Queensland for the golf day, I was delighted to have the chance to catch up with Wendell. I spoke to him, asked him how he was going, and suggested if he did switch codes he could be a success in the 15-man game. Sure, I had some reservations too. I think I mentioned to him he would need to do something about learning to kick. But when your business partner is trying to sign him up as a client, you are not exactly going to detail, chapter and verse, all you think he needs to do to fix his game. Especially when the bloke is arguably the leading winger in rugby league, a guy who had played in premiership winning teams and in Test matches for the Kangaroos. How do you think my appraisal of his expected shortcomings would have gone down? So I made small talk. Yes, as he said in his book brought out in early 2003, I did suggest he could be a success. But it was hardly the big sell from me in a bid to get him on to the company's books. I have always left that side of the business to Daryl. And I did, as he again detailed, offer to help him with improving any facet of his play that might make his transition a little easier. That offer, incidentally, has never been taken off the table. It still stands today.

To his credit, Wendell did tell us back then that as far his future was concerned, in terms of a possible move to rugby union, that there were a couple of companies wanting to manage him and we were one of them. He said we were 90 percent chance of securing him. Clearly, that is not a done deal, and we accepted the situation, hoping he would choose Campese Management to act for him when he felt the time was right. But what Daryl decided is that we would only act for Sailor in dealings with the ARU. We were not going to get involved in dealing with the Broncos as well. I don't know if that cost us in the end, but Wendell eventually went with another management group.

As a newspaper columnist, I was naturally enough asked to express my opinions on Sailor. He did not take kindly to suggestions that I thought he might struggle with some aspects of the game. Sailor said he'd be happy to play against me on the wing every day of the week because he'd use me as a doormat.

In his book he seemed to intimate that the reason I had a go at him, and the basis of my future analyses of his performances was, in effect, a form of payback. It appears he is under the misapprehension that it was all linked to him turning down Campese Management and opting to go elsewhere with his business. In all honesty Wendell, the business is going pretty well. Not securing your signature was never going to make or bust us. It was not that important in my life that I would embark on some sort of revenge campaign to discredit you. Besides, the Australian selectors are not exactly disciples of mine. It might have furthered your cause to have my constructive criticisms aimed in your direction.

Sailor said in his book: 'There was worse to come. After I was picked to play my first Test against France in June 2002, Campese bagged me in his column.' He quoted my words from *The Australian* newspaper and, in fairness, I will reproduce parts of it here so people can make up their own minds.

'The methods for selecting Test players must have changed if this Australian side is anything to go by. For example, Wendell Sailor was caught out of position time and time again last weekend against the Maori and yet he gets named. It just seems Wendell has been given a red-carpet ride to Test selection. To become a dual international is obviously a great achievement but when you look at previous dual internationals, like Michael O'Connor, they were exceptional players who performed week in and week out. I cannot see Wendell in that mould. I'm still amazed to think there were players in Super 12 this year who performed consistently at a high standard – like Andrew Walker – and they're overlooked. Yes, Wendell's big. Yes, he's strong and, yes, he's getting paid a lot of money. So maybe we want to see some return on that investment. But does all that justify why he's been selected.'

Essentially, what I was saying is that I believed there were, on form, other players who should have been chosen ahead of Sailor. As for the 'return on the investment', let me pose these questions in my defence. If Wendell was a no-name winger who had played all his life in rugby union, working his way through the ranks, would the form he showed in the 2002 Super 12 series been good enough to earn Test selection? I would be surprised if any selector, hand on heart, answered in the affirmative. Equally, I wonder whether another player, say an Andrew Walker, would have had so many people leaping to his defence if had missed, as Sailor did, the two tackles in the Sydney Test against France in that first few weeks of his international career.

Let me also point out that Wendell was not chosen for the Tri-Nations series that followed. Surely that suggests the selectors, in hindsight, felt he was not ready for the upper echelons of Test rugby. Perhaps I could have phrased my words a little better when linking the size of Sailor's pay cheque to his premature elevation to the Test team. I just think the massive publicity over his signing and the huge reputation he brought across with him might have had the selectors thinking they needed to see if they could fast-track any potential he had for making a splash in rugby union. But they never admitted to that. If they had, perhaps they would have eased the pressure on Sailor. Then again, they would have left themselves open to the claim that they were giving away Test jerseys rather than making players earn the right to wear the Wallaby gold.

So, as the Wallabies prepare for the 2003 World Cup, what do I think of Wendell and his impact on the game in his second season since waving goodbye to rugby league? Let me preface this by saying I thought he was a fantastic rugby league player. I watched and admired his efforts for the Brisbane Broncos and for

Australia. He was obviously comfortable in that game. He knew it inside out. He also knew his own strengths and how to inject himself into the game. He had the strength and the pace and the tackle-busting qualities that made him an absolute standout.

Rugby union, as Wendell now admits, is a completely different game. It requires a different set of skills and a different outlook. Unlike in rugby league, where there is no pressure in running the football because if you're tackled you simply get to your feet and play it, the demands on your decision making in rugby union are far more excessive. You have to be careful you don't get isolated and at risk of turning over possession. There is less predictability and structure to the game. In rugby league, they will bash it up a couple of times and then swing it wide. A winger always knows, almost to the exact play, when he is going to get the ball. In rugby union, those moments are far more difficult to prepare for and you have to be willing to come off your wing in search of the pill. This all takes time to load into the brain before it is spat out instinctively. Even a Queensland teammate of Sailor, winger Ben Tune, said while watching the former league great in action during his first season, you could almost see his brain ticking over before he made his play. That hesitation was, in part, to be expected. Sailor is more a programmed player than a natural instinctive footballer in the way of another convert, Lote Tuqiri. So he was going to take a while to come to grips with the game.

I do think Wendell has now proven himself as a Test quality footballer. I have no hesitation in making that statement. He has come a long way since we saw a bloke on the right wing who looked ill at ease, especially in that Test against France when he was twice beaten on the outside in defence. Who was using whom as a doormat that day? But if you ask me would I have Wendell Sailor in my World Cup starting side for the Wallabies, the answer would have to be 'it's touch and go'. But I would definitely find a place for his former Broncos teammate Tuqiri. Let me explain. There was a lot in the way of comparisons made between Sailor and Jonah Lomu when the ex-Kangaroos star came across to rugby union. But Lomu, unfortunately struck down earlier this season with a recurrence of a career threatening kidney ailment, remains a more explosive runner than Sailor. At the same time, the days of the out and out power runners are starting to look a bit limited. Defences are improving each season. Players are more adept at taking opponents head on in one on one situations. Remember the 1995 World Cup semi-final between England and the All Blacks when Lomu ran roughshod over the Poms to score four tries? In one of his tries he brushed past four defenders and trampled England fullback Mike Catt, who was left looking like he'd been wrestling a steamroller. As great as Jonah has been, it is difficult to imagine him scoring a similar try against the modern-day England, whose defence has been finely honed.

Wendell tried a 1995 Jonah in his first interstate game in 2002. He got the ball with room to move and had one Waratahs player in front of him, halfback Chris Whitaker. As game as they come, Whits weighs about 80 kilos. Wendell has an advantage of about 25kg. So he attempted to run straight over Whitaker, who felled him like a treecutter taking the chainsaw to a mighty oak. In the position he was, with the ball in hand and the line in sight, Wendell should have crossed the white strip. He should have tried an in and away on Whitaker and made a beeline for the corner. He relied on brute strength and failed. Since then, he has made massive improvements.

The try he scored against NSW in the Super 12 season of 2003, taking the ball from the kickoff and setting off from his own quarter on an 80m surge, was great. The try from his own in-goal against Wales was obviously a special effort. I can't recall too many tries at Test level being scored by players running 105m. And his solo effort against England at Telstra Dome, when he took the ball at first receiver and came back on the angle, through some tiring Pommie forwards, was a score that best indicated he was coming to grips with the required angles that allow you to get in behind a rugby union defence. It was also a run smacking of confidence, which Sailor, when he first came across from league, was clearly lacking. He talked it up in those early days, but underneath must have been doubting himself. Not doubting his ability, but his sense of place and timing.

After the June Tests in 2003, he could say he earned his place in the Australian side, but he is not yet a great winger, not in the same class as Sailor the rugby league sensation. Whether that will come to pass in the future is yet to be seen. I have my doubts because I feel the game of rugby union is moving now towards a return to skill rather than power. Because defences have improved so much, the wheel has turned and the re-defining of the attacking side of the game will provide the next breakthrough to success. Wendell also has to work on the kick in behind him and his own ability, or lack of it, with the boot. The Welsh coach Steve Hanson made a point of it after the Sydney Test where Sailor made his scything run down the right touchline. Hanson suggested everyone in the international rugby community realised Sailor was not adept at kicking a football. He recommended Sailor work on the art before he was pinned into a corner by opposition sides. I am not saying Sailor is alone in having areas of his game that require further work. I had weaknesses too that I attempted to rectify over the years. Like the high ball. The All Blacks realised taking the bombs was not one of my strengths and they tried to work on me in that area. But it is more Sailor's approach to beating a man that leads me to predict his rugby union achievements will be surpassed by Tuqiri. Lote has it all.

Unlike Wendell, who tends to tuck the ball under his arm and run through anyone in his way, Tuqiri has real flair and finesse. He demonstrated in his first few Super 12 games, with the limited possession he got, that he is a player blessed with rare skill. The try he scored in South Africa against the Sharks, when he dribbled the ball past his opponent, ran around him and regathered to score was a real breath of fresh air. It was a terribly complex manoeuvre he attempted. Running at pace and putting just the right weight behind the kick is very a difficult assignment. He did it so easily, Tuqiri made it look simple. Only the best players can do that. Even in the Brisbane Sevens at the start of 2003 he showed deft little touches and an understanding of where he needed to be to support the ball carrier or be in a position to make the play. Unlike Wendell, he does not rely only on strength. He thinks outside the square. He has the speed and the step and the vision to create havoc. He is just what rugby needs. The difference between the former Brisbane Broncos teammates is that Tuqiri can create, Sailor is a finisher.

When Mat Rogers came on the scene in 2002, having played rugby union some 10 years earlier as an Australian Schoolboys five-eighth, he played some terrific rugby at fullback for NSW. He is a brilliant runner of the ball but has not been fully utilised, by NSW or Australia. There have been reasons for it, namely an inability of the Waratahs midfield to get him involved more, a string of injuries and, at Wallaby level, because his first bunch of Test caps were as a second half sub. He probably should have been even more advanced than he was as the Australians prepared to go into the World Cup. He needed game time, and he needed a permanent position. I mean, it was a bit ridiculous that after some 18 months in the game, Rogers was still being shifted around the backline having played wing, fullback and centre. Ironically, the position I believe he is best suited to is the one he has yet to play at the highest level. But more about that later. That must have been very frustrating for him. He has so much talent and Rogers looks like the type of player who will really kick on once he has a defined role to play.

But of the three prized recruits, I think Tuqiri will turn out to be the pick of the bunch. He is still very raw and he is still very young, despite the credentials he has now built up in two football codes. What he needs, while he is on the wing, is to have an outside centre who is capable of giving him the ball with some room to move. An outside centre with the ball distribution skills that Wallabies of the past who filled that position had by the bucketful. Annoyingly to me, there was a long period of time there, from the mid-1990's on when it seemed Australian selectors were quite happy to have centres who could tackle better than they could pass. That causes a real problem for your back three because they are so reliant on the midfield players giving them the launching pad. This sounds ridiculously simple but in all the mumbo jumbo you hear as the years roll on, this same philosophy still applies. Get the ball to your wings when the bloke at the end of the line will have time and space, and hopefully a one-on-one situation to size up. If you can do that, then the winger should do the rest. That was the beauty of Lomu. Apart from his incredible power, he was also incredibly fast and nimble for such a huge physical specimen. One-on-one he was simply unstoppable. There was a classic point in case in the Bledisloe Cup Test in Sydney in the year 2000. It was that superb game of football many people later claimed was the greatest Test ever played. And it was sealed when the All Blacks sent the ball to Lomu on the left wing with only Wallabies five-eighth Stephen Larkham to beat. Lomu whistled around him, avoided the despairing attempted diving tackle and waltzed over for the matchwinning score.

I get the feeling Tuqiri will do the same if the Wallabies can present him consistent opportunities. Tuqiri has the speed and vision to go with the strength. He is not as big as Lomu, but I would guess he's quicker, he can put on a step and he can change angles. He has the full bag of elusive tricks.

When the Wallabies get their personnel properly sorted out, I have no doubts they can be the best backline in the world. Here is the ultimate backline for me, from what the Wallabies had available from the start of the 2003 international season. At fullback I would plump for Chris Latham. He always seems to be cast as the fallguy when something goes wrong. There is this talk of him making the big mistakes in the big games. But he reminds me of me in some ways. The less ball he gets, the more frustrated he gets, the more mistakes he makes. Latham is the best attacking fullback in the world. He plays the game the way I thought coach Eddie Jones wanted it played. We kept hearing about this change in style and how the Wallabies were going to evolve into an electrifying backline-driven outfit capable of burning opposition sides with attacking brilliance. If they do, then Latham will come into his own. People have criticised him for committing blunders. But he makes a valid point in saying if you try to get involved in the game as often as he does, then you will tend to have a higher error count, given the number of touches you get on the ball. If the Wallabies are serious about moving the ball, Latham has to be there. I would have Tuqiri on one wing and Wendell Sailor on the other. I would not have gone with Wendell, until he started finding his try-scoring touch in 2003. He scored that beauty against England in Melbourne and another against South Africa in the opening Tri-Nations Test in Cape Town. I have also been a long-time fan of the mercurial Andrew Walker. But his mid-season signing with rugby league was a clear indication he sees his future elsewhere. Perhaps he knew he was out of favour with the selectors. The reason I would have had Walker as an option is that I favour a policy of picking a back three where the entire trio can, at a pinch in Tuqiri's case, play at fullback. The interchange qualities of your back three can be very important. In 1991 when the Wallabies won the World Cup, we had a back three of Marty Roebuck, myself and Rob Egerton from Sydney University. At club level, we were all fullbacks. In 1999 it was a similar situation with Matt Burke, Joe Roff and Ben Tune. Few people seem to realise Tune has played quite a bit of football in the centres and, I'm sure, could also handle fullback.

At outside centre, I would play Roff. He has size, pace, can make a break and can offload as well. A perfect fit for the position. Inside centre goes to Elton Flatley. He is an under-rated footballer. Not brilliant by any means but very consistent and he can shovel the ball for my strike players out wide. Flatley would also give the team a goalkicking option which makes the selection of Matt Burke unnecessary. My five-eighth would be Mat Rogers. I have said it before. I think he has a great natural feel for the game, can run comfortably in heavy traffic and shapes as an ideal playmaker. George Gregan or Chris Whitaker completes the picture at halfback.

The reason I pick that backline can be answered in one word – attack. Look at the scoring potential there. It is full of players who are so unpredictable, an opposition would not which way they were going. And in defence, which even I have to acknowledge is a major part of the game these days, they can all hold their

Here's to Bill…celebrating the 1991 World Cup final win with assistant coach Bob Templeton.

Inducted into the Australia Hall of Fame in Melbourne with some of this country's most respected sporting greats in 1999.

Making an appearance on the *This Is Your Life* program for author Bryce Courtney.

You're kidding coach…I enjoyed my time playing under the tutelage of Mark Ella at Milan in the early 1990s.

Heavy-hitting champagne drinkers…to my left is Silvio Berlusconi, the Italian prime minister and the richest man in the country, while AC Milan soccer manager Fabio Cappello stands to my right. This shot was taken in 1992, before Berlusconi moved into politics.

Sweet success…a win for the NSW Waratahs during my final season. The teammate is five-eighth Scott Bowen.

Left: Playing golf with former Australian rugby league captain George Peponis, cricket greats Bob Simpson and Alan Davidson and former Wallaby John Ballesty.

Right: Enjoying a dinner in Italy with Wallaby mates Tim Gavin (front left) and Mark Ella (front right). We were all tied to the Milan club at the time.

A favourite pastime…I had my golf handicap as low as six. But there's no way I can play off it now.

Left: In Sardinia for a tribute match for Italian internationals Marcelo (far left) and Massimo (far right) Cuttitta. That's their dad in the tie.
Right: You do it this way…turning my hand to coaching in Japan on one of my many visits there over the years.

Left: Kind words…an autographed photo from singer Phil Collins.
Right: I have always been a car fan and relished the chance to drive in the celebrity race at the Australian formula one grand prix in 2002.

Campo meets God…AFL hero Gary Ablett carried the ultimate nickname. This was a promotional shoot in Melbourne in 1994 before the Wallabies played Italy.

Back in Milan, outside the Duomo Cathedral, after the 1991 World Cup.

ground. Still, attack should hold sway in a selector's thinking. After all, isn't that what we have backlines for, to score the tries after the hard work is done by the forwards. During the Rod Macqueen coaching era from the late 1990s, it seemed the scoring of tries played second fiddle to preventing the opposition from scoring any. Teams seemed to be built around stopping the other side, not creating chances for yourself. If I was a coach, I would go in with the attitude of scoring so many points the challenge for the opposition would be to try and score more.

Sometimes I think coaches forget those basics. They blind themselves, and everyone else, with these statistical printouts of player performances which, to my humble way of thinking, do not always shed as much light as the coaches like to portray. I was fascinated, for example, by Eddie Jones' defence of Sailor after his 2002 Test against England at Twickenham. The British journalists gave Wendell a frightful going over, as did one News Limited journalist, Bruce Wilson, who suggested rugby union sell Dell back to rugby league. There were not too many people raving about Sailor that night. But Jones did. He came out quoting how Wendell had so many touches on the ball and carried it x-number of times. What a load of crap. The bottom line should have been, on how many of those touches did he do something constructive with the ball. And, on other touches, was it noted how hesitant he was about taking on the defence. Statistics can be twisted and turned to suit any argument and Jones managed to massage them nicely after that Test in London.

But I do wish Sailor all the best for the rest of his rugby union career. If he ever needs any help or assistance, I'm only too happy to offer my services. I said that from the start, from the first day I met Wendell at the Twin Waters resort, and nothing has changed despite the words exchanged between us. Will he be a great? I have real doubts. But I have always been prepared to pass on anything I can to wingers in this country who feel as though I could be of some benefit to them. I hope some of them do. After 101 Tests, albeit with a few of them at fullback, I would like to think I am qualified to give some insight into the wing position. Not that I'll hold my breath waiting for the call from Wendell. On the Wallabies tour to the UK in 2002, I stayed in the same hotel as the Australian side in London. I don't know if I had ever seen a more sour-faced bunch of Wallabies in my life. They looked as if the world was about to fall apart on them. This was, you might recall, the week after they had been beaten by Ireland in Dublin, in what was Australia's first loss to the Emerald Isle in 23 years. So that might explain the glum expressions. I saw Wendell walking past at one stage and said hello to him. I got a 'hi' in reply but no more. That was the last time we spoke, and that's disappointing.

When I was playing, there were people waiting for me to fall every week. Every dropped ball, every missed tackle, every kick that failed to find touch, they always managed to find their way into the papers. It annoyed the hell out of me but what can you do? If I was worried about some of the things Wendell gets worried about, I would never have got out of bed. All I can say now is: Wendell you still have the chance to prove me wrong. I'm happy to accept that and I'll be only too willing to eat the humble pie.

BYE BYE BOB

Were any of Dwyer's fawning disciples ... ready to mention they might have been a bit premature in trying to carve me up?

There are moments in life you deeply regret. Calling for Bob Dwyer to be replaced as NSW Waratahs coach during the 2003 Super 12 season is not one of them. It was time for change. The Waratahs were not improving. Dwyer had been there for almost three seasons. He was in his sixties and I dared to say what plenty others were whispering behind their hands. NSW needed a new man at the helm, a younger coach with new ideas, and a fresh enthusiasm for the game.

But to go into print in my Daily Telegraph column with those ideas was difficult. Despite what people might think, I do consider the possible fallout before making statements of that sort of magnitude. I also like to be honest. Maye that's my downfall. I'm not one of these off-the-record types who will criticise and backstab but say nothing in the public arena to ensure my nose is clean. I detest that sort of forked-tongue approach. And so I called for Bob's head. Here's what I wrote:

'The time has come for the NSW Rugby Union to face reality and part company with Waratahs coach Bob Dwyer.

It is all going pear-shaped this season with three home losses and yet another defeat to arch rivals Queensland. Make no mistake. The Waratahs have done their dash. They will not make the semi-finals.

Dwyer did a great job for a couple of seasons. He took the side to the semi-finals last year but was also re-signed for a further two years just before the Waratahs imploded at the end of May.

They conceded 96 points to the Canterbury Crusaders and another half-century to the Brumbies a week later. But Bob, by then, was untouchable.

To be fair, a lot of NSW officials probably thought he was still the right man for the job anyway. But the signs this season have not been good.

The Waratahs should have improved since last year. Instead, they appear to have gone backwards, despite their recruitment of top talents like Lote Tuqiri and Nathan Blacklock.

So who is going to wear the blame?

The NSW Rugby Union has to bite the bullet, cut Bob's contract short at the end of this season and get in some new blood, some fresh ideas, a young coach with a long-term future.

There are up-and-coming Australian coaches around the place. It's just that most of them have had to go overseas to get experience at the professional level.

I can reel off three to start with – Ross Reynolds, Michael Foley and Brian Smith. They are all in the UK. They are all players from the past two decades, in Foley's case as late as 2001, and they have a sound knowledge of how the modern-day game is played.

On the home front, there are younger coaches waiting in the wings, as part of the support staffs at the Waratahs or the ACT Brumbies.

The Waratahs won't make the semi-finals this year so, if you remove the financial considerations from the equation, why persist with Dwyer into 2004?

Bob has had a great career. He first coached Australia in 1982 and, even before then, led Sydney club Randwick to a string of first grade premierships.

But what does he have left to give?

I'm not saying the coach is entirely to blame for what has happened this season. But when teams win, the coaches are hailed as heroes. So if they lose they have to bear a fair brunt of the responsibility.

Others in the past have had to do so when the Waratahs have failed to aim up in Super 12.

And one thing NSW continue to show is that they have a problem with their big-game mentality. If it was not for guys like Chris Whitaker, who performs week in and week out regardless of the result, the Waratahs would be in an even worse state.

I just can't fathom why one week NSW go wide to their weapons like Lote Tuqiri and Mat Rogers then ignore them the next. The Waratahs used their big guns against the Sharks in Durban and gave them a spanking.

Against Queensland, how many times did Tuqiri and Rogers get the ball with room to move. And I'm not talking about returning opposition kicks. I'm referring to what the midfield did, or did not do, to create opportunities for them.

And so to this week. How will the Waratahs fare against a side that dished them up 96–19 last season? They will have to be scarred by that defeat.

They will also be nervous about their past two home losses, given they led both matches against the Stormers and Queensland at halftime, only to be run down after the break.

It reminds me somewhat of last season when the Waratahs lost against the Crusaders. I thought they would bounce back the following week. Instead, they crumbled again and got flogged by the Brumbies.

I have a nasty feeling we might see them beaten well again on Saturday night.

That would make four home losses this year. Totally unacceptable. And someone will have to wear the blame. As you know already, I think that person should be Bob Dwyer.'

My fears of a flogging against the Canterbury Crusaders were unfounded. The Waratahs came out and, against the odds, pulled off a great victory. But it did not change my mind on the coaching job. And don't get me wrong. It was a tough call to make because Bob and I went back a long way. He introduced me to Test rugby in 1982, when I was a teenager and a host of experienced Wallabies opted out of the tour to New Zealand. Dwyer took a chance on me. I like to think I delivered. He was also the one who encouraged me to leave the ACT and go to Randwick.

The first time he mentioned it to me, going to Randwick that is, I was just 18. It was 1981 and Sydney had played ACT. It was also the first time I had played against Mark Ella, although I had played against his brother Gary in an under 21's match earlier that same year, as a curtain-raiser to a Sydney-World XV game. Dwyer said I could not go through my career without experiencing the way Randwick play rugby. It would suit me, he smiled. And, you know, he was right. Some of my most enjoyable rugby experiences would have been in the club ranks down at Coogee Oval when I finally moved to Sydney at the end of 1986.

Alan Jones was the Australian coach at the time and thought I'd be better off keeping Canberra as my base. Jonesy suggested I start up my own brand of clothing and open a shop. He was telling me to think of life after rugby and to start preparing for my future. I said no and went to Randwick. Looking back now, was it the right decision? From a rugby perspective, certainly. I loved my time at Randwick. But who knows what might have happened on the commercial front if I had started up a clothing line down there, and had it firmly entrenched by the time the ACT Brumbies hit the Canberra sporting marketplace with a bang in 1996. But I'm more than content with how things have panned out. I think the rugby I learnt to play at Randwick is the kind of rugby everyone should be lucky enough to experience once in their lifetime.

But I digress. As I say, Bob was the one who brought me into Test rugby. He was also the bloke to drop me 13 years later, after the failed 1995 World Cup campaign in South Africa. It would be fair to say our relationship was put under more strain by the events of the time. But that paled into insignificance compared to what happened when I made the suggestion in 2003 that the Waratahs go in search of a new coach.

Fox Sports asked me to be part of their commentary team for a Super 12 match the following month. The Waratahs were playing the Chiefs and, as it turned out, they needed to score only four tries and win to reach the semi-finals. But Dwyer made it clear in the countdown to the match that he wanted no part of any interviews with his former winger — me. He also told a Fox Sports producer he did not want me talking to any of his players. I was never quite sure whether that request came from Bob alone or from the players. In all honesty, I don't really care. If they wanted to react so churlishly to comments in my column, there was nothing much I could do.

I remember standing in the players' tunnel at Aussie Stadium well before the game. The Waratahs were heading to their dressing room after arriving at the ground. I just stood there, watching them file past, when Bob walked by. I said 'g'day', he replied 'hi' without stopping and didn't look too happy. Such is life.

Twenty minutes later, having recorded a pre-game prediction

from out on the ground, I walked back up the tunnel and was standing there with one of the Fox Sports directors. This bloke asked Bob if he would be available for an interview. Dwyer replied: 'With who?' The director told him Phil Kearns. Dwyer said OK. What I had written had obviously hurt him. That was not the intention.

When Bob returned from overseas, where he coached at Racing Club of Paris, Leicester and Bristol, he took over a Waratahs side that had been branded, with justification, as the perennial under-achiever of Super 12. Bob took on a two-year appointment and set about improving the team. He was the right man for the job at the time. NSW were a rabble. They needed a high-profile boss who would bring success immediately. Dwyer, with all his experience, was able to do that.

He also has the most finely-tuned sensors when it comes to unearthing young talent. Everyone knows the story of how Dwyer brought Tim Horan, Phil Kearns, Jason Little and Tony Daly into the Test side as virtually untried rookies in 1989. He plumped for youth and they went on to help win the 1991 World Cup. There have been countless other examples over the years, and a number during his most recent stint with the Waratahs. Dwyer took a punt on rookie flanker Rocky Elsom. He graduated from Super 12 unknown to Wallaby contender in almost record time. Milton Thaiday was another recent acquisition, brought down from Lismore where he played rugby league after the coaching staff studied videos of him in action.

So there were certainly positive aspects to Dwyer's reign, especially when he took NSW to the semi-finals in his second year. The only problem was, NSW Rugby Union officials, so cock-a-hoop about finally having the franchise in the playoffs, went off too early and re-signed Bob for a further two years. He put pen to paper before the last round match against the Canterbury Crusaders in Christchurch. The game will go down as one of the darkest nights in Waratahs history. They were squashed like bugs on a windscreen as the Crusaders made one rampant attack after another to run up an unbelievable scoreline, 96-19. A week later the ACT Brumbies put the cleaners through them by rattling up a half century of points. That would have been the time for administrators to sit back and think whether the Waratahs would go much further under Dwyer. As it turns out, they missed the semi-finals in 2003 when they could not score those four tries they needed while beating the Chiefs in Sydney. It was the same game at which Dwyer made it clear I was not his favourite columnist, despite protestations earlier in the week that he never read my stuff.

My belief that Dwyer had to go was really set in concrete after the NSW-Queensland game, also in Sydney. The Waratahs are still waiting to beat Queensland in a Super 12 match but they had their chances in this one. The fact they could not go on with the job suggested to me there was something amiss. The Reds had been at the foot of the table and the Waratahs were well placed for a back to back shake at the finals. Then Queensland came out and defied the formguide, as they have in the past. There is a different mindset there. The Queenslanders want so badly to win just that one game every year. They could lose the rest and still consider, with a sole victory over NSW, that the season had been a success. They're strange that way but it's a mindset NSW teams have to, one day, make a real attempt to confront. It is surely that little brother mentality, the chip on either shoulder approach that has them fired up so efficiently. NSW tend to be a much calmer collection of individuals. Is it a lack of desire compared to the Reds? Maybe, and while it can be a difficult situation to overcome, given the Queensland obsession for beating NSW, more work has to be put into the mental side of a Waratah team's preparation. Dwyer, naturally, dismissed any suggestion the Waratahs were out-hungered by the Reds. But the post-match comments, especially from the Reds, tell a different story. Reds skipper Toutai Kefu remarked: 'They just don't get it, do they?'

As the 2003 season started to wane after what had been such a promising start, I came out and suggested NSW might need a new coach. It is amazing what happens when you have a few words to say. I spoke about the sport I love and pretty much became the enemy. My comments, as I have outlined, were made in the week leading up to the Sydney game against the Crusaders. It was the first time the two sides had met since that 96-19 result of the previous year. And right through the week I was vilified for speaking out as I had. Bob took the high moral ground and said he didn't care what Campo said. It sure didn't seem that way on the night of the game.

As it happened, the Waratahs scored a famous win. They exorcised the ghosts of Christchurch by toppling the defending champions with a last gasp penalty goal from five-eighth Shaun Berne. Another product of the Randwick club, as was his dad John, an international centre way back in the 1970's, Berne had been brought back to NSW after a couple of seasons in the UK. And he must have learned to kick over there because he had no reputation as a superboot in Sydney. Against the Crusaders, he was rated only a stopgap — until that mighty thump from almost halfway. While there were some people around the place who thought that result was the perfect answer to my column of a few days earlier, and who felt with that one victory Dwyer had shored up his position, I did not see that the situation had changed dramatically. I also took great delight in the Waratahs win. I am a former NSW player, I loved playing for the blue jumper, I want to see them do well. There was no sense of death-riding them against the Crusaders. As far as I was concerned, I had made my point about the coach. I didn't need to have it backed up with a Waratahs loss. As I say, one win, or one defeat, was not going to determine whether my judgment call was right or wrong. It also annoyed me that commentators were trying to spin that the performance was somehow a payback to Campese. Here's what I said the Tuesday after the match:

'NSW coach Bob Dwyer was clearly upset when I called for his head last week. A few players were also miffed by my stance that Bob should go and the Waratahs were washed up as Super 12 contenders this season.

The following night I watched what would have to be their best performance of the season, beating the Canterbury Crusaders to edge back into the tournament top four.

So let me offer my congratulations. It was a terrific win, and over a quality opponent. The faithful at Aussie Stadium have been waiting a while to see that this season.

But do I retract my comments? On Dwyer, no. On the Waratahs prospects, we will have to wait and see — there are still five games to the playoffs.

My issue with Dwyer is that the time to blood new talent has arrived, to bring in a new voice and new ideas. Dwyer has, in his own words, been coaching at the senior level for 26 years. It is time to pass on the baton.

One victory, as good as it was, does not change my thinking.

I also hope my honest appraisal on the eve of the Crusaders game was not a motivating force for the Waratahs. If it was, it can only be a sad reflection on their standing as professional footballers.

They are paid to play at their best every week, not rise only when they get needled in the press.

If they want me to give them a hard time every week to make them play better, I'll oblige, but I'd rather they just go out, with no more urging from me, and serve up the humble pie every week from here until the semi-finals.

While it might surprise Bob and his players, I want to see the Waratahs succeed. Why would I waste my time making suggestions — ways I think they can improve — if I wanted them to sink without trace?

Going back a couple of weeks, I seem to recall taking issue with the fact the Waratahs were having problems with their handling, yet they continued to train in daylight. I wondered why they were not training at night.

Coincidentally, they did the following week.

If Bob took that suggestion from me or it suddenly dawned on him, weeks into the series, that having a session under lights might be a good idea, I don't know. But at least the Waratahs were moving in the right direction in terms of preparation.

The questions now to be answered are: can NSW go on with the job and how can their form fluctuate so madly from one round to the next?

The Waratahs were, the week before playing the Crusaders, beaten by the team that had not won a game before coming to Sydney and still sits at the bottom of the table.

The Queensland Reds put in a gutsy effort against the Hurricanes on Friday night. Bottom line, they lost. They are now one from six with the solitary victory against a NSW side which turned around seven days later and toppled the four-time champions.

Figure that one out.

Is it a problem with the coaching staff?

Perhaps.

Is it something to do with players' enthusiasm? NSW lose two of their most experienced footballers, Matt Burke and Mat Rogers, replaced by two youngsters on the rise in Milton Thaiday and Morgan Turinui.

Thaiday and Turinui turn out to be two of the best on the paddock. Does that say something about them, or the players they are replacing?

Rogers complained the other day that NSW were being harshly criticised. When teams perform to half their potential, I believe they leave themselves open to criticism.

And if NSW, given how well they played against the Crusaders, look at some of their other performances this season, then they have little cause to whinge. Just get out there Friday and belt the Hurricanes. The praise will come soon enough.'

It amazes me how sensitive players and coaches can be these days. You say something that might bruise the ego and look out. You have managers on the telephone complaining. You would think some of these blokes were Hollywood stars. What they should do is make an honest analysis and appraisal of their on-field performances before they start bitching about comments from outsiders.

That whole episode with Bob and the coaching job really opened my eyes. Those who follow the game closely have probably worked out why. For the rest, I'll explain. On one hand we had Bob and his merry band of backroom men not only talking down my suggestion that he step aside, but they were also trying to make out I have no idea what I'm talking about.

Then, presto. Bob decides he's going to stand aside as coach and take on some other position which I don't really understand in full but it keeps him within the Waratahs system. Not only that, but he reveals he was in discussions with the NSW Rugby Union to change his role at the Waratahs when my column calling for his dismissal was printed. So how, in hindsight, did I get it wrong? People were taking pot shots at me for daring to suggest Dwyer be replaced as head coach when Dwyer himself, in secret negotiations, is working towards the same goal. Did anyone bother to revisit that? Were any of Bob's fawning disciples in some sections of the media ready to mention they might have been a bit premature in trying to carve me up? It's just amazing what the spin doctors can do these days. On one hand, when the column first came out, you had Bob dismissing it with a laugh, suggesting no-one takes much notice of what I have to say. But NSW Rugby Union chairman Dilip Kumar saw fit to turn up to training to lend his support to Dwyer. One hundred percent behind the coach, he beamed. If only everyone knew what was going on behind the scenes. I don't know if Dilip was in the loop at that time.

It is disappointing to me that my ties to the Waratahs are getting more frayed with each passing season. If I had treated the players like gods, become a yes man, some sort of lapdog who would only tell them how good they were, perhaps things would have been different. If I had not spoken my mind, if I had gone easy on them, if I had not mentioned what others were thinking but dare not say, then perhaps the Campese name, in the inner sanctum, would not be so sullied. But where is the evidence of all these so-called frivolous attacks? Can someone point out the errors of my ways? Have I been so off the mark that my credibility is shot? I don't think so. All I know is that people say I've always got a comment or an opinion. That might be true. If that comment or opinion is also reasonably close to the mark most of the time, then what the hell is the problem?

One player I have rarely, if ever, criticised in that NSW team is halfback Chris Whitaker. If the Waratahs had 15 of him, they would be getting nothing but praise from me. Whits is tough, he's skilful, he takes on a workload Hercules would baulk at. He never complains, even when spending the best part of an international season warming the Test bench for George Gregan. Whitaker is the ultimate professional. He prepares himself with a minimum of fuss, he goes about his business at a consistently high level of performance and he leads by deed. You never hear him bleating about referees or gesticulating with whistle blowers out in the middle. He rarely loses that look of composure. If you zoomed in on the face of Whitaker throughout the course of a match, you would never tell, from his demeanour, whether his side was comfortably in front or getting the mother of all hidings. That is professionalism for you. And if NSW did not have Whitaker, they would have lost plenty more games over the past few seasons. Hopefully in the future there will be others prepared to step up to the plate as consistently and courageously. It is what the Waratahs need if they are to become a dominant franchise on the southern hemisphere provincial scene. With the number of players they produce, the history of the place and the big town support, NSW should be an ongoing rugby dynasty.

When Dwyer moved sideways in the Waratahs organisation, a former Randwick, NSW and Test teammate of mine, prop Ewen McKenzie, took on what has been tagged the poisoned chalice of coaching. NSW coaches do not have the longest of life spans within the organisation. Chris Hawkins was their first Super 12 coach. He was bumped after one season. Matt Williams, who went on to coach the Leinster province in Ireland and was taking up the Scottish post after the World Cup, managed to stay in the job for three years. Ian Kennedy was the next in line. Like

Hawkins, he was given just one Super 12 campaign before the administration hooked him from the coaching stage. Dwyer succeeded Kennedy and, as I mentioned before, was the right bloke for that particular time. There had been too much turmoil in the NSW ranks. They needed a settling influence and the experience of Dwyer was always going to provide that.

Queensland, by comparison, were never keen to install a revolving door to the coach's office at Ballymore. Bob Templeton, what a great man he was, coached the Maroons for what seemed like a lifetime. When he departed they brought in John Connolly in 1989. 'Knuckles' was not everybody's cup of tea, but he maintained the proud heritage and traditions of Queensland rugby. Principally, that meant he hated NSW, he rallied the troops for every interstate battle as though it were war, and he did, especially in the early to mid-1990's, bring the state enormous success. They were, having won the Super 10 the previous year, the heavyweight provincial outfit in the southern hemisphere, when the game went professional in 1996. Connolly stayed in the job until the year 2000 until the Queensland board decided it was time he departed. Former Wallaby hooker Mark McBain took over and lasted two years before Andrew Slack, a favourite son in Queensland and my Test captain on the Grand Slam tour to the UK and Ireland in 1984, was handed the reins for 2003. As it was with Dwyer, the name Campese was not recommended for mentioning within Slack's company. Again, it came back to a column, and another call for change. Here's what I wrote on May 9, 2003:

'Andrew Slack is a favoured son in Queensland, and deserves to carry that status. He's a great bloke and was a great leader when he was captaining the Wallabies.

But it's time to gatecrash the party. He isn't the man to coach the Reds.

If people think I was tough on Bob Dwyer this season, then it's only fair to give an honest appraisal of the man whose side will, regardless of this weekend's results, finish below the Waratahs on the table.

Despite that, they will probably get more players into the Wallaby team — on reputation in some cases. So what does that say for how the Reds have gone this season?

There is a chance, if the Reds get well beaten by the Highlanders tomorrow night, that they endure their worst finish ever in Super 12. I know hypothetical situations can be tedious, but here goes.

Should the Stormers beat the Cats, the Sharks beat the Bulls and the Chiefs beat the Waratahs, the Queenslanders would finish 11th on the ladder. They would beat home only the Cats, coached by a mate of Slack's, fellow Bananabender Tim Lane.

How does that happen when the Reds have so many Wallabies in their side. Count them. Two in the front row, two in the second row, two in the backrow. There's six in the pack.

From five-eighth to fullback they have genuine Test contenders, when fit, in Flatley, Kefu, Herbert, Sailor, Tune and Latham. All Wallabies too. A total of 12 in the side.

What excuse can be given.

And worst of all, the Reds are not even playing decent football. Their match against the Sharks the other night at Ballymore was Valium without the prescription.

Slack came in saying he was going to change the way the Reds play. He was going to have them playing a brand of rugby embracing all 15 players, and using the obvious strengths they had in their back three with Sailor, Tune and Latham.

It sounded good. Better than the kick and keep it in the forwards stuff we have been so used to from the Reds. But we're still waiting for the transformation to happen.

I read the other day where Slack was suggesting you would have to have only half a brain to realise it was always a good option to get the ball into Sailor's hands.

Instead of talking the coaching philosophy, he should have had the Reds doing it.

Isn't that the job of a Super 12 boss.

I said a few weeks back when calling for Dwyer to be replaced at the Waratahs, that if a team is not doing what the coach wants, if they are not responding to his style, then there can be only one option.

Get rid of the coach or get rid of the players. And I can't see the Reds ripping up all those playing contracts.

Showing Slacky the door will not happen. But I wonder how Mark McBain is feeling right now.

He was the Reds coach for two seasons. In his rookie year, he got the Reds to the semi-finals. In his second season he got the punt, even though Queensland finished fifth with seven wins — the same number as the third-placed Brumbies who went on to make the final.

So Slack is elevated to the role and the Reds, heading into the last round, are sitting with four wins from 10 games. Two from eight before stringing together back-to-back victories over the Cats and Sharks over the past fortnight.

That is not a good season, and certainly not as successful as when the Reds were playing under the much-maligned McBain.

If there were positive signs for the Reds, if they were moving in the right direction and playing a brave new style, you could perhaps excuse their results as a painful, but necessary, transformation for the team.

But they are not playing with panache. I pitied the people who paid to watch the match against the Sharks. There are still some great players in that Queensland side. They should be have done so much better.'

Some two months later, Slack did a Dwyer. He stood down from the job. But unlike Dwyer, he did not want to move elsewhere in the organisation. I think it took plenty of guts for Slack to walk away the way he did. He said he was not enjoying the job and, if that's the case, why persist? Obviously, he could have kept taking the money and toughed it out for another year or more. But he is a principled man, Andrew Slack, and he decided he wanted out. The man in the hotseat for 2004 will be former Test flanker Jeff Miller. A man who has spent that last few years in administration. But he was also a very important part of the 1999 Wallabies coaching set up. That side won the World Cup and Miller probably had a greater hand in the work done to get them there than he was ever accorded after the tournament. It will be interesting to see how he goes in the head coaching position because coaches, in the end, have to shoulder the responsibility for the performances of their sides. Clearly, not every coach has the same cattle to work with, and cannot deliver a title year in year out. If that was the sole measure of keeping your coaching job, then 11 of the Super 12 provinces would be placing advertisements for a new man at the end of each season. But you can, looking at a side on paper, work out roughly whether they are entitled to be considered as contenders, fringe dwellers or just making up the numbers. And the Queensland side Slack had in 2003 should have been contenders. They kicked into gear midway through the tournament but it was, by then, too late.

My argument against Dwyer holds the same for Slack. Why were they not able to get the best out of their players?

It will be interesting, on the NSW front, to see how Ewen McKenzie handles the role through 2004. The Waratahs administration did give him a hand by securing two Wallaby second rowers in Justin Harrison and David Vickerman. It was an area the Waratahs had struggled with for some time. Dwyer, without doubt, would have appreciated the chance to have two quality ball winners in his lineout. For the Waratahs, though, the challenge is to get the best out of what has been such a quality backline. I might not hold coaching certificates nor be up on the latest buzzwords in the game. But if you had given me Chris Whitaker, Mat Rogers, Matt Burke, Lote Tuqiri and Morgan Turinui to work with during 2003, I think we could have come up with something in the way of tactics and skills that would have made them a far more significant danger than they were in Super 12.

The pressure on McKenzie is to make sure the Waratahs do progress. Not in some airy fairy way, where the coaching staff will trot out a basketload of statistics and try to blind us all with science. The proof will be in the Super 12 pudding. Can they, for one, return to the semi-finals after their one and only visit in 2002. And can they, two, finally bring the trophy to Sydney. We will have to wait and see but I do hope McKenzie plays the style of rugby the Aussie Stadium crowd is desperate to see.

Heading off on a slight tangent, given I am discussing McKenzie – who was Eddie Jones' coaching co-ordinator with the Wallabies – I am wary of this modern tendency to promote from within when it comes to rugby coaching positions. It is like they want clones across the board who will all work in a similar manner and to a similar style, so when players reach Wallaby level they are not undertaking a crash course in new patterns of play. I consider that an awfully dangerous way to go. What if the bloke at the top, the Australian coach, does not have it right? What if he is following a style of play that is either outdated or simply ineffective? What then happens to the rest of our representative rugby structure?

Let's see some more instinctive play. It always annoys me when you see runners heading out on to the field, disguising instructions from the coach behind their delivery of a water bottle. Everyone seems to do it and, to me, it is a reflection of how programmed our current players have become. Dwyer, to give him credit, does encourage players to try things out of left field. He does not take the wind-up toy approach to the same extent that other coaches do and hopefully Ewen McKenzie will also avoid being too restrictive. There is nothing more soul destroying than to take away one's right to think. At the same time, the Waratahs have to look at getting their backline right. When you have a back three like they did in 2003, it was bordering on criminal not to give them more ball.

McKenzie was a tight head prop in more than 50 Tests for Australia. He knows how to be tough. With luck, he will also know how to be creative. They nicknamed him 'The Missing Link' during his rugby playing days. I only hope that moniker will hold true and he can provide the bridge the Waratahs need to cross if they are to win a Super 12 title. NSW have the talent.

WORLD CUP WONDERS

Thank God for the Australians and the Kiwis. Where would the game be today without a World Cup competition?

We stood facing the one-deck western grandstand of Concord Oval as the national anthems were played. Sixteen years on, if the Wallabies reach the same point in their 2003 World Cup campaign, they will form a single line, side-by-side, and sing along, just as we did all those winters ago, to Advance Australia Fair. And that is where the comparison will end.

To understand just how far rugby union has burrowed its way under the skin of the Australian sporting public, I can offer no more striking analogy than the 1987 World Cup semi-final and the yet-to-be-played semi-finals of the 2003 tournament at Telstra Stadium in Homebush. The state-of-the-art venue, home to both semi-finals at the fifth World Cup, is only a few kilometres inland from where we met France for a place in the decider of the inaugural global showdown. So close and yet a world away.

In 1987, there were just 18,000 people to watch us lose, at the death, a Test match still hailed as one of the greatest ever played. We could not even raise the house full sign at a suburban ground where the capacity was a tick over 20,000. Less than two decades on, a stadium that was purpose-built for the 2000 Sydney Olympic Games will hold close to 90,000 spectators. And, even then, the semi-finals to be played on those back-to-back days in mid-November could have been sold out many times over. Such was the expected demand for two of the prime knockout matches, the Australian Rugby Union had to implement a ballot system to distribute the sought after tickets. Back in 1987, I would never have thought it possible for the code to come so far in such a relatively short space of time. If it had also been suggested that Wallaby players over the same period would progress from earning nothing to having contracts worth up to $450,000 a year, be receiving $10,300 per Test and be standing to earn around $100,000 in bonus payments if they retained the World Cup title won four years earlier in 1999, I would have sent for the men in white coats to take the deranged prophet to the nearest sanitarium. But fact in this sport can be stranger than fiction.

The 1987 World Cup was a tournament on trial, an idea tabled by Australian and New Zealand officials at the International Rugby Board and only accepted begrudgingly by boffins in the northern hemisphere. The Australian Rugby Union had to underwrite the event, so lacking in confidence was the game's world governing body that the concept would fly. In some ways, they might have been justified for having their doubts, especially about staging the event in Australia. The game here was still a minor sport, with nowhere near the profile it enjoys today. There was hardly any money in the game and, by that, I mean limited sponsorship revenues, only smallish gate takings because there were so few Tests played each season, and nothing in the way of broadcasting rights. The ARU had a staff you could count on two hands and players were in the game only for the love of the sport. Against this backdrop the tournament was split in two, with pool games being played on either side of the Tasman. Here in Australia, matches were limited to Sydney and Brisbane. They were considered the strongholds for the game in this country and, more pointedly, were perceived as the only cities where reasonable crowds could be attracted. Not that the fans rolled up in their masses. An inability to sell out Concord Oval, a quaint if undersized suburban ground, was evidence of the ambivalence with which the Australian public greeted that first World Cup. The tournament, however, with New Zealand downing France in the final at Eden Park in Auckland, proved successful enough – it even turned a profit of around $1 million – to convince the IRB the plan was worth proceeding with, on a four-yearly cycle. Thank God for the Australians and the Kiwis. Where would the game be today without a World Cup competition?

The first World Cup was a forgettable one for me on a personal basis. I had a haematoma in my left leg and while scans showed up nothing, it definitely hampered me during the event. So did an ankle complaint that I had checked out during the tournament, only to be told there was no structural damage. As it happened, doctors eventually found a cracked bone around the joint when the World Cup ended, and I had to be withdrawn from the tour to Argentina later the same year — the trip that would mark the final days of Alan Jones' reign as Wallabies coach. It was also a gut-wrenching disappointment from the entire squad's perspective when we were beaten by France in the semi-final with one of my old mates Serge Blanco scoring the try that killed us off. We had won the Grand Slam in the UK and Ireland in 1984. We had won the Bledisloe Cup in 1986 on New Zealand soil, a feat only achieved once before, by Trevor Allan's tourists in 1949. So we entered the tournament with justified confidence. There were some comfortable wins en route to the quarter-finals where Ireland were seen off without too much difficulty. But then it boiled down to us or France for a place in the final. We still had the nucleus of those previously successful sides on board and we had trained hard leading into the game. When it came to the crunch, though, we could not deliver. We gave up a soft try on halftime and Blanco's brilliance, even though he was on the end of a sweeping French movement and had a straight run to the line, was enough to see them advance. We were a shattered side. I remember how quiet the dressing-room was as we reflected on what had happened. While we had our heads down, cursing ourselves for the odd mistake and the French for spoiling our World Cup party, our conquerors walked out on to the middle of Concord Oval, with darkness descending, and led their celebrations with song.

We were lacking something during that campaign and certainly our preparation had hit a few snags. Sydney guys were wandering off to go to work when we were in the harbour city. We were also training in the afternoon, rather than the morning, which was not conducive to some players who felt they were going stale by lounging around hotel rooms all day. But if we are honest with ourselves all these years later, we have to accept that perhaps the hunger had waned a little after the previous successes under Jones. The bottom line is we just weren't good enough and, even if we had beaten France, it is highly unlikely we could have put away the New Zealand side that went on to take the championship.

The 1987 World Cup was played under a different structure to those that followed. There were no qualifying matches as the organisers set up an invitation-only event with 16 nations accepting the offer to play. There were four groups of four teams each with the top two in each pool advancing to the knockout stages. By the time the World Cup was over, no one doubted the All Blacks had replaced us as the best side on the planet. They were unbelievable, bringing on stars like winger John Kirwan and flanker Michael Jones. They were prototypes for the next generation to follow and mimic. Kirwan was quick, powerful and a prolific try-scorer. Jones was simply an outstanding footballer, one of the best I have ever had the privilege to witness. New Zealand became very much the innovators of international rugby. No one could get anywhere near them. The Kiwis were just so far ahead.

Organisation off the field left a little to be desired in the first World Cup but it was always going to suffer teething problems when the inaugural organisers had to start from scratch. There were no previous blueprints for them to work from. There were no precedents for the fans either, who embraced the event in only lukewarm fashion. The evidence of that came in our semi-final against France when we failed to fill Concord Oval. Long-time supporters had grown to love the Sydney Cricket Ground as our NSW Test venue and there was, I suspect, an element of spectator backlash when the World Cup games had to be shifted to Concord Oval. It was unavoidable for Australia to play their games at the inner-west venue rather than in the eastern suburbs where the game was traditionally strongest. The first rugby union international had been played at the SCG in 1899 and it was still in use until 1996. But for World Cup games, clean grounds needed to be provided and the SCG, with existing perimeter advertisers, could not meet the requirement. So we headed out to a redeveloped Concord Oval and stayed there for two seasons until the Sydney Football Stadium opened for business in 1989.

It is amazing to think just how far rugby union has come. The transformation is incredible. But rugby union these days is run as a business, not as a sport. And the World Cup is a blue chip part of the equation. Unfortunately, the money generated from the tournament does not always go where it is needed most.

Between 1987 and 1991 interest soared, perhaps because the second tournament was staged in the UK, Ireland and France. The profile of the game over there was massive. Britain was swept up in the excitement, even more so when a very boring English side made its journey all the way to the final. Australian audiences had not really been bitten by the World Cup bug four years earlier. We, for instance, did not play games in Melbourne or Perth or any other major capital city or regional centre outside of NSW and Queensland. Rugby was pretty much a no-go zone for those areas.

The standard of play from 1987 to 1991 also improved, I think, as the game evolved and new patterns of play and tactics were devised. Fortunately for us, Australia returned to the forefront of the game after coach Bob Dwyer took the gamble on a batch of new faces and revamped the side. He introduced a young second-rower by the name of John Eales in World Cup year but had also elevated centres Tim Horan and Jason Little, prop Tony Daly and hooker Phil Kearns during a two seasons build-up. Without going into too much detail, the 1991 World Cup was my most memorable campaign in an Australian jumper. I scored six tries in as many Tests and was named the player-of-the-tournament. For some reason I always seemed to play better overseas, in Britain especially, and on this occasion the theory was definitely borne out in my performances during the pool rounds and the sudden-death matches. People still ask me about the pass over the shoulder for Tim Horan to score in the semi-final against the All Blacks, but I would say the try I scored prior to that, by beating John Kirwan and Sean Fitzpatrick to the line, was more personally gratifying.

The Australian side in 1991 took the game to a new level, as we had in 1984, with an attacking style synonymous with

Wallaby sides of the past. The difference was, with both those sides, that we had the forwards to provide us with a steady stream of possession and a rock-solid platform from which to launch our scoring assaults. I still maintain we did the game a favour by beating England in the Twickenham final of 1991. There is no doubt other teams around the world copy what makes the best sides successful. Had the Poms beaten us that afternoon in London, the 10-man game England had adopted throughout the tournament might have been the standard others would mimic in the years to follow. Ironically, the English decision to move away from their staid approach and try to run us off our feet in the decider backfired on them. If they had persisted with what had come natural to them in the games leading up to the final, they might just have snatched the Webb Ellis trophy.

The success of the World Cup was further entrenched by the 1995 finals in South Africa. Touching on our failed campaign briefly, having covered it elsewhere in this book, we were ambushed in the opening game by the Springboks and never really recovered. We had not expanded our game. We were playing the same style we had in 1991, and other countries knew what to expect. The South Africans brought to the table a new physical brand of rugby we were not equipped to handle as they dished us up at Newlands. Eventually we crashed out in the quarter-finals to England. It had been a rocky road for the Wallabies.

Leading into the tournament there was great anticipation because this was South Africa's first crack at a World Cup. They had been allowed back from isolation when the apartheid era was ended and, as a superpower in the game, they were primed to show the international community they were capable of competing again at the very highest level. Like the Springboks, the All Blacks had embraced a new physical approach as well. Thanks mainly to one man — the massive winger Jonah Lomu. He had made his debut the previous year as the youngest ever All Black, but had not made the impact he would at this World Cup. His power running game was something rugby had never previously witnessed. He was a giant of a man but also exceptionally quick.

After we departed the tournament, the Poms were left to play New Zealand in a semi-final. Jonah crushed them almost single-handedly with four tries. Nobody had seen anything like it before. He made experienced internationals look like schoolboys the way he brushed past them on the way to the tryline. And so it came down to the All Blacks against the host nation in the final. It was a fitting finale. The high-octane All Blacks against the combative South Africans who had been adopted by the President Nelson Mandela. I will say this now, without fear of overstatement. That day at Ellis Park in Johannesburg will go down in my memory as rugby's match of the century. It was not necessarily the most skilled game of rugby. But the atmosphere was overpowering and it will never be repeated. Here we had a post-apartheid South Africa, and a black president stepping on to the ground before the game wearing the Springbok jumper once associated only with the white minority in the republic. It was unbelievable to hear the crowd salute Mandela as he met the teams before the match with the No.6 on his back — the same number the South African captain Francois Pienaar wore into the final. Those who were at the ground will also agree that the flyover by a jumbo jet with Go Bokke written on its under-carriage was one of those almost surreal experiences. The plane emerged silently from nowhere — the boom of its engines would be heard only after it could be seen — and flew across the ground at low altitude. All this at a time when rugby was said to be bringing the country together as one. It was a potent emotional cocktail. And it was fitting the Springboks and the All Blacks would fight out the final. It could not have been a better script.

New Zealand were hot favourites, and were entitled to be after some of the magnificent rugby they had played. All the talk in the days leading up to the match centred on Jonah Lomu and how the Boks could possibly stop him. The newspapers ran page after page of suggestions, from the most technical advice to the simple solution of arming South African players with elephant guns. Watching the game, I felt the All Blacks blundered in the way they used Jonah. They seemed so confident he would just run over the top of the Boks they continued to send the ball in his direction, and a posse of defenders followed. He was shut down by sheer weight of numbers. What the All Blacks should have done was use him as a decoy on most occasions. It would have opened up opportunities for other players and, more importantly, would have discouraged the Springboks from sending so many defenders in his direction. Once the pressure eased, they could have brought him into play, no doubt with the same sort of devastating effect he had on the Poms in the semi-finals.

The impact of Jonah Lomu was something world rugby had never seen before and I doubt we will ever see again. He was, if given any room to move, an unstoppable force. He would simply run over the top of people, as he did to Mike Catt, the England fullback, in the semi-finals. Jonah was before his time in many respects. At almost 120 kilograms he was the first of the muscled-up wingers. And he started a trend that still exists today. Opposition sides went looking for hulking speedsters just to try and counter the Jonah factor. Then professional rugby arrived and players were fulltime practitioners of the game. They all got bigger, faster, stronger and defences improved out of sight. Jonah's power game was never going to be quite as effective as it was in 1995. He was still an exceptional attacking weapon. But the unstoppable tag was eventually removed. The All Blacks themselves did not help Lomu maintain his mystique. Instead of using him sparingly as a stormtrooper, they had him hitting the ball up in midfield. Effectively, he was a battering ram. What a waste of such extraordinary talent.

Considering the dramas of the 1995 World Cup, with talk of the World Rugby Corporation swirling in some circles, whispers about professionalism coming from other quarters, and the dream final match-up capturing the world's attention, there was hardly any need for further controversy. But it certainly appeared, shortly after the Boks had been crowned the champions courtesy of a dropped goal from South African five-eighth Joel Stransky — a fantastic kick forever to be remembered. There were claims from the New Zealand camp that several players had suffered food poisoning the night before the final and coach Laurie Mains suspected foul play in the hotel's kitchens. I remember being told in Cape Town, before our tournament opener against the Boks, to be wary during the tournament, that the South Africans would do anything to win the World Cup. The words came from a South African. I am not precisely sure what he meant. But I do not for a second go along with the deliberate poisoning conspiracy theory.

I prefer to think of that day as an afternoon when all the planets were aligned for the Boks. It was almost as if they were destined to win, that fate had intervened in every possible way to make sure South Africa would be celebrating their first World Cup by lifting the trophy, given to their skipper Pienaar by President Mandela. The former political prisoner had given the

Boks his full support and the world, New Zealand excepted, wanted to see that faith repaid.

For Australia the 1995 World Cup was a major disappointment and a learning experience. Looking back we had too many injured players, had some of our leading guys, me included, unable to match their deeds from the past. And we had not really changed our style. Opposition sides knew what to expect from us and the game had changed. It had evolved into a more physical contest and we were not up to the mark when it mattered. Especially in that opening game against the Springboks in Cape Town.

Two years on the Wallabies were still struggling to recapture that dominance on the world stage. The 1997 Tri-Nations campaign was enormously painful, for the players involved and for the rest of us watching from the outside as a once proud side seemingly came apart at the seams. There was a flogging in Dunedin where the All Blacks led 36-0 at halftime and went on to win 36-24. Then the worst of all, that Test in Pretoria against South Africa when the Boks won by a record scoreline of 61-22. I remember Australian Rugby Union boss John O'Neill letting rip on the players, basically claiming they had not been worth their money on the night. There was a real sense of trouble in the camp. Clearly the players had lost confidence in coach Greg Smith even though, as we all discovered later, his health was seriously on the decline. Rod Macqueen stepped into the job for the end-of-season tour that year to Argentina and the UK. His initial trip was hardly five-star material either. The Wallabies lost one of two Tests in Argentina and it seemed, some 24 months out from the next World Cup, that Australia would struggle to be any sort of force.

But the turnaround over the next 12 months was quite

incredible. The Wallabies made a clean sweep of the All Blacks in a three-Test series and from there they launched into a World Cup year that would bring the ultimate success. To review that season fills me with mixed emotions. I remember acting out the haka for an advertisement, and copping flak. I offered an honest appraisal of the Wallabies leading into the tournament and that managed to put me offside with a whole bunch of players. One observation, more than any other, raised the Wallabies hackles. I referred to Daniel Herbert, the massive outside centre in the Australian team, as a battering ram. How else would you describe him? He played a very direct and confrontational role. It was what the coach wanted. But by describing him in such a manner, and suggesting he was one-dimensional in attack, I bruised the boys' pride. My argument was straightforward. The Wallabies had lost the flair in their game. They did not rely on skill in the backline, only this brawn-before-brain mentality.

Even now I find it hard to grasp why we had to take our game to that extreme. It did not sit comfortably with me that Australia was playing rugby in such a manner. Yes, they ended the tournament as champions. But as I have stressed elsewhere in these pages, the Macqueen methods left a lasting, and not too pleasant, legacy for his successor Eddie Jones. You cannot argue with success. But you don't necessarily have to like how that success is achieved. Rugby to me is about entertainment and in the professional era perhaps more so, given the players are well-paid and the spectators are forced to fork out big dollars to watch them in action. Macqueen was a coach who favoured robotic patterns. He coached me in 1991 and 1992 at NSW and the second of those seasons was one of my least enjoyable in the game. I would have to say Macqueen was the one coach I found whose views on rugby were most diametrically opposed to mine.

Defences had, looking at it from his perspective, advanced considerably and he hit on a style he believed would be most successful. Never take the ball too far from the pack and develop the ability to control possession.

The Australia-Ireland game in that 1999 World Cup was unbelievably boring. The Wallabies led 6-0 at halftime and eventually won 23-3, scoring two tries to nil. Watching paint dry had never looked more appealing. In the semi-finals, most people look back with rose-coloured glasses at the spectacular dropped goal five-eighth Stephen Larkham launched from almost halfway. It came in extra-time and Australia went on to win a bruising contest 27-21. But do you know what my abiding memory of that match is? The fact that 48 points were scored but the 100 minutes, including the extra-time, passed without a single try. There could be no more defining moment to show just where the game was at that moment in history. Defence ruled, and the Australians, by tournament end, had conceded just one try in their six-match campaign. The sole try, incidentally, scored against their second-string team by the USA in Limerick.

In remembering the 1999 World Cup success it would be churlish not to praise the Wallabies for what they achieved. But, while delighted to see Australia back at the top, I did not take a great deal of pleasure from the way they went about reaching the summit. Admittedly their 35–12 win over France in the final was the most comprehensive in World Cup history, with Ben Tune and Owen Finegan scoring tries in the decider. As a spectacle, however, it was not a game for the time capsule. And if you wanted to release a video of highlights package from that 1999 World Cup, the goalkickers and dropped goal masters would have figured more prominently than any collection of sweeping backline movements. Call me old-fashioned. Call me out of touch. The Wallabies had devised the most effective way of winning in an era when increased fitness and strength had helped develop defences to the point where attacks were struggling to beat down the brick walls. But it did not mean I had to embrace the philosophy as well. Blind Freddy could see the Wallabies were not the carefree exponents of the running game they had been over several decades. And it makes me wonder, looking back now, why the Australian team was so prickly about being branded by yours truly as a side that fostered muscled up robots.

Perhaps a lot of that angst was superficial. I remember heading home from the 1999 World Cup and stopping over in Singapore. I ran into a player who had been part of Macqueen's successful side. A guy I had previously played Tests alongside. I asked him why there was no intent from the Wallabies to run the ball when they had the strikepower out wide with players like Ben Tune, Joe Roff and Matt Burke. They could have done even more damage to opposition sides by bringing those three into the game more than they ever threatened to during the campaign. He confirmed what I already knew. 'It was safety first, mate,' he said. 'No-risk rugby. It's what the coach wanted.'

Even in 2001, when the Wallabies had won three Bledisloe Cup series in succession, had the World Cup under lock and key and boasted an assortment of other trophies in the cabinet, any move towards flair appeared to be discouraged. An unfair generalisation? I think not, and I offer up in my defence the first Test against the British and Irish Lions that year. Queensland fullback Chris Latham, still among the best attacking fullbacks in the world, was dragged out of the game and not seen again in the Australian starting side for 357 days. He paid the price for being a flair player. Latham was prepared to risk mistakes to make something happen. It was not what Macqueen and perhaps Eddie

Jones, wanted. For all his success, and for that I do congratulate him, Macqueen always struck me as a coach who was scared of his teams having a go. Thank God I wasn't playing in his days as Wallabies coach. Then again, he probably feels the same way about me. I get the impression the David Campese approach to try different things would have been blunted pretty quickly. He might have had me locked in chains and bolted away in a room somewhere. Maybe I would never have been given an opportunity under Macqueen. As I say, we are not on the same wavelength when it comes to rugby.

The structured style Macqueen favoured quickly came into vogue in other countries apart from Australia. It was that old copy-the-winners routine. But at home I think we suffered for it as our provincial sides started heading the same way. The basic skills of backline players suffered because they were not called on to display the trickery and speed of hands so vital to Wallaby sides in the past. It is one of the great ironies of professional rugby. Players were fulltime, training every day, and being paid for it, yet they lacked the rudimentary skills of the part-timers who had gone before them. If you doubt me, give yourself this brain teaser. Come up with a best ever Wallaby XV. Extend it even to selecting a World XV. How many current players, from the Wallabies or elsewhere, would you include? I went through this exercise late in 2002 while doing a series of speaking engagements with former England captain Will Carling, former All Blacks skipper Sean Fitzpatrick and former Springboks leader Francois Pienaar. We discussed it over the odd glass of wine and struggled to find any current players worthy of inclusion.

Hopefully that will change by the end of World Cup 2003. If it does, let me suggest the additions will come from the All Blacks. They are taking the game out of its boring cycle and returning a wonderful attacking edge to the code. The game has come full circle again. The teams prepared to run the ball are those looking most likely to penetrate defences. We saw the All Blacks in their opening two matches of the 2003 Tri-Nations series run up 50 points against both South Africa and Australia. And it came on back-to-back weekends, one in Pretoria and the other in Sydney. Watching wingers Joe Rokocoko and Doug Howlett run from the back field, to watch them communicate with Auckland Blues teammate, fullback Mils Muliaina, was sheer poetry. Hopefully the Australians will be able, in some way, to emulate the free-wheeling Kiwi approach. It is our only chance of retaining the Webb Ellis trophy.

TIME FOR CHANGE

We owe it to Fiji, Tonga and Samoa, and to Argentina, to accelerate their attempts to turn themselves into genuine contenders.

When powerbrokers from the Big Three sit down in 2004 to consider the future direction for the game in the southern hemisphere, there must be consideration given to including the Pacific islands and Argentina in all major tournaments. The current 10-year broadcasting rights deal between News Corporation and the three heavyweight nations of Australia, South Africa and New Zealand (SANZAR) was struck in 1995. When it ends at the close of 2005, the time will be right to expand competitions like Super 12 and the Tri-Nations series beyond current SANZAR boundaries. I am not sure how the figures will stack up in terms of television revenue. But for the good of the sport, and to ensure its continued global spread, we have to look further afield. The SANZAR board and broadcasters will open negotiations in 2004 on what they want for 2006. They will need the time lag in between to sort out the mechanics of any changes made. And changes there should be, by extending the hand of partnership to the South Pacific and Argentina.

Super 12 has been incredibly successful. With five teams from New Zealand, four from South Africa and three from Australia, the concept has been widely embraced. The profile and coverage of the game has increased unbelievably and Australia, in particular, has benefited greatly from the introduction of regular top-quality competition for elite players. Imagine if we were back where we once were, with just two provincial teams, an annual interstate series, and some friendly matches against overseas teams. Sure, the Super Six and Super 10 tournaments set the agenda for what was to follow. But they never provided the week in week out three-month preparation our players now receive before they head off on international duty.

South Africa and New Zealand were never going to struggle in the professional era. They had their domestic Currie Cup and National Provincial Championships to harden and develop their emerging talent. We had NSW, Queensland, to a lesser extent ACT and club competitions in Sydney, Brisbane and Canberra. I still maintain we need to rebuild the club premierships in those three centres and have more representative players on deck in a bid to ensure the up-and-comers get a taste for what might lay ahead. But I also feel we owe it to Fiji, Tonga and Samoa, and to Argentina, to accelerate their attempts to turn themselves into genuine contenders on the world stage. That's what this game needs going forward. More and more teams capable of competing at the highest level. Take Samoa as an example. They announced their arrival as an international force in 1991. No-one knew what to expect from them going into the World Cup because the islanders had not been one of the 16 teams invited to the first competition four years earlier. The Samoan side was also chockful of players based in New Zealand. Not all of them were playing at a provincial level either, so the South Pacific newcomers were not tipped to make too many ripples. So much for the pre-tournament predictions. Samoa gave us a shake-up in Pontypool and beat Wales at Cardiff Arms Park in what was one of the most uplifting days for the game – the Welsh will disagree – of the 1991 championship. They went on to make the quarter-finals before going down to Scotland at Murrayfield.

Four years later, in South Africa, the Samoans again qualified for the last eight before South Africa took them apart on the way to the title. But in 1999 the islanders failed to reach the top eight and, for mine, that signalled a decline where there should have been further development in Samoa's playing stocks and standards. Heading into the 2003 World Cup, they had the great former All Black flanker Michael Jones involved. Of Samoan descent, Jones has been telling anyone prepared to listen how the South Pacific islands need help. The problem is, who's listening? In the professional environment of the modern game, the Samoans — and the Tongans and the Fijians for that matter — will suffer unless they are given the chance to boost their rugby revenues. It is simple economics. If they don't raise money, they can't pay their players. And if they can't come up with the cash, the players will baulk at pulling on the national jumper. Especially now that the International Rugby Board has brought in its one-nation-for-life rule.

Jones gives a hypothetical example: there is a young player of Samoan descent growing up in New Zealand with an exceptional talent for the game. He is approached to play for Samoa. What does the player do? Accept the invitation and be tied to Samoa for the rest of his playing days, potentially earning very little from the international game? Or does he knock back the land of his roots to pursue a dream of representing the All Blacks, and the fame and fortune attached to the jersey with the silver fern? The player, of course, might never reach All Blacks status. He might be a fringe-dweller throughout his career. He might play Sevens for New Zealand or for the New Zealand A team and that alone would prevent him from turning back and playing for Samoa. His hoped for international career might pass without ever playing a Test. Some people might say tough, that decisions like that are part and parcel of professional sport. That might be so, but where does it leave Samoa? A country like New Zealand can afford to lose the occasional player to the island nations. The reverse, however, does not apply. The South Pacific countries need all the talented players they can find to keep rolling over their playing rosters. But what will most of these young kids in New Zealand do when confronted by a situation like the one above. I'm betting the vast majority will turn down certain Test selection with Samoa to keep alive their All Black dreams.

As Jones points out, the IRB needs to embrace and foster the islands, where the game is followed with as much passion, if not more, than it is in places like South Africa and New Zealand. But does the IRB really pay any more than lip service to the Samoans and their South Pacific mates. Jones certainly doesn't think so and he is at the coalface of the whole issue. These are rugby strongholds that are slipping behind because of the over-riding consideration in the modern game – money. They need more of it and the only avenues open to them are the IRB through grants and law changes or the SANZAR countries through an invitation to take part in any expanded versions of the Super 12 and Tri-Nations series. I would not hold my breath on the IRB helping out, so the onus will fall to Australia, New Zealand and South Africa.

What are the answers? Obviously a place in the elite southern hemisphere competitions. At this stage, it would have to be as individual nations (Samoa, Tonga or Fiji) or as a combined South Pacific team at Super 12 level. If that works out, then a combined South Pacific team could be included in the Tri-Nations and one or all of the individual islands could be offered a spot or spots in the expanded Super 12. If only one spot was available, then the islands could stage a Super 12 qualifying series to determine which nation goes through. The qualifying series could even be played in New Zealand where most of the players would be based. The revenue for the matches could be pumped into the combined islands' coffers. Clearly there are shortcomings. Would the islands be competitive first-up? Perhaps not. But I remember South African supremo Louis Luyt saying exactly the same about the ACT Brumbies before they were launched as part of the new-fangled Super 12 competition in 1996. The Brumbies, in a lovely touch, knocked off Louis' Transvaal heavyweights in one of their opening games and finished just one win out of the top four. They were in the final the following year.

The moral to that story is, you sometimes have to take gambles in this game. Off the field as well as on the paddock. The South Pacific islands are too important to the culture of this great game to let them wither now. We need their flamboyance and their missile-like tackling styles. They bring excitement and fun, and pain on occasions, to a game that needs players who are not worldwide clones of each other. The IRB also needs to get in on the act. They like to make out how supportive they are of the island nations. Well, to me, their track record looks pretty ordinary. Where is the growth of the game in Samoa, Tonga and Fiji? Where are the results that show the game's governing body is helping these people stay pace with the superpowers in the professional age? I have seen very little evidence of it, and nor has Michael Jones judging by the way he speaks so passionately about the cause. Someone needs to listen to this man, whose credentials remain unchallenged. Apart from being a gentleman of sport, he is remembered as an on-field legend.

What I do find concerning is that as the Pacific islands seem to be struggling for recognition and assistance from the IRB, there is a real determination from the men in the ivory towers to push the game along in places like Germany and other backwaters of Europe. Would it not be better to shore up the strengths of the code first, the grass roots areas like the Pacific islands and Argentina, before trying to transplant the game into countries where it will never be anything more than an alternative sport? I would be making a big push into the United States and Canada as well. Rugby union could become a major code in Canada. As for the US, it can be a fringe sport and still attract the sort of advertising and broadcasting revenue that would leave some of our major nations in the shade. Japan too offers a land of opportunity and at least the IRB was moving in the right direction by having the Orient in line as a World Cup host in 2011. But taking a World Cup there is not enough. We need to improve the standards in these other countries.

Argentina has done extraordinarily well given they have no set place in the global jigsaw. The top European sides have the Six Nations and the second-tier in Europe play underneath that championship. Australia, South Africa and New Zealand have the Tri-Nations. Argentina relies on one-off campaigns against these countries, and heading into the 2003 World Cup were placed seventh on the rankings, ahead of Scotland and just behind Ireland. How much better could the Pumas be if they were playing annually in a structured competition like the SANZAR jewel in the crown?

So let me ask this question. What is the IRB's long-term plan for the game? If they have one, why have we not been charmed with the blueprint? If they are keeping it under wraps, why? My bet is rugby has become this uncontrollable moveable feast for the administrators in Dublin. They are reacting to issues that rise up on a regular basis, rather than being pro-active, setting the agenda and moulding the game in an image that the masses will find most appealing. To my way of thinking, that means more competitive World Cups, and greater diversity in Test match scheduling while still retaining traditional tournaments like the Six Nations Championship, the Bledisloe Cup and Lions tours.

If we don't head in that direction we'll become like cricket where there is only a handful of top-flight nations and the rest are cannon fodder. Blow out scores do no-one any good, especially in World Cups. Why will the minnows have any incentive to keep turning up? Sure, there is the argument that they are happy just to share the spotlight with the very best every four years. But why should we settle for that?

It is not an easy problem to solve but, if it was, there would be no need for the IRB. They are there to give the game leadership, to make the tough decisions and to steer rugby on a course that will allow it to flourish and prosper further in the future. You sense it needs a good clean out before that will happen. Get rid of some of the deadwood, and the old crusty survivors who have been there for the best part of a century. Get some young blood into the running of the game, get the players and coaches involved in helping to re-write the law book and let's make a serious bid to lift the standards of some second-tier nations so we have a genuinely understandable, global and competitive game. If that can be done, then rugby will build a profile in the international sporting community far in excess of what we have at present.

What we have to accept from the outset is that this game, and professional sport these days, is about entertainment. On one hand the IRB want to be the great protectors of the game's traditions. It might be a sweeping statement, but you can just picture the boffins rubbing their hands with glee and mouthing 'bravo' when they watch a match packed with scrums, lineouts and rolling mauls. All these have a place in the game, I am not denying that. But if we want to turn our sport into an arm-wrestle up front, where the technical side of the forward battle might warm the purist but leave the general populace cold, then forget these fantasies about the code becoming a mega-hit around the world. A game of pub darts would be more interesting.

In the modern age, sport must entertain or be marginalised. It needs to be speed and movement. Rugby can deliver on both fronts, if the referees get their act together and the IRB provides them with a lawbook that is not only easy to read but simple to implement as well. That is one significant problem with the current rules and regulations. Referees can find a dozen or more infringements at any breakdown. It is simply a matter of which one he chooses to penalise.

Referees have too much control at the moment and a lot of it comes down to the way the laws are worded. It allows too much room for that buzzword of 'interpretation'. There should not be any grey areas for referees. The laws should be altered to make them simpler for players, referees and spectators. As I mentioned before, the laws at the breakdown provide nightmares for referees. Maybe there are too many of them. Surely we can devise some way of reducing the number of possible infringements by re-working the regulations around that whole tackle area. At the moment the responsibility of the tackler is to get away from the ball-carrier immediately and the tackled player has to release the ball simultaneously. But there are so many variables at work. The tackler can sometimes be pinned to the ball carrier by other players coming in and there are times when the tackler gets to his feet standing over the guy in possession but he still has his hands on the ball making it impossible for the player on the ground to release. They are little subtleties that can be missed in the speed of the game and it makes a referee's job a nightmare. They miss plenty and it can have a major effect on a game. Why did we have coaches talking about the need for referees to enforce the tackle law to the letter to ensure attractive play at the World Cup? You don't hear coaches in other sports airing concerns about match officials on the eve of a major competition. That should be warning enough to the IRB that we need to get this issue addressed once and for all. It is fine for the traditionalists to say the complexities of rugby are part of its attraction. But I have heard few people outside the inner circles of the game praising the technicalities of our game. If the IRB is happy to maintain that quirky aspect of rugby, fine. But it could be so much better.

The game's top brass seem to concentrate more on trivial matters, like halfbacks not putting the ball in straight at a scrum. Referees are instructed to pull up lineouts if the ball is not thrown straight down the middle. I can understand that if one side is trying to take advantage of the contest for possession. But can someone explain to me why a defending team should be given a scrum when they don't jump at a lineout and the hooker throwing it in is half a foot out in accuracy? The defending team was never disadvantaged in the first place because they had conceded possession by not jumping for the ball. Likewise in the scrum. When the ball is at the feet of the No.8 and the front-rows come up, why re-set the scrum? The ball is about to come into play and then the game has to come to a stop for a boring re-set. Sure, referees are only playing to the laws, but it does the sport no good as a spectacle.

I know with the above examples I am calling on referees to show a little bit of empathy for the game, to referee to the spirit of the laws rather than to the letter. And earlier I spoke of breaking the laws down to make them more simplistic so referees do not have judgment calls to make. But this is part of the dilemma for the IRB. They have to find a happy medium somewhere and it should mean, after the World Cup, sitting down and having a thorough review of the laws. Work out where we want the game to head and structure the laws accordingly. But always taking into account that rugby, as a professional sport, is also in the business of entertainment.

I have no doubt part of the frustration for teams during the international season of 2003 leading into the World Cup was caused by over-zealous referees. They were out to impress because they had assessors in the grandstand scoring their performances. World Cup selection for them was at stake. It was also evident that the assessors were basing their scores on how many correct decisions were made. In other words, the more penalties a referee could find, the better he must have been doing his job. Ask the spectators what they thought. All the fans want to see is an attractive spectacle, not one dominated by the bloke in the middle and his whistle. In future, perhaps the IRB should announce its panel of referees a few months in advance of the tournament. Then they can relax into the mid-season internationals and not be paranoid about missing the odd infringement and having their scorecard marked down because of it. Leading teams playing under those referees can also sort out any problems they might have with a particular referee they are likely to encounter when the World Cup rolls around.

As for law changes elsewhere in the game, I do side with the traditionalists and give a thumbs down to any suggestion that rugby does away with kicking out on the full from inside your own quarter. It is an intrinsic part of the game and also a skill. In fact, I would even consider looking at the rugby league rule known as the 40–20 and introducing a similar regulation to our game. In the rival code, it rewards any kick from inside your own 40m that finds touch, on the bounce, inside the opposition quarter. The team putting the ball into touch is rewarded with a scrum feed. Rugby could offer the same, with an attacking lineout where the ball goes out. Some students of the game might be horrified by the suggestion, thinking I am encouraging more kicking in the game. But what I am encouraging with this idea is the chance for an attack to break up defences more easily than they can at the moment. For instance, wingers would have to weigh up whether they drop deeper in defence to counter any attempt of a 40-20. If they do, then the attacking side has the option to run the ball, knowing if they get it wide quickly enough the defence could be caught short because the winger has dropped back out of the frontline. If the winger stays up and the kicker is successful in finding the line with a 40-20 then the chances of a try will also be increased by the formation of an attacking lineout inside the defending team's 22. It's worth a thought.

It might also encourage some of the supposed superstars of the modern game to fine tune their skills with the boot. It is a bugbear of mine in this age of fulltime professionalism that we have players in key positions who cannot kick with both feet. The game might be faster and the players stronger but the skill levels have certainly not improved. Tactical kicking, when you look at how defences have improved in recent years, could in the end help us to produce a more attacking game. Having defences in two minds is the key to making breaks and if you can keep defenders guessing by employing the occasional kick, then you can create the hesitancy that will allow the ball runners to do the damage.

There have also been left-field calls to reduce the number of players on the field. To get rid of flankers and turn our game into

Wedded bliss…Lara and I on our big day at George in South Africa in January, 2003.

On the run…the front cover to the menu for my tribute dinner in 1995.

All in the family...my father Tony, Lara, me and my mother Joan after I received my AM at Government House in 2003.

On holiday with Lara at the Great Wall of China

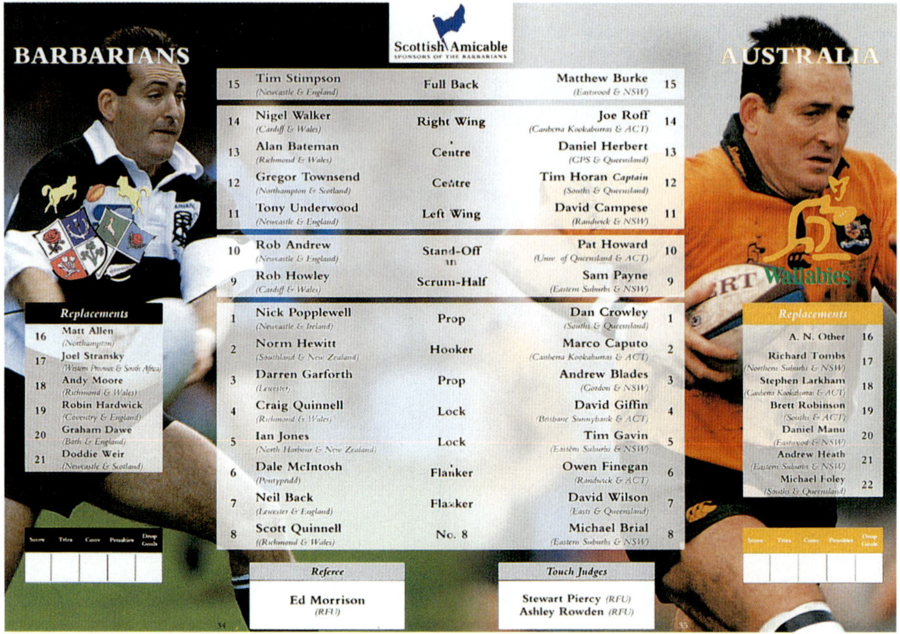

Scottish Amicable
SPONSORS OF THE BARBARIANS

	BARBARIANS		AUSTRALIA	
15	Tim Stimpson *(Newcastle & England)*	Full Back	Matthew Burke *(Eastwood & NSW)*	15
14	Nigel Walker *(Cardiff & Wales)*	Right Wing	Joe Roff *(Canberra Kookaburras & ACT)*	14
13	Alan Bateman *(Richmond & Wales)*	Centre	Daniel Herbert *(GPS & Queensland)*	13
12	Gregor Townsend *(Northampton & Scotland)*	Centre	Tim Horan *Captain* *(Souths & Queensland)*	12
11	Tony Underwood *(Newcastle & England)*	Left Wing	David Campese *(Randwick & NSW)*	11
10	Rob Andrew *(Newcastle & England)*	Stand-Off	Pat Howard *(Univ. of Queensland & ACT)*	10
9	Rob Howley *(Cardiff & Wales)*	Scrum-Half	Sam Payne *(Eastern Suburbs & NSW)*	9
1	Nick Popplewell *(Newcastle & Ireland)*	Prop	Dan Crowley *(Souths & Queensland)*	1
2	Norm Hewitt *(Southland & New Zealand)*	Hooker	Marco Caputo *(Canberra Kookaburras & ACT)*	2
3	Darren Garforth *(Leicester)*	Prop	Andrew Blades *(Gordon & NSW)*	3
4	Craig Quinnell *(Richmond & Wales)*	Lock	David Giffin *(Brisbane Sunnybank & ACT)*	4
5	Ian Jones *(North Harbour & New Zealand)*	Lock	Tim Gavin *(Eastern Suburbs & NSW)*	5
6	Dale McIntosh *(Pontypridd)*	Flanker	Owen Finegan *(Randwick & ACT)*	6
7	Neil Back *(Leicester & England)*	Flanker	David Wilson *(Easts & Queensland)*	7
8	Scott Quinnell *((Richmond & Wales)*	No. 8	Michael Brial *(Eastern Suburbs & NSW)*	8

Replacements (Barbarians)

16	Matt Allen *(Northampton)*
17	Joel Stransky *(Western Province & South Africa)*
18	Andy Moore *(Richmond & Wales)*
19	Robin Hardwick *(Coventry & England)*
20	Graham Dawe *(Bath & England)*
21	Doddie Weir *(Newcastle & Scotland)*

Replacements (Australia)

A. N. Other	16
Richard Tombs *(Northern Suburbs & NSW)*	17
Stephen Larkham *(Canberra Kookaburras & ACT)*	18
Brett Robinson *(Souths & ACT)*	19
Daniel Manu *(Eastwood & NSW)*	20
Andrew Heath *(Eastern Suburbs & NSW)*	21
Michael Foley *(Souths & Queensland)*	22

Referee
Ed Morrison *(RFU)*

Touch Judges
Stewart Piercy *(RFU)*
Ashley Rowden *(RFU)*

The team lists for my last match in Australian colours, against the Barbarians in Cardiff in 1996.

Sevens heaven…the victorious Australian team after we won the Paris Sevens in 1998.

A new team...the World Cup commentary experts for radio station 2GB. From back left myself, Andrew Moore, Jason Little. Front: Alan Jones and Ray Hadley.

On my way...looking for an opportunity during my last season in the Wallaby jumper.

The David Campese World XV that played the Australian Barbarians at the Sydney Football Stadium in 1994.

A vintage centre…sharing a drop of red with another Test centurion, Frenchman Philippe Sella.

Light my fire…running with the Olympic torch before the 2000 Games in Sydney.

Bronze medal winners…the Sevens team that finished third at the 1998 Commonwealth Games in Kuala Lumpur.

Accepting my Australia Medal from the NSW Governor Marie Bashir in 2003. The Governor's husband, Sir Nicholas Shehadie, once held the record I am now honoured to have…for making more Test appearances than any other Australian player.

rugby league without play-the-balls. The reasoning is fitter, faster, stronger players are closing down attacking opportunities. Again, I side with tradition. We don't need to cull any players. We just need to get smarter about the way we play the game and attempt to prise open defences. This is a simple game, one we sometimes make too structured. The flair disappeared from the sport, especially in Australia, when we went to a no-frills style to achieve the success we did from 1998-2001. It worked. It was right for its time. But the cyclical nature of this game has brought us back to the need for flair. If we develop enough players with the footwork to stand up their man, then the impression that we have too many players on the field will fast fade. New Zealand showed that in Pretoria during the 2003 Tri-Nations series. They smashed up the Springboks 52-16, running in seven tries with a wonderful style of play built on winning quick possession and freeing up the exceptional ball runners they had out wide. I didn't see the Kiwis complaining that South Africa had two too many players on the pitch. If anything, they could have done with an extra couple. They had no answer to the pace and precision of the All Blacks.

The Auckland Blues were the same during the Super 12 series. To my mind they were the team that turned the game on its head at the start of the World Cup year. They went away from the norm of recent seasons. Even the All Blacks of 2002 were playing a rigid sort of game. It was a style based on the Canterbury Crusaders, who ground down their opponents before putting them away. The Blues didn't worry about the grinding side of things. They just went out there, bayonets attached, and slaughtered rivals with brilliance. Carlos Spencer at five-eighth was brilliant, and they had that exhilarating back three of Doug Howlett, Joe Rokocoko and Mils Muliaina. Providing their forwards did the donkey work expected, the backs had too much polish. It was no surprise, but it was a major relief for me, that they won the Super 12 title. In this game, people follow winners, and I wait now for teams around the world to embrace the same attack-based game the Blues brought back to rugby. They did, of course, have the advantage of fielding perhaps the fastest fullback-wings combination the game has ever seen. Rokocoko is supposedly the quickest in their side, faster even than Howlett who once dreamt of being an Olympic sprinter and has clocked a 100 metres time of 10.76 seconds. But there was more to the Blues than blinding space. They had a creativity about them that allowed them to exploit the speed out wide. The same sort of individuality that has been lacking, and not encouraged by coaches, for some time. Eddie Jones wants to do the same with the Wallabies and, for Australian rugby's sake, we should all embrace the approach. This game is up against rugby league and Australian football. Unless we give the paying spectator value for money, they will go elsewhere.

Perhaps the most radical suggestion I have for improving rugby as we move into the future is the re-structuring of the northern hemisphere schedule so we have a global season. When the attempted takeover of the World Rugby Corporation was launched in 1995, that is what they had in mind. Obviously to align the seasons between north and south, those above the equator would have to play in summer. In Europe, I think the proposal would be a real positive. Instead of playing in sleet, mud and freezing temperatures which did, for more than a century, encourage teams to play 10-man rugby, they could take to the field in dry conditions with the sun on their backs. Those two factors alone would help encourage a more attacking approach. I should stress here that England have on occasions showed they are capable of playing a wide game. But in the club scene over there, the forward contest still dominates and it comes back to the wet and wild climatic conditions in which they have to play the game. At present, the make-up of the seasons never really allows for a fair comparison when teams travel out of their own hemisphere. Take the 2002 November Tests where England beat Australia, New Zealand and South Africa in successive weeks. A superb achievement but there was still the whiff of doubt over the Poms' triple treat. They met an Australian side that was supposedly fatigued after a long domestic season. The Kiwis had taken an experimental side across and the Springboks were seemingly at the end of their tether. Apart from Super 12 and the Tri-Nations, their players also had to come through a tough Currie Cup campaign. So there were excuses for all three against England.

It is the same when the English come down under. It is usually at the end of a frightfully long season for them while the home teams are at the start of their international matches. One team fresh the other starting to flag.

What better way to even up the contests than having both teams playing at the same point in their seasons. There would be no doubts then, no excuses. If the Poms managed to knock off the three southern hemisphere powers back-to-back at Twickenham, then they would rightfully claim they were, at that point in time, the best team in the world. The home ground factor would be the only variable. But results, given everything else is equal, would then shed light on just how much playing on familiar territory means to sides like England.

The most appealing aspect to having Europe shift seasons, though, is the effect it might have on their week in week out football. I'm convinced, from club level up, playing in better conditions would help develop better skills and eventually lead to better competition. And all those things equal more spectator appeal. It would also take rugby union out of direct competition, at least for a few months, with the number one code of soccer.

Visitors to my shop always come up with weird and wacky ideas and another I have heard in recent times is that the number of points for a try should be lifted from five to six or even seven. I honestly don't see the need for such a move. In many cases it is not through lack of effort that teams are not scoring tries. It is through lack of skill and confidence. The best example I can think of is the NSW Waratahs in their final Super 12 match of 2003 when they needed to score four tries against the Chiefs from New Zealand to advance to the semi-finals. It was irrelevant whether tries were worth five or fifty-five points that night at Aussie Stadium in Sydney. The Waratahs could not reach the number required and a place in the final four was lost. The argument of course for lifting the value of a try is to encourage teams to attack the line rather than shoot for penalty goals. But in this game, things are not always what they seem. Sure, the encouragement to attack would be there. But so too would the desire of defending sides to concede more penalties, realising to sacrifice three would be chicken feed compared to giving up almost a double figure score if their opponents collected a try and a conversion. For that reason I would not tamper with the try-scoring value, or the three-point reward for penalty goals. If you reduced the value of penalty kicks, then defending teams again would be more inclined to offend. If the lawmakers want to tamper with any part of the current scoring method, then perhaps they could look to drop the worth of dropped goals. I don't think we want a situation where two dropped goals are worth more than a try. It gives too much incentive for teams to take a negative approach once they reach the attacking quarter.

From a philosophical viewpoint, we also have to accept this

game is on the path to irreversible change in terms of the people who play it at the highest level. When I first came into the Wallabies, there were lawyers and professional people throughout the side. Take a quick flick through history. Have a look how many doctors and captains of industry have captained the Australian side. Most of the players to have donned the national jumper have also been products of the private school system. I was one exception. There were others, but not too many when I was around. So when you combine those two factors, it is understandable that rugby union in Australia carried a reputation for being the game of the tweed coat and leather patches brigade. That is changing – and dramatically. Private schools will continue to be the primary nursery of the game, but it will attract kids from the government system too, because they will see the code as a potential career.

For the same reason, talented rugby-playing kids from either side of the education system who intend pursuing a professional career – be it as a doctor, lawyer, stockbroker or whatever – will have a tough decision to make when they leave school. Do they go for the bucks outside the game or try to make it as a fulltime footballer? If they choose the latter, there is another issue that needs addressing, and I have to commend the Australian Rugby Union for moving on the right path with this one. Players need education about what awaits them after rugby, and what they need to do to prepare themselves. The ARU advises players on potential tertiary qualifications and offers career counselling. I think they should be even more hardcore with it and write into players' contracts that they must pursue something, be it a job or study, outside the game. Players these days have too much time on their hand. Too much dead time to waste their money or get into trouble. And I don't necessarily mean fighting or off-field incidents involving others. I'm talking about trouble for themselves, be it with drinking or gambling. If guys are in their early twenties, with pocketsful of cash and plenty of hours in the day to fill, temptations will touch them. The ARU needs to beware.

DOWN TO BUSINESS

The high-powered British businessman Nigel Ray offered me enormous money to go and play with the Saracens club.

My playing career has been lovingly boiled down to three minutes of video highlights. It's a package I will usually have played to an audience before a public speaking engagement. Fifteen years of sweat and slog and a lifetime worth of enjoyment are crammed into those fleeting moving pictures. It is also a timely reminder, every time I see it, of how time marches on. But I like to think I have moved on with it. Where my life was once dominated by boots and balls, training and try-scoring, it now has a more sedate, if no less draining direction. Over the past decade my business interests have grown substantially and, I hope, over the next five years will expand and flourish even further.

The seeds of my post-rugby existence were sown in late 1991, when I returned from our triumphant World Cup campaign. Sitting down to dinner one night with my good friend, now business partner, Daryl MacGraw, he asked me what I would like to do when I eventually gave the game away. Daryl suggested even then it was time to start planning for the future. He was working for Tooheys, I had just decided I would stay in Australia after the Channel Ten television network came up with an offer that ensured it would be worth my while to remain at home. Before Ten came to the party, I had seriously considered retiring from international rugby and moving to Italy. There was a position available with a golf resort in some sort of ambassadorial role. These, remember, were the days of amateurism. Playing for the Wallabies was not paying the bills. As the night progressed and the wine flowed, I told Daryl owning a sports store really appealed to me. The following day he was scouring Sydney looking for opportunities. He found one in St Ives, on the city's north shore, and within months I had my first shop. My new role in the retail trade did not hold back my rugby. I continued sharing my time between Australia and Italy, playing most months of the year and still getting a huge kick out of the game. But I also had the comfort of knowing the foundation had been laid for when I eventually decided to hang up the boots.

In 1996, there was a chance for me to move to England on a fulltime basis for a couple of years. The high-powered British businessman Nigel Ray offered me enormous money to go and play with the Saracens club, where Tim Horan would eventually head when he retired from Test football four years later. It was a major temptation, I will not deny that, but two factors eventually convinced me to turn down the deal. One, I did not know whether I would handle the weather in England. In Italy, it gets cold. But it is not so consistently grey or miserable as it is in the UK. Two, I was a bit concerned that if I took myself out of the Australian environment for two or three years, I could lose significant business opportunities. By the time I returned, or so I figured, I could well miss the boat. The business argument was the clincher. I rang and told Nigel I would not be wearing the Saracens jumper.

It was also in 1996, after my last tour to the UK, and my last game for Australia against the Barbarians in Cardiff, that a young sporting hopeful came to meet me at Heathrow Airport in London before I flew home. His name was Mark Webber. You might know him now as Australia's latest formula one motor racing star. But, back then, Mark was struggling to make ends meet as he chased his dream of breaking into the four-wheeled big-time. I had played with Mark's dad Alan at the Queanbeyan Whites way back at the start of the 1980's and, because of the connection, I was phoned by a mutual friend to see if I would meet with the young bloke and perhaps steer him in the right direction as he sought out sponsorship possibilities. I had heard of him, in a vague sort of way. The Queanbeyan network sticks solid and my mum was certainly well versed in what Mark was achieving in Europe. I had no problem with meeting him and was impressed by his desire to succeed. I returned to Australia then headed back to Europe trying to convince Australian businesses over there that he was worth supporting. In the end, some money was organised for Mark and he was able to keep his overseas base. From there his career went into orbit. Those dealings with a young Mark Webber also convinced Daryl and I we should expand our interests and it led to the establishment of Campese Management Group. Our list of clients includes the swimmer Alex Popov, golfer Brett Ogle and basketballer Lauren Jackson. We did not want to be restricted to rugby union players and it's good to have that mix of sports stars under the umbrella. It has been a fruitful experience too. We started with three employees on the books at CMG. We now have 13.

Once my Test career ended, the business continued to grow in other areas as well. We opened the Canterbury shop at the Rocks in partnership with the New Zealand-based sportswear manufacturer and eventually went it alone by buying the franchise. There are also shops at Warringah Mall on Sydney's northern beaches and one at the QVB building in the city centre. A further arm to the business is our hospitality side, which has included the rights to stage events during the 2003 World Cup. As we continue to diversify, there is no doubt I am indebted to the efforts of Daryl MacGraw, who has run Campese Management Group and was the catalyst for my move into the business world. He advised me to get my post-rugby life in order well before I finished playing and it was the sort of counselling that has enabled me to be in the position I am today.

I do consider myself extremely lucky to have also rubbed shoulders and made acquaintances, even friends, of some powerful corporate identities, both here and overseas. Most have offered a word of advice, some an offer to help me out on the business side. Either way, it has been part of the learning experience for me. Bob Mansfield, the Telstra chairman who was kind enough to pen the foreword to this book; Ted Pretty, a Telstra executive; James Strong, the former Qantas boss; Nick Shehadie, a former Wallaby prop, Lord Mayor of Sydney, boss of SBS television and a member of the SCG and Sydney Football Stadium Trust — all these people and so many more have enabled me, in Australia, to become more corporate savvy in recent years. Overseas, I count former British and Irish Lions winger, Heinz boss and media proprietor Tony O'Reilly as a friend. He's a guy who played Test rugby and excelled at the highest level. But those lofty sporting achievements pale into insignificance compared to the impact he has had on the business world on a global basis. He has a great aura about him and I enjoy the times we catch up when occasionally in the same city, like during the 2000 Sydney Olympics when Tony played the most gracious of hosts in his corporate suite at Telstra Stadium. We continue to keep in contact and he encouraged me to go ahead and write this book, to give my perspective on the game since retiring from action in the middle. Another interesting character is Silvio Berlusconi, who was an Italian media magnate and the owner of the A.C. Milan soccer club when I first met him, before his corporate career carried over to politics and led him to the highest seat of power in his country. Berlusconi was also the benefactor of the Milan rugby union club where I played and Mark Ella coached. I found him to be a guy who just loves his sport. He had fair taste in houses too. I was invited to his villa a couple of times. The producers of that TV show *Lifestyles of the Rich and Famous* – if it's still being shot – don't know what they're missing. While I was playing in Italy, Berlusconi invited me to a couple of A.C. Milan games and, on one occasion, I recall presenting him with an Akubra hat. Just a bit of an Aussie keepsake for him. Our eyes for fashion were obviously turned in different directions. I never saw him wear it.

But the man who has had most influence on me, apart from Daryl, as I try to make a name for myself off the field, would have to be my former Wallabies coach Alan Jones. He has been enormously successful in his own right as the breakfast king of Sydney radio. He has always been available when I need advice, and brought me on board at 2GB as part of their World Cup commentary team.

Even though I don't in any way consider myself a business guru, I can see the comparisons between a successfully run sporting team and a cutting edge company. In sport you need a good coach and the cattle to succeed. In business you need a wise head at the top and quality staff. If there are elements of the business that just don't pull their weight then it's very difficult to be successful. One of the differences, though, is the need to create the right impression. When I was playing rugby, being part of a team, it was also more acceptable than it would be in the corporate sector, to speak your mind. The verbal blasts I have given in the past, when it comes to rugby, have all been aimed at improving standards. But in business, I think you have to be a little more circumspect. It comes with the territory. Perhaps I might have to pull back a little on the public comments too. I'm sure a few coaches and players around the place wish I had done that some time ago. It doesn't mean I'll be backing off in my newspaper columns. I have always been honest and always will be. I don't want to compromise the ideals I've held throughout my life. What I might do though is restrict my availability when all arms of the media come knocking for a comment. I know I'm outspoken and I know the papers, radio stations and television networks are aware of it too. That's part of the reason the phone rings so often with interview requests. But if I want to have respect in the corporate world, I can't foster any perception that I'm just a former player more interested in commenting about modern day trends in the game rather than getting down to post-rugby business. There is no escaping the fact I will always be, even in the corporate community or should that be especially in the corporate community, David Campese the rugby player. But I would like to tweak that recognition factor just a little. I would like people to see me as David Campese the rugby player who has also made a successful transition into business. That is my challenge over the next few years. To continue the growth of our various pursuits, make more deals, expand my own education in the corporate world and command respect for my efforts away from the rugby paddock.

Your choices in life are often simple. I could have retired and been content with what I had achieved as a player, meandering through the rest of my years while holding on to the memories of a time when rugby was my one and only priority. But I do have a naturally competitive streak. I guess that comes as no surprise given I played Test rugby for 15 seasons. So when the time to retire came, I did not want to just drift away. I would like to think in the years since I stopped playing the transition to business has progressed relatively smoothly. I like to think Daryl and I are a bit like opposing five-eighths. I'm the ideas man, the bloke who's prepared to take the high-risks in the backline. Daryl is more the percentages player. He's the five-eighth who provides the steadying influence. The bloke who puts the ball into touch when you need to clear your line. I'd be more inclined to say damn the consequences, let's run it. And if anyone mentions the 1989 Lions third Test, so help me . . .

But in business, as in rugby, I consider myself to be exceptionally fortunate. I have met good people, people of influence, friends and associates who have helped shape my life after rugby. Helped shape who I am today.

BEST OF THE BEST

I don't believe we ever saw the best of Mark Ella. He was gone too quickly, retiring at age 25.

Comparisons are always odious in sport, perhaps even more so in rugby union. Trying to line up players from different generations is virtually impossible because nothing quite remains the same. The opposition varies, so too the teammates. And in our game combinations are so vital. For instance, how would the great halfback Ken Catchpole have fared behind some of the dominant packs of the 1980s and 1990s? He might well have been the greatest player rugby has ever seen, in any country. Likewise Mark Ella, if he had hung around long enough. Mark retired after the Grand Slam tour of 1984. He was just 25 years of age. What did we miss out on because of his premature exit? I'll go this far and say we never saw the best of Mark Ella. He was still improving, still developing what were already masterly skills in the five-eighth position. But at 25, he was nowhere near his peak. He had, after all, only been a first-choice Wallaby selection for two years. In 1982, after the first Test against Scotland at Ballymore, he was dumped for Paul McLean. His brother Glen was dropped too. They came back for the tour to New Zealand that same season, which just happened to be my entry to the international ranks.

Looking back to those days, to the Bledisloe Cup glories of 1986 and 1994, to the World Cup in 1991 and even the occasional down times, I consider myself unbelievably fortunate to have achieved what I did in the game. To have played Test rugby for so many years, 15 seasons in all, was immensely satisfying. I devoted myself to the game. More than once I uttered the words 'rugby is my life' and every time it was said with feeling. Which brings me back to comparisons. It is not one of my favourite topics but I do understand that people love debating these sort of issues. Whether Ella was better than Lynagh (Mark gets my vote every time). Whether Tom Lawton or the hooker that replaced him, Phil Kearns, contributed more to the code in Australia (thumbs up to Tommy). It is all so subjective. There are no right or wrong selections and I also have to admit my mind over a decade has seen my opinion sway on occasions.

But at the risk of upsetting former teammates and the galaxy of international stars I played against during my career, I have decided to choose two sides. One is what I consider my all time favourite Wallaby XV – from players whose careers crossed mine somewhere between 1982 and 1996. The second is my Dream International XV – drawn from the players I played against during the same period.

When I look back, I tend to think I was lucky enough to witness what was roughly three generations of Wallaby teams. There was that side of the early 1980's when a few of the old hard heads were still around, the side of the mid 1980s which enjoyed so much success under the coaching of Alan Jones, and the team which went on to win the 1991 World Cup with a great sprinkling of rising talent alongside some long-serving but still world-class players. It sort of ended there because many of that 1991 side hung on until the end of my career. As you have read in the previous pages, it was one of the reasons our 1995 World Cup campaign went pear-shaped.

But enough of the time wasting. Time to announce the Campese Selections. And we'll start with the Australian All Stars.

FULLBACK — ROGER GOULD

He was a great player, and I don't use the word loosely. He was also exceptionally helpful when I first came into the side.

Roger was a big bloke for a fullback, had the most massive calf muscles I have seen on any footballer, and could punt a ball into a different post code. But he was also an attacking weapon from fullback like we have probably not had since, until Chris Latham brought that same sense of involvement to the position. He timed his runs into the backline perfectly and, because of his size, caused panic in rival defences. His own defence was sure and safe. Gould really was the complete fullback package. Even Alan Jones admitted as much in Wallaby Gold, the History of Australian Test Rugby. Alan says of Roger: 'My best player, I think, was Roger Gould. If your defensive line is going to hold up, the opposition are going to roof it, and you've just got to have someone who's absolutely rock-solid. Gould was flawless. He was a freak. He just did wonderful things.' He was also a terrific team man. I will not forget the support and encouragement he gave me when I first came into the side.

RIGHT WINGER — BRENDAN MOON

Here was a player unique in his own way. He scored 14 tries in 35 Tests and really was a quality finisher.

Brendan was blessed with great pace. Not really a creator but give him a chance and he would score. His running style was especially impressive. He looked like a genuine track sprinter. He also had good strength and his defence was sound. A bit like Gould at fullback, he was the all-round performer. But again, like Roger, he could give defences the worst of nightmares. I enjoyed playing with Brendan and it was a great shame when he broke his arm in the opening international of the Grand Slam tour in 1984.

He was replaced during the England win and had to fly home. The squad at the time took the news really badly. That shows how popular 'Benny' had been. He did come back from the injury and played three more Tests in 1986, against France and Argentina twice.

OUTSIDE CENTRE — GARY ELLA

This was tough, really tough, because I played with so many quality outside centres. Saw them at close quarters too given they were generally the ones delivering the final pass to send me away up the touchline. Jason Little was obviously a standout performer, Andrew Slack filled the role for the first few years I was around, Matt Burke and Joe Roff had a dabble in the No.13 jumper and so did Brett Papworth before he left for rugby league. Others to play there during my time included Anthony Herbert, Daniel Herbert, Dominic Maguire, Brad Girvan, James Grant, Michael Cook and Richard Tombs.

But my vote goes to Gary Ella, who made his Test debut on the same day I did, against New Zealand at Lancaster Park in Christchurch on August 14, 1982. Gary was a magnificent support player and the best centre I ever saw in terms of making room for his fullback and wingers. He was aware of creating opportunities for others rather than trying to make them for himself. Not many outside centres have adopted that same approach in the modern game. In terms of his support play, you always knew he would be there. He was not the quickest of centres, not after the knee injury he suffered in his early days. But he made up for it with his angles of running, the timing of his passes and ability to give the wider runners room in which to manoeuvre. One thing about Gary Ella. He never crabbed across the field or crowded his wingers.

INSIDE CENTRE — TIM HORAN

There was that unfortunate time in 1995 when my name was mud with Tim Horan supporters. I had suggested the selectors overlook Tim for the World Cup that season because he had just overcome a knee injury that could so easily have ended his career. My thinking, as I've already outlined, is that he would take a long while to get back to his best, if he ever did. Horan did go to the 1995 World Cup but it was at the tournament four years later where he really made his impact. As a teenage centre in 1989, it was obvious Horan had tons of ability. His passing game was not as developed as perhaps it should have been, but he was exceptionally gifted.

He was very quick, had great acceleration and was extremely elusive. He could pick a gap, hit it and be through before the opposition could shut him down and, like Gary Ella, was an outstanding support player. I suppose that goes without saying after his try in the 1991 World Cup semi-final against the All Blacks in Dublin when I tossed him the ball over my shoulder. I knew he was there. I had heard the call.

In 1999, he was simply inspirational. He carried the Wallabies in the semi-final against South Africa, consistently breaking their line in what turned out to be a tryless match. And to think the same morning he could hardly get out of bed, so badly was he affected by a virus. He would have worked well in tandem with Gary Ella.

LEFT WING — DAVID CAMPESE

Sorry, but I could never part with the No.11 jumper. I wore it in my first Test, which I started on the left wing, and continued to wear the double-one even when I moved to the right wing. According to the game's numbering system, I should have been in 14 by then.

FIVE-EIGHTH — MARK ELLA

This was the easiest selection of all. Mark is the only player who belongs in the Australian five-eighth jumper if I am sole selector. It is daylight to second place. As I put forward at the start of this chapter, I don't believe we ever saw the best of Ella. He was gone too quickly, retiring at age 25. If I had done the same, I would never have played beyond the 1987 season. I just could not imagine giving up that young. Sure, he made a comeback down the track, but not to the Test side. He walked away having played only 25 internationals. But it was enough to have him acknowledged worldwide as one of the true magicians of the code. What made Mark Ella so good? His grace and the time he always seemed to have to execute whatever it was he was planning to do. But let me deal first with the areas of his game that went largely unrecognised.

Mark was a great tactical kicker. It's just that he preferred to run most of the time. His front-on defence was also a cut above many other five-eighths. But it was his running ability, his creativity and flair, and his support play which set him apart from other Wallaby pivots that came before or after him. The football would pass through his hands so quickly en route to the centres you would sometimes swear he got it there by some telepathic process. The ball never seemed to touch his fingers. He gave his outside runners just so much space. And he would be there to take the ball back from you. He knew the short cuts. He would predict where the wide ball carriers would end up and make a beeline for the same spot. He would be jogging along and suddenly be there at your shoulder. It was freakish. I don't think I've ever seen a player like him. And I doubt I ever will again.

HALFBACK — NICK FARR-JONES

When Nick came on the scene in 1984, on that Grand Slam tour, he was certainly not arrogant. But there was a real sense of confidence and self-belief about his play. He didn't start the trip as the number one halfback. That honour had fallen to Phillip Cox. But Nick soon turned around the thinking of coach Alan Jones. He knew what he was doing, despite his inexperience and he had the demeanour you would expect from a senior figure in the team, not some Sydney University rookie who was making his first Wallaby tour. I developed a very solid on-field relationship with Nick over the years. He would always know when I wanted the ball on the blindside. He was adept at the little kick over the forwards, giving me the chase through. Or sometimes he would simply run my way, a tactic that was also successful given he was a big halfback and difficult for the defence to take one on one. He also had a marvellous pass, even if Mark Ella did come up with that priceless gem on the Grand Slam tour when he said to Nick: 'You just throw it, I'll catch it.' There was a lot more to the Farr-Jones pass than an aimless toss in the direction of his No.10. Down the track, Nick became captain, the best I played under. He led by example and had such a presence about him on the field.

NUMBER EIGHT — PETER LUCAS

This was another extremely tough choice when you consider there were two long-serving players in this position who gave such great service to the Wallabies during my time in the game, in Steve Tuynman and Tim Gavin. My last Test coincided with Gavin's farewell when he played in the second-row in the game against Wales at Cardiff Arms Park on December 1, 1996.

But my selection is out of left field, a guy with whom I played my first three Tests on that 1982 tour to New Zealand. Peter Lucas only played three times for Australia, during that series against the All Blacks. He deserved to play plenty more. This bloke was devastating. A fantastic runner of the ball with a sidestep to match most centres and the ball skills to go with it. He was tough, a big hitter in defence and opposition sides always knew he was on the paddock. Lucas was a surprise omission from the 1984 Grand Slam tour. He really was one of the unlucky players of his generation, and that is taking nothing away from Tuynman who came into the side and carved out a memorable career for himself.

OPENSIDE FLANKER — CHRIS ROCHE

Even though he played in the days when teams usually ran their flankers in a left and right formation rather than as openside and blindside, he was the forerunner to all those great ball pilferers like Jeff Miller and David Wilson. Roche was absolutely everywhere on the field. His work at the breakdown was brilliant. He would be at the bottom of every ruck but still find time to get to his feet and charge off to the next one. He was a fox terrier mixing it with the bigger breeds in the forwards. But he never let his smaller stature get in the way of winning turnover ball. He was small but dynamic and one player who, given the training and preparation of modern day international sides, would easily slot into the current era.

BLINDSIDE FLANKER — WILLIE OFAHENGAUE

How lucky were we that this former New Zealand schoolboys representative eventually decided to settle in Australia? Willie O was the original impact player. Built like a tank he had the engine of a sports car. Willie was unbelievably strong and he took no backward steps to anyone. I remember in the 1991 World Cup quarter final that an Irishman belted him early. Willie didn't flinch but then proceeded to hammer every man in green when he could line them up in defence. He was enormously important to our success at the tournament and he is one player I can genuinely say instilled fear in the opposition. Even more impressively, he had rivals running scared whether he was on the attack or preparing to make a hit on some unsuspecting ball carrier. For such a big guy he also had very subtle skills. He did not run straight lines all the time, he had good footwork and could offload a pass. Like Roche, he would fit into the modern game with ease. The current training techniques and fulltime professionalism would have made him an even more dangerous player. What a thought. I'm sure Eddie Jones would love to transport this bloke into his World Cup side. At his best he was simply unstoppable.

SECOND-ROWER — STEVE CUTLER

I started with Skylab in the under 21 scene and he really matured over the years. Standing more than 2m tall, he was always destined to be a world-class lineout forward. There were question marks over whether he would stand up to the physical nature of Test football, but he quickly dispelled any doubts once he was given the opportunity at Test level. Cutler matured into a very valued member of the Australian side under Alan Jones. His ball-winning expertise was crucial in an era when lineout jumpers had to do all the work themselves. There was none of this lifting business with an array of forwards propelling second-rowers into orbit to make a catch. Cutler had the height and the athleticism to carve his own niche in the game. He had some terrific battles with All Black stars like Andy Haden and Gary

Whetton and rarely did he finish on the losing side of the lineout ledger.

SECOND-ROWER — JOHN EALES

Imagine Eales and Cutler working in tandem in a time when lifting was outlawed. You would never lose a lineout. Eales should have had some of his impact dulled when the International Rugby Board did allow jumpers to be assisted. But it was the mark of his greatness that he continued to be a dominant force in the game. He would have been even more revered, if that's possible, had those law changes never gone through. But Eales was more than a lineout forward. Who will forget his try-saving tackle on Rob Andrew in the 1991 World Cup final. He came out of nowhere to mow down the English five-eighth. He did a lot of work around the paddock which went unnoticed and the same could be said of his captaincy. I only played under Eales for one season, his first in the leadership role in 1996. But he grew into the job and became a statesman of sorts, in the same way Nick Farr-Jones had done when he skippered the Wallabies. Eales was always that steadying influence, the unflappable forward who would win lineouts, make tackles, find time to kick crucial goals and still deliver the on-field speeches that mattered. It is only in his retirement, I think, that the real merits of his captaincy have been acknowledged. A case of 'you don't know what you've got till it's gone'.

TIGHTHEAD PROP — EWEN McKENZIE

The Missing Link he was christened and he never said much out on the field. Never got rattled either. He just went about his job in a thoroughly professional manner. He scrummaged well, he made his tackles but he was also a very under-rated support player in attack. He followed this plan that when he saw the ball going wide and the chance of a break emerging, he would not try to chase the play, he would simply run as fast as he could up the middle of the field. The idea was when, or if the movement headed back inside, he would be on hand to carry on the attack. At Randwick club training it was also a frequent occurrence for us to play touch football and McKenzie had a highly developed set of ball skills. He just never got the chance to show them that much in the middle of a Test battle. Ewen has now moved into coaching and will be at the helm of the NSW Waratahs in 2004. I wish him well.

HOOKER — TOM LAWTON

The Turtle could be a one-man wrecking ball. He was the first of the oversized hookers but relied on more than his size to make an impact on proceedings. He was quick for a big man and powerful in the scrum but he never shirked his duties as a support player or in defence. There is a famous photo of Serge Blanco going across to score the matchwinning try in the 1987 World Cup semi final at Concord Oval in Sydney. The Australian who made a gallant cross-field chase and launched a despairing dive in an attempt to prevent Blanco scoring was Tom Lawton. I recall too, on the 1984 Grand Slam tour, during a non-Test match, how I made a break and looked on the outside for support. Who happened to be there? Our trusty hooker. Lawton would have also been a great success in the current climate, with Australia searching for a hooker who can throw the ball consistently straight at lineout time. Lawton could hit a 10 cent piece from 20 paces. He hardly ever erred in accuracy. It was always a pleasure to play with the Turtle.

LOOSEHEAD PROP — ENRIQUE RODRIGUEZ

It could never happen these days with the new one country for life eligibility regulations. But back in the early to mid-1980's. Topo Rodriguez was a man in demand. In 1983 we had played against him when Argentina toured Australia. The Pumas had brought with them a scrum of such devastating power that our forwards were digging up the Ballymore turf as they tried to repel the might of the visiting pack. Rodriguez was at the forefront of that scrummaging assault and 12 months later we were happy to welcome him into our side when he decided to settle in Australia. Our scrum, if my memory serves me correctly, never went backwards again for years to come. Topo brought not only his individual talent, but the strategies that would help us develop an attacking forward platform. His role in the emergence of the Wallaby forwards as a world-class outfit should not be forgotten. And it all came together that day in Cardiff, on the 1984 tour, when our scrum managed the pushover try against Wales.

As for the International XV, there is a distinct French flavour to my selections. I make no apologies for it, even if some of the players in my side might be considered in some way inferior to more household names in their respective positions. To me, though, the exercise was not about assembling the biggest names from my years in the game. It was about building a team that you would gladly sit in the grandstands and watch week after week for the rest of your life. A team to entertain, to marvel at, to surprise and thrill you. The 15 names I finally settled on would do all that, and more. No matter how many times you might watch them, they would always leave you wanting an encore. This team is flair and flamboyance, and filled with some of my favourite players.

It was never designed to be a sterile collection of players based on how long they had been around, or how many Tests they had played. Although, one of my choices for the centres, Philippe Sella, was well qualified on those counts as well. So here is the Dream Team 1982-1996.

FULLBACK — SERGE BLANCO

A graceful Frenchman who was so relaxed on the field you had to wonder whether the cool facade was an act. It made him even more remarkable that what you saw with Serge is what you got. He just loved playing the game. He felt an affinity with rugby. And he was blessed with such incredible ability, he will always be remembered as one of the greats of any era. Blanco could make something out of nothing. In 1990 we played France in a three-Test series at home before a tour of New Zealand, and Serge scored one of the greatest international tries during the second game in Brisbane. He carried the ball about 80m for the score and never once looked like he was getting out of second gear. Because of that languid running style, Blanco was deceptively quick, as we found out that afternoon, and had witnessed three years earlier when he grabbed the matchwinning score in the World Cup semi-final. Incidentally, isn't it strange that when the greatest Tests of the past 20 years are mentioned, they are always the games that involved players of immense attacking talent? Penalty goal shootouts are for the birds. They are dull, boring and a major turn off. But who could forget the Blanco try in in 1987 or the Jonah Lomu strike in 2000 when he crossed in the left corner in injury time to give the All Blacks a 39-35 win at what is now Telstra Stadium in Sydney. But back to Blanco, and he was a very casual player. Nothing fazed him. He had his good days and he had some bad. Such is the way of a player prepared to take risks. In my mind, every footballer should strive to be just a little like the former French captain.

RIGHT WING — JOHN KIRWAN

He was at the peak of his powers at the 1987 World Cup. The astonishing try he scored against Italy, when he fielded the ball from a kickoff inside his own quarter and threaded a path through the defensive line before outstripping the cover, was pure class. In that sort of mood, JK was unstoppable. He was big, he was strong but he had other tricks in the repertoire too. His fend was a beauty and he had the in-and-away manoeuvre mastered at an early stage in his career. As a finisher, there were few better than Kirwan at any time in rugby's history. He eventually went across to rugby league, but only when his best days were behind him. Devastating with the ball in hand, Kirwan was a dominant figure for a long time.

OUTSIDE CENTRE — PHILIPPE SELLA

One of the beauties of the French game, and to some extent, the reason for their fluctuating fortunes during the years I played against them, was that they had such an unstructured style. They were the masters of ad lib rugby. There was a real emotion to the way they approached the game. When things fell into place and their confidence peaked there was simply no answer to their brilliance. Sella embodied this French artistry. He had blinding pace and, because of his wonderful vision, was a support player almost without peer. It is a mark of his standing in the game that he became the first international player to reach the landmark of 100 Tests. Even more remarkably, he managed to achieve that honour when the French were renowned for chopping and changing their sides on a whim. There has always been a lot of off-field politics in French rugby. But the class of Sella always ensured he escaped the selection tinkering.

INSIDE CENTRE — JONATHAN DAVIES

Before anyone tries to correct my supposed error in judgment by pointing out this little Welsh magician was a five-eighth or fullback, let me explain the reasons for installing him in the No.12 jumper. His extraordinary footwork would make him a constant danger in attack and his ability to kick in general play would provide further options in the midfield. Davies had an unpredictability the modern-day Welsh side would gladly welcome back to their ranks. His step was sharp and incisive and he had the ability to create for his outside backs as well as take any half opportunities himself. Well-rounded players like that, guys who have so many choices available to them when the ball sits in their hands, are the key to any successful backline operation because they keep defences second-guessing. A one-dimensional player is incapable of putting defenders into panic. They know what to expect and they can shift the pressure to other points of the field. With Davies, you were constantly on your toes. By creating hesitancy in the opposition, he would be indirectly ensuring time and space for wider runners. Those traits in a playmaker can often be overlooked – except by the teammates who benefit.

LEFT WING — JEAN BAPTISTE LAFOND

In other parts of this book I have described the impact Jonah Lomu has had on rugby since his phenomenal performances at the 1995 World Cup. Jonah is a one-off. We might never see a player of his ilk again. Not with modern defences being better equipped to handle runaway juggernauts. But Jonah was power and pace. There was never great subtlety to the way he played. Not surprising, given he could stampede his way through half a dozen defenders without overly exerting himself. But on the selection criteria I have drawn up for the Dream Team – principally that players be equipped with a range of skills that make for sporting entertainment – then I go with another shock choice in Lafond. In 1983 on the Wallabies tour to France, Blanco missed the first Test in Clermont-Ferrand and this bloke took over at fullback. He was destroying us until an Australian forward knocked him almost into the grandstand with a hit that dislocated Lafond's shoulder. With Blanco at fullback in my side, I'll slot Lafond on to the wing, ahead of his countryman Patrice Lagisquet, another gloriously talented runner of the ball. Lagisquet made his debut in that 1983 series and shocked us with his raw speed. We learned later he had once clocked 10.8 seconds for 100 metres.

FIVE-EIGHTH — HUGO PORTA

His unerring accuracy with the boot is what earned this Argentinian a reputation as one of the game's greatest flyhalves. His tactical kicking was unbelievable, he could kick goals from everywhere and long-range drop goals were one of his specialities. But Porta was also a fine midfield general who could move the ball wide when required. That part of his game was seriously under-rated. Porta and Mark Ella are the two best players in the No.10 jumper I have ever had the pleasure to watch.

HALFBACK — DAVE LOVERIDGE

A truly dominant figure behind a good New Zealand scrum. He was calm under pressure and had a well-crafted kicking game. But the speed of his service is what wins him Dream Team selection.

Having put together such an array of talent in the threequarter line, all I want the halfback to do is get them ball as quickly and cleanly as possible. Loveridge would be the man.

NUMBER EIGHT — MURRAY MEXTED

So many players come into contention here. England's Dean Richards was a tower of strength for the British Lions in 1989 while Frenchman Laurent Rodriguez was a great ball runner. Then you have the queue of Kiwis knocking at the door. Wayne Shelford and Zinzan Brooke were banging loudest. But I eventually settled for Murray Mexted. He read the game so well and had that raw-boned strength to cart the ball forward and consistently carry his side over the advantage line. He was also a great team player. Mexted came into the All Blacks side in 1979 and stayed until 1984, playing 34 consecutive Tests. His father, a No.8 as Murray would be, also played for the All Blacks.

OPENSIDE FLANKER — JEAN PIERRE RIVES

What he lacked in size – Rives weighed only 83kg – he more than compensated for with heart. The flowing blond locks were his trademark but the former French captain was no showpony player. His workrate was outstanding and he was constantly on the front foot encouraging his forwards to join him in the next ruck battle. He was always in the thick of the action, never scared, but a downright nuisance for opposition teams. Rives was an inspirational skipper. He was ready to give as good as he got on the paddock and it was rare not to see him finish a game without blood trickling from somewhere on his head. But the man who later took up sculpting and has had his works exhibited extensively, was first and foremost an inspirational leader. It showed in his career longevity, from 1975 to 1984.

BLINDSIDE FLANKER — MICHAEL JONES

This guy was the prototype for a new generation of backrowers when he starred at the 1987 World Cup. He was fast, strong, a phenomenal runner and defender. He pretty much had it all. He was all over the field and virtually impossible to contain. It's good to see him still involved in rugby, helping out with the Samoan side. Michael was one of the nicest blokes you could ever meet and it was a pleasure to play against him. I don't know if he would say the same thing about us Australians if he knew how we used to plan to nullify his brilliance. We would go out there with a plan to keep him on the bottom of rucks if we happened to find him there. Nothing dirty. Just hold on to him to stop him getting back on his feet and harassing the backline further. If anyone succeeded, we'd suddenly find more room out wide. Unfortunately, it never happened enough.

SECOND-ROWER — ANDY HADEN

A man mountain in the All Blacks side when I first came into the Wallaby team in 1982. He was tall, mean, streetwise and a great lineout forward. When it came to trying to tame the All Blacks in those days, Haden was the most dangerous beast of all. He was clearly world-class and the All Blacks thrived on his experience and confidence. Having tight forwards of that calibre are crucial to any great side. They are the engine room bosses. They stoke the fires for the rest of the team. Haden was like that for the All Blacks. I'm just glad I got the chance to play against him, four times, during the 1982-83 seasons.

SECOND-ROWER — PAUL ACKFORD

This guy was so tough and durable. A real workhorse in the pack. It's just a shame he was a Pom and not an Aussie. It is even more disappointing to reflect on his finest moment against us – the Lions series in Australia in 1989. For obvious reasons, I get a bit sick looking back on that particular three-match part of Australian rugby history. Still, Ackers is worth the painful revisit to that 2-1 series loss. He was one of the flint hard Englishmen in that Lions pack and they physically destroyed us up front. Like Wade Dooley and Mike Teague in particular, two other Poms from that pack, he was very determined and extremely aggressive. He was also a money man at the lineout.

TIGHTHEAD PROP — GARY KNIGHT

Much was made of the fact that when we got to New Zealand in 1982, I really had no idea that All Blacks winger Stu Wilson was this legendary figure over there. I made the now infamous 'Stu who?' reply when asked for my opinion of his rugby prowess and made what you might say was an immediate impact in New Zealand. Thank God they didn't ask me what I thought of Gary Knight. I had never heard of the Kiwi prop but to insult him might have made my life hell on the field in the three Test matches that followed. But if I did not know of Knight before the tour, I certainly knew all about him as the trip progressed. He was another of the All Blacks hard men of the era. An uncompromising forward who was high on technical knowledge but low on mercy for rivals. A prop who would have excelled in any generation.

HOOKER — DANIEL DUBROCA

Another Frenchman, and this one a natural born leader. He was also a playmaker of sorts. He captained France in that memorable 1987 World Cup semi-final at Concord Oval and I have to say he marshalled his players brilliantly on the day. Keeping a French side in check would be no mean feat, but Dubroca had the total respect of his Test match teammates. He was aggressive, powerful in the scrum, and was vital to the success of the French side at that time.

LOOSEHEAD PROP — STEVE McDOWELL

A black belt in martial arts, this All Blacks front-rower was not to be messed with, especially if it involved some spindly Wallaby winger. McDowell was part of that dominant All Blacks side of 1987 and was in the side we beat four years later in the World Cup semi-final at Lansdown Road in Dublin. Like Michael Jones, he was before his time in his particular position. McDowell brought this amazing mobility to the front-row but maintained the strength that allowed him to be a world-class scrummager as well. He also had that ruthless streak about him, as so many of the All Blacks did through the 1980s. If you were on the wrong side of the ruck, you could expect McDowell's studs to tattoo your back. But that was fair enough. It is as the game should be. A bit of legal rucking, as long as it's well away from the head, never really hurt anybody. You would never dare say the same about a McDowell tackle. He was a master of rattling your ribs.

MARRIED LIFE

When Lara decided she'd stick it out,
I realised I'd have to change.
Change my selfish ways.

For almost 20 years my life was devoted to an obsession. I wanted to be the best rugby union player possible, and that meant a selfish approach to how I lived, trained and prepared myself for each and every game. Cutting corners was never an option. I dedicated myself to training, to the gymnasium, to skills session, to eating right and, when I enjoyed some down time, to playing golf or watching movies. I did what I wanted when I wanted away from rugby. It was the only way to keep going season after season. While other players were complaining of feeling tired or not wanting to train, I always revelled in the opportunity to get a football in my hands. And I was prepared to make sacrifices off the field, behind the scenes, to ensure I was ready to play each week of each month of each year. For a long time I played for six months in Australia and the other six months in Italy. That is not to say other players did not make sacrifices. Of course they did and, in many respects, it was even tougher for them. Most were trying to juggle their football careers with serious relationships, engagements, marriages and even children. That I stayed single for as long as I did was not chance or fate. It was a decision. An indirect one, I have to admit. I did not sit down and say to myself 'I won't be getting married'. But I was conscious of not letting anything interfere with my rugby. It was selfish and — surprise, surprise — it did not endear me to any women I did meet. But I could live with that because I lived for my rugby.

There were times when I wondered whether the bachelor life might be mine well into the future. When you play a sport — eat, breathe and live that pursuit — and travel a lot, you can become a very self-absorbed type of person. As an international rugby player touring the world, you are looked after to the extreme. You never have to prepare meals or wash your own clothes. There are medical and physiotherapy staff on hand whenever needed. You train, you play, you eat, you sleep. If you like sightseeing, it is an option. If you play golf, there is always time (even more so now it seems) to get on the course. You are spoiled. I have no problems with admitting that. And, to me, while living that sort of lifestyle, I thought it better not to have a partner. Mind you, I'm sure there were women who would have felt I was not for them either. They would not have appreciated having to fit into my life somewhere below playing, training and travelling. But I always regarded distractions as potential dangers that would take me away from my major priority, and that was making the most of my rugby career.

Then I met Lara in 1997. We met in a gym in South Africa when I was over there with the NSW Waratahs. There were a couple of nights out and Lara really made an impact on me. My career was obviously winding down at that point, and my last Test had been played the previous year. But Lara came from a sporting family and realised the demands and commitments involved. Her brother Dale has been a top cricketer for a decade and played for South Africa on a frequent basis. Another brother Brett was a professional cricketer and his twin Boyd was also a well-respected sportsman. Martin Benkenstein, Lara's dad, was an all-rounder, having played cricket for Rhodesia. He was also a top competition squash player. Her mum Lorna was also a sportswoman and is now an avid golfer. But while Lara and I stayed in touch with each other it was not until 2000 that our relationship — and now fate does intervene — really took off. I was in South Africa for a number of speaking engagements and was boarding a plane in Port Elizabeth to fly to Durban. Lara just happened to be at the airport at the same time. Later the same year, Lara came out to stay with friends during the Sydney Olympics. Maintaining a long-distance relationship after she went home was a strain on both of us but it would be after Christmas 2001 before we decided it was time to see if we could make a go of it as a long-term couple. Lara came to Australia to stay.

It is amazing how things happen in your life. I was selected for the Wallabies at 19, went on to play 101 Tests, retired, moved into business and then found Lara. I have been exceptionally lucky. When Lara, who was a successful marketing executive in South Africa decided to give me a chance and head to Australia, and then stuck it out once here, I realised I'd have to change. Change my selfish ways. Moving to the other side of the world must have been such a culture shock and life change for her, it was only right the dedication I once gave to my sport now belonged to her.

We were married at the Fancourt golf resort in George, along the Garden Route in South Africa, in January 2003. It was a fantastic day, especially with the large number of friends from Australia who made the trip to be part of our day. In my personal life, rugby people have never really been among my closest friends. There are some exceptions. Former Wallabies coach Alan Jones, former Randwick coach and rugby celebrity Jeff Sayle, and my old mate Duck, who is so passionate about the Galloping

Greens he had their logo tattooed on his arm. They were all there. So was former Springboks coach Ian McIntosh, who's a close friend of Lara's dad — what a small world — while another mate of Martin's who attended was the great South African cricketer Garth le Roux.

It was especially nice for my parents Tony and Joan to make the trek and enjoy the South African experience with us, and Lara's parents. We had guests flying in from the US and from Italy, as well as from Australia and from all parts of South Africa. It was unforgettable. African dancers came down from Johannesburg to perform before the ceremony, which included an address by Reverend Cronje, the brother of the late South African cricket captain, whose tragic plane crash occurred in the hills behind the resort.

They call those first few months after marriage the honeymoon period. Well, approaching our first anniversary, the honeymoon continues for me. And we already have a family, of sorts. Demi, a Staffordshire bull terrier, has been with Lara for years. After emerging from quarantine, which upset Lara as much Demi, she settled in really well. One of a kind is Demi. I was never one for pets when I was growing up or playing rugby. I could never afford the time to properly look after them. Obviously that has all changed. We have a second Staffordshire now, who goes by the name of Tyson. Big, bullish, I think it suits him. As long as it doesn't give him any ideas about biting people's ears.

As for the longer-term future and the obvious question of children, it will, in the end, be my greatest challenge of all. To raise a son or a daughter, perhaps both, and instilling in them the values and principles you pick up in your own life. It makes me wonder why I was so worried about leaving a life of playing rugby behind. There is so much more awaiting Lara and I into the future. It has allowed me to set new goals and look at life from a completely new perspective. But I have to be a former footballer for just a moment and observe that whatever children we do have, I'll be astonished if they don't find their way into sport. The genes demand it, on both sides, and I will certainly encourage them in whatever pursuit they do decide to follow. Although I don't know if I would necessarily like a son to play rugby union. I don't know that I would want him to play a game and continually be compared to his old man. If he does want to play, that's fine. If he doesn't, I'll again be happy. My nephew Terry, who also carries the name Campese, had to put up with comparisons when he was coming through the ranks. Not that it seems to have had any negative effect on his football. He's happy having just signed a new three-year contract with the Canberra Raiders rugby league club. And I'm delighted to say Campese Management Group handled the negotiations. Not that it was too tough an assignment for us. The Raiders were keen to have him on board and regard Terry as one of their most promising stars of the future.

And, so, after so many years of trying to entertain people, trying to be the best footballer I could possibly be, and living my life with the next rugby exploit on my mind, the landscape has dramatically changed. From the shy and naive Queanbeyan kid who graduated into the Wallabies, I have now moved into the world of business and the life of a husband and, hopefully, one day a father. It has been such a journey, such an extraordinary ride. Sometimes you have to sit back and take a check on where you've been and where you're going to fully appreciate what has come your way. I know I've been lucky. I like to think I've created some of that luck and others have contributed to the rest of my good fortune. Especially now.

I have had so much enjoyment, and been fortunate enough to meet so many interesting and powerful people both here and overseas, and will continue to do so as the years roll by. I would like to thank everyone involved in rugby for making my career so memorable to look back on now that I'm no longer playing. That even includes all those media types who loved to have a crack at me at various times. To those that I have since annoyed with my outspoken comments about the game, I apologise not for what I have said but for any pain it may have caused. I don't ask that everyone agree with me, and I know a lot of people don't, on a regular basis. But I will always defend my right to have an opinion. And I can guarantee you, those opinions do come from the heart. I am not into hidden agendas or vendetta campaigns or any other sly manoeuvres to undermine anyone playing or coaching in the modern game. I have made mistakes in the past, shot my mouth off when I was playing. I put my hand up and admit to it. But these days I do think I'm more subjective, because I'm not as personally involved as I was when I was pulling on the boots. Time will tell and those who read my columns or listen to my radio commentaries will judge whether I am fair or unfair, on the money or out of touch. But one thing is for sure and certain. I love this game, I always have. It dominated my life for such a long time. My life has now changed but rugby rolls on, season after season, spawning new players, new kids with dreams. I have had my time and was lucky enough to live out all my ambitions and then a few more. But rugby is still in my blood and will always be there. It will never leave me and I wouldn't have it any other way.

FEARLESS PREDICTIONS

It has taken Eddie Jones a long time, perhaps too long, to get his team and his blueprint into place.

The World Cup on home soil. There has been no bigger rugby event ever staged in this country. And it will be a long time, perhaps two decades or more, before we see the tournament in Australia again. On that basis, I wanted to lay out, prior to the opening game, how I figured the 20 teams would shape up during competition.

There is one fact beyond dispute. By November 22 one man will have stepped forward in front of a sellout crowd at Sydney's Telstra Stadium. The World Cup final will have been decided and the skipper of the winning nation, in the most unforgettable moment of his sporting career, will be handed the golden trophy that crowns his team as the best in the game. All the sacrifices and the planning, all the years of hard work and training will, in that split second, be rewarded with the ultimate prize. It is a feeling only a select few in the game have experienced. David Kirk as skipper of the All Blacks in 1987, Nick Farr-Jones of the Wallabies in 1991, Francois Pienaar for South Africa in 1995 and John Eales as Australian leader in 1999. For the next winning captain and his players, it will be a day, perhaps the day, to savour. I can vouch for that, because I was lucky enough to be part of that Australian team to win the second World Cup. And make no mistake. Luck does play its part in the outcome of a World Cup. We had our share in 1991, when Ireland almost tipped us out in the quarter finals. In 1995, South Africa survived a semi-final scare against France. And the 1999 Wallabies won their semi-final in extra time. Only the first World Cup champions, the All Blacks, were basically untouchable. They were on a different level to everyone else in 1987.

So what of 2003? Leading into October there were, for me, five teams, maybe only four, who deserved to have realistic expectations of success. In order, I would have to say they were New Zealand, France, England and Australia. For most of the year I was tipping France to win their first global title. As the season unfolded I became less sure, especially after the All Blacks emerged with a bang. I still maintained the side that brought a new style to the game, with the skill to back it up, would be best equipped not only to win the title but to shape the way the game might be played in the future.

For those needing a reminder the pools looked this way:

Pool A — Australia, Argentina, Ireland, Namibia, Uruguay
Pool B — France, Scotland, Fiji, Japan, United States
Pool C — England, South Africa, Samoa, Uruguay, Georgia
Pool D — New Zealand, Wales, Italy, Canada, Tonga

NEW ZEALAND

How could you not be impressed by what the Kiwis have done at provincial and international level this year? They have played fantastic and entertaining rugby and are deservedly favourites to carry off the Webb Ellis trophy for the first time in 16 years. John Mitchell strikes me as extremely shrewd coach. He played hardball with his players last year and left most of the senior blokes at home so he could experiment with new faces on their end-of-season tour last year. He also played hardball when he settled on his sides for this season's domestic Test campaign. Taine

Randell was the All Blacks skipper to Europe last November. But Mitchell could not find a place for him in the 2003 squad. Just as he jettisoned fullback Christian Cullen and hooker Anton Oliver during the year.

The Mitchell selections worked a treat, even though he came in for a caning from the New Zealand media when he first turned his back on Randell, Cullen and Oliver, another former All Blacks captain. The Kiwis won the Tri-Nations series and I get the feeling they will taste success again in the competition that matters most. There is still a sprinkling of key, experienced players in the All Blacks squad. But they have also brought on some exciting youngsters whose enthusiasm knows no bounds. They have transformed this side with names like Rokocoko and Muliaina thrilling crowds in the World Cup countdown. What I like about the New Zealand challenge is how they've gone about establishing this electrifying running game. I love it. They run the ball with such precision and confidence. They have players coming at all angles and their counter attack is just spectacular if they get room to move at the back. The Brumbies style game people adopted after 1999, based on ball retention and no mistakes, has reached its use by date. And no one has accelerated the introduction of a new wide-running alternative better than Mitchell's mob. They are not only catching opposition defences unaware but they are attacking with such express pace on the flanks that there is little rival teams can do to shut them down once the slightest opening appears. Their backs play the game at a pace others will struggle to match. They also have such enthusiasm and passion about what they're doing. Defensive rugby has been the bedrock of successful teams in recent seasons. Fortunately, the All Blacks are moving us away from that era.

But it is not just the outside backs that excel in this side. They are strong across the backline. They utilise all their players behind the scrum. They don't have to rely on just one individual and that, as a combination, makes them even tougher to contain. New Zealand run when they can and kick when they have to, and are very well drilled. Maybe we will see another side to them when the pressure comes in the World Cup. Some of the young guys might not be able to handle the pressure if things get tough. If their confidence is dented, their games could fall apart because confidence is vital to the high-risk game they play. That is the danger for the All Blacks. To throw the ball around they need to be brimming with self-belief. Otherwise the mistakes can creep in and the decision making can falter. But whoever does beat the All Blacks should go on and win the title. New Zealand should play South Africa in the quarter finals and, if they advance, Australia in the semis. England and France will be on the other side of the draw if the preliminary matches go as expected.

ENGLAND

The Poms came to Australia and New Zealand in June and did what many thought was beyond them. They beat both countries to confirm the form that brought them a Six Nations Championship Grand Slam earlier in the year. England also displayed a style of rugby Australia and New Zealand found foreign. They were the ultimate team unit with no glaring weaknesses. Five-eighth Jonny Wilkinson is clearly their linchpin but they do have an attack that utilises all 15 players and their defence is great. They also have the best captain in international rugby in second-rower Martin Johnson. He leads the forwards magnificently and is such a calming influence on those players. He has that real aura of leadership about him. His team look to him for inspiration. And they have a fair way to tilt their heads back if they want to search the Johnson features. The former New Zealand under 21 forward is a giant of a man. With Jonny Wilkinson at No.10, they will be extremely hard to beat when it gets to the pressure games. He has the best tactical kicking game in rugby and is also the finest goalkicker. If points are at a premium, Wilkinson can emerge as the matchwinner.

England coach Clive Woodward has also done his homework on other sides and devised his side's tactics accordingly. When they played the Wallabies in Melbourne and beat them 25-14, they knew what the Wallabies were going to do, who their key players were, and it showed. England can mix it up, which is also important. They used the maul effectively against New Zealand but also have fine finishers on either wing if they decide to take the ball wide. It might sound crazy coming from me, the proudest Pom-basher of all, but they are going to be an extremely powerful force in this World Cup. With two provisos. One, that they don't get carried away with themselves. And two, that their aging forwards do not pack it in during the heat they are likely to experience during the six weeks of the event. The age factor has to be a concern to Woodward. The upside is they are all vastly experienced and hardened Test players. The flip side is players can hit the wall quickly at the tail end of their careers, and once the slide starts, it is usually unstoppable. Summery conditions and hard grounds then will be the major worry for the Poms. If they can survive that and a pool match against South Africa, they will surely book a semi-final date with France.

AUSTRALIA

There is enormous pressure on the Wallabies and they need no reminding that back-to-back World Cup victories have never been achieved by any nation. Part of the reason for that, I'm sure, is that successful sides tend to carry too many of the title-winning side into the next World Cup. New Zealand suffered for it in 1991, as did the Wallabies squad that I was part of in 1995. I hope history does not repeat itself this time around but I fear the Wallabies did hold on to some of the old timers for too long. During the Tri-Nations series there were experienced players not aiming up. They were playing too far below their best. It also took a while after 1999 to reshape the team. Some of the older stars left in their own time during 2000 and 2001. But Eddie Jones, who took over from Rod Macqueen for the end of year tour two years ago, was left having to start from scratch and at the conclusion of the Tri-Nations series in August he was still experimenting trying to find his best combinations. To me, that is asking for trouble with no further games until the Argentina match that second Friday in October.

My other concern is that Jones has been talking about turning the Wallabies into a more potent attacking side ever since he came into the job. But it has taken him a long time, perhaps too long, to get his team and his blueprint into place. Time together as a side is crucial and plenty of these Wallabies have not chalked up many hours together out on the playing paddock. The attacking game Jones wants in place will take the Australians away from the crash-ball philosophy they embraced during Rod Macqueen's reign. These days it is called a 'direct' game. A nice way of saying 'boring'. But, again, Jones did not fast-track his master plan. Even against South Africa in Brisbane in the middle of the Tri-Nations, they were falling back to what they knew best, and that was keeping the ball closer to the pack rather than flinging to the genuine gamebreakers out wide.

The Wallabies' performances have been grossly inconsistent this year and a lot criticism has been headed Jones' way over the style of game the team is playing. They have some great individual flair and a raft of talented players. But after the losses to England and New Zealand, changes were needed. I also think we should have had a few trial games organised between the last Tri-Nations match on August 16 in Auckland and the November 10 date with the Pumas.

The Wallabies look to be struggling with this new concept of how Jones wants them to play. Moving from the rigidity of the Macqueen generation to a more ad-lib style does not seem to have flourished and it reminds of a television show I was watching a few months back with Lara. It was called *Australian Idol*, and went through the selection process for all these pop star wannabes. On one night, every contestant had to get up and sing the song of their choice. On another night, they had been given 24 hours to prepare themselves to perform another song — this one given to them. The transformation was incredible. When they had their own well-rehearsed song to sing, they sounded great. When having to sing the song given to them with one day to learn, many of them dropped the ball. They couldn't remember the words or sang off key. It just goes to show you: when you get taken out of your comfort zone your performance can be affected dramatically. It happened to the hopefuls on Australian Idol and I suspect it has been happening to the Wallabies this season. They were once programmed to do certain things on the field and they did them very well. But once they were asked to ad lib or create, they were not quite the same side.

Australia will need flair and a bit of unpredictability to make real headway in the tournament. Although, barring a disaster in the pool rounds, the Wallabies should have a comfortable quarter-final match-up with Scotland followed by a semi-final almost certainly against the All Blacks. The weakness of this

Australian team could be their pattern of play. They have become predictable and, unless they change, will struggle to make it two in a row.

FRANCE

The only side to make the World Cup final twice and lose. But I think the French are in with a real chance of going one better in this tournament. When they came to Australia in 2002, without a number of leading players, they looked like a team that could cause havoc in the World Cup. A disappointing Six Nations campaign and two losses to Argentina in June too a bit of gloss off their build-up but their coach Bernard Laporte has continued to experiment heavily. When they put their number one line-up on the field they will be tough for anyone to beat — if they click. French sides in the past have been blessed with talent but have failed to show the discipline or consistency to make them world beaters.

Their discipline over the last couple of years has improved considerably and after the defeats in Argentina they went to New Zealand, made more changes, trialled a few youngsters and still gave the All Blacks a run for their money. That was impressive. A major hurdle for the French will be to keep their heads together over six weeks away from home. They have demonstrated in the past they can play well at home and beat anybody. But the travel factor and the need to put in high-level performances game after game at the World Cup are the question marks hanging over them.

One aspect of French rugby I have always enjoyed is their ability to look so relaxed when things are running their way. They can unleash a display of sustained brilliance when you least expect it, like in the 1999 World Cup semi-final against the All Blacks when, after struggling early, they exploded with a second half effort that earned them a berth in the final. There is an enormous depth of talent in France and when they play with traditional flair, and have their forwards running crazy out in the backline, they can strike fear into the hearts of any opposition.

I only hope when the pressure comes on that the French won't fall back into their old bad habits. When they get rattled they lose their shape and start giving away silly penalties at crucial times. They need to be patient in defence and back themselves in attack. And one thing you know will not be missing from their play is passion. As long as they direct that passion in a positive manner, they will cruise into the semi-finals. From there it is anybody's guess. The French are not renowned for following the script.

SOUTH AFRICA

The republic's Super 12 teams set a disappointing tone earlier in 2003 with disastrous campaigns in the provincial tournament and the Springboks were just as sluggish. While they beat Scotland twice and Argentina with a late three-pointer, South Africa never looked impressive. Even when they beat the Wallabies in Cape Town, against all expectations, there was nothing brilliant about their victory. They relied on a smashing midfield defence. That might work for you occasionally but teams will find a way to combat it. In the return match at Suncorp Stadium in Brisbane, the Wallabies did not find the missile-like De Wet Barry so much of a handful. They stood deeper and the pressure valve was released.

The Boks have lost a lot of senior players in recent seasons to the UK, where the value of the pound compared to the rand is so attractive it is difficult for their top blokes to say no to any lucrative offers. At least their coach Rudolf Straeuli had the good sense to entice a couple back for their World Cup campaign with prop Rob Kempson and utility back Thinus Delport returning home to take part in the June Tests and Tri-Nations series.

But Straeuli still faced a battle to transform this side into genuine world-class competitors. Their passion can never be questioned. Nor their commitment. Their skills levels though are down. So is their sense of innovation. Brent Russell, used off the bench so effectively against the Wallabies in Cape Town, is a matchwinner. A player of rare flair with the pace to capitalise. But he is also inclined, as he showed against the All Blacks in Pretoria where the Boks were smashed, that he can also turn in the occasional shocker. The New Zealanders pressured him and he did not respond. He was back to the bench the following game.

The South African pattern of play has been non-existent at times. It looked as if their players were not sure how they were supposed to build a score, apart from an unhealthy reliance on the boot of their five-eighth Louis Koen. While they have a combative forward pack, there is not much doing behind the scrum. They were heading into the World Cup probably realising in their own minds that unless they could knock over England in Perth on October 18, their challenge would be in ruins. A likely quarter-final with New Zealand would not be their idea of fun.

Clearly, on the back of the allegations that came out of their Brisbane clash with the Wallabies, there are still discipline problems within the Springboks camp. And there was no doubt the Australian accusations of biting, eye-gouging and spitting will have been noted by referees. If the Boks are to again revisit their incredible achievement of 1995, they have to pull off an upset like they did in the opening game of the third World Cup when we were the unfortunate targets of their ambush.

IRELAND

The Irish deserve a lot of credit for their re-emergence on the world scene in the past couple of years. Admittedly the presence of two players who would walk into any World XV – centre Brian O'Driscoll and hooker Keith Wood – have been the arrowhead of their renaissance. But Ireland also changed its domestic infrastructure to ensure players had the chance to earn a living as a professional player at home. When the game first went pro back in 1996 they lost so many of their leading guys to British clubs. The European Cup for them has been a godsend. While they are still a level below the very best sides, Ireland provide more than nuisance value. They showed that in 2002 by beating the Wallabies in Dublin in what was their first victory over Australia in 23 years.

But depth is a problem in Irish rugby and they continue to bring in imported players rather than working on the grass roots level to develop the next generation of Test team members. Australians like John Langford and Jim Williams spent a few seasons in Ireland. There are a bunch of other Aussies there too, some of them worked into the system by former NSW coach Matt Williams before he was invited to take over as Scotland coach after the World Cup. Even now, Munster has signed Kiwi fullback Christian Cullen when they should be looking to grow their own.

When touring Australia and New Zealand in the middle of 2003, without Wood and O'Driscoll, the Irish were not quite up to the mark. They had reached a Grand Slam decider with England some months before but were well and truly lapped by the Poms who racked up 40-plus points. It demonstrated how much more the Irish still have to improve before they can genuinely threaten the game's major powers on a consistent basis.

One disappointing aspect of the World Cup finals draw was Ireland's placement alongside Australia and Argentina, the seeded sides, in Pool A. It was, to a certain extent, Ireland's own fault. They were beaten by Argentina in a playoff to decide which country went through to the quarter-finals in 1999. Having lost that game, the Irish were forced into qualifying for the 2003 event. No wonder they tagged it the Pool of Death with one of the eight best teams in the world consigned to missing the knockout stages this time around. If the Irish have a weakness apart from their lack of depth, it would be the absence of a big game mentality. And you really only create that from enjoying consistent success. To be a top tier nation they will need the luck of the Irish.

ARGENTINA

On their day the Pumas can cause havoc. They have done since they first came to Australia in 1983 and surprised us in Brisbane with a scrum that included a bloke named Enrique Rodriguez. Topo became the rock of our pack the following year when we won the Grand Slam in the UK and Ireland. Under the current International Rugby Board regulations, which allow a player to turn out only for one Test nation during his career, Rodriguez would never have made the major contribution he did to Australian rugby.

One thing about Argentina, aside from that victory at Ballymore 20 years ago, is that traditionally they don't travel well. They are incredibly tough to beat at home but on the road their record is not great. It's a major hurdle for them. Being away from friends and family does not always sit well with the South Americans. There are other obstacles they have to overcome. They still carry in their squad a number of home-based players who are still only semi-professional, not fulltime footballers like the guys who have taken up contracts in the UK and France.

They can play a good style of rugby and have shown they are no longer so reliant on forward power, even if the pack remains the mainstay of their tactical approach. Argentina has always produced marvellous goalkickers like Hugo Porta and, at the last World Cup, the tournament's top points-scorer Gonzalo Quesada. Maybe it's the soccer influence, with the round ball game incredibly popular, especially around the capital of Buenos Aires. But they tend to give away easy points as well. Discipline is not usually found in abundance in Pumas teams. When they get frustrated they can let themselves down badly. If they back themselves, play with confidence and use the skill in their threequarters, they can put a scare into any side.

Halfback Agustin Pichot is world-class. He's a very exciting player and leads them by example. But Argentina can lean on him too much in some cases. The Pumas pre-World Cup form was excellent, beating France twice and losing to South Africa on the bell. It was a game they could and should have won. At least it gave them further confidence.

SCOTLAND

The Scots have really struggled to deliver any world-class players on the international stage for a number of years. Without those top-drawer stars you can never expect to win a World Cup. Everything the Scots do is workmanlike. They are bringing on some young players, especially in the pack. But icons like the Hastings brothers, Gavin and Scott, are long gone and no-one has ever managed to replace them in the backline. They were terrific footballers and had a huge role to play in the British Lions' series win over Australia in 1989. So did their coach Ian McGeechan who was in charge of that Lions side. He steps down after the World Cup.

What he will need, what the Scots have been crying out for, is a talisman, just as Keith Wood and Brian O'Driscoll fill that role for Ireland. They play a lot of buzzsaw stuff. They get around the ground quickly, are very competitive at the breakdown and they can shift the ball quickly. Determination levels are high but they need the touch of class they used to get from Gregor Townsend. I speak in the past tense because Townsend is no longer the force he once was when his running game would unlock defences. Outside of him they don't really have much in the way of individual brilliance. Another downside for the Scots is that they haven't developed the winning habit. When you head into a tough six-week campaign with seven matches facing you en route to the Holy Grail, it's nice to know you have been able to string together a whole series of wins in the past. Scotland just don't know what that's like.

WALES

Two words describe their chances of victory whenever Welsh players run out for a Test match these days. Good luck. And they almost always need it given their appalling results of recent years. It is a crying shame this once proud rugby nation has been reduced to such a rabble. They have struggled ever since they toured Australia in 1991 and had their backsides spanked. At the after-Test function in Brisbane they even started belting each other. Welsh rugby, as an international force, has still not recovered.

Whether they ever can is also open to debate. They have a small population, a small pool of players. Ironically, they have been paying their guys extraordinary sums of money since the game went professional but they have had little joy for the investment. If they started out as a blue-chip commodity they are now a two-dollar shelf company and teetering on the brink. A loss to Italy in the Six Nations Championship undermined them further, although there are some very promising under 21 players starting to come through. Hopefully the worst of the storm is over for Wales. But don't get too excited about the prospect they might one day revisit their halcyon era of the 1970's. They had so many great players back then. Stars who would walk into a World XV, and most of them in the backline. It must be gut wrenching for some of those guys, like Gareth Edwards, Gerald Davis and Barry John to witness how far the back play has declined in their country. These days they would be lucky to have a single player in the world's top 90.

When they visited Australia in 2003 it was obvious how far off the pace they were and how they also lacked the physical development of the Wallabies. What happened to those big packs and classy backs that were once the Welsh trademark? For mine, the last great backline player they produced was Jonathan Davies, who was in the Wales team when I played my last Test at Cardiff Arms Park in 1996. I know Neil Jenkins is the leading points-scorer in world rugby. But he was a great goalkicker, not a great player. The well of talent has really dried up.

ITALY

It is a quirk of the World Cup that in five tournaments since 1987, Italy has been grouped in the same pool as New Zealand on four occasions. Even more quirky is the fact that the All Black winger who tore them apart in the inaugural global showdown is now coaching the Italian Test side. John Kirwan was a sensational player and he's turning out to be a pretty reasonable coach as well.

I hear only good reports about him from my Italian connections and securing a win over Wales in the 2003 Six Nations was a great achievement for him. Even if Wales were awful.

There was a period just before they were given entry to Europe's top competition that Italian rugby was in a very healthy state. But then most of the quality players that had started building this impressive international record retired, and it has taken a while to bring on the next generation. There are still some old heads there but Kirwan has done his best to meld into the mix some up and comers.

Even though there have been some disappointments in recent seasons, Italian rugby has still come a long way from when I first went over there in the mid-1980s. The standards then were quite poor. They have picked up immeasurably and their domestic competition no longer has to carry that demeaning tag of Spaghetti Rugby. By the same token, many of their leading players now ply their trade in France. The money is obviously better.

One of the problems you encounter with any Italian side is getting them to play as a team. They can start playing one out as individuals. Kirwan knows it. He played for many years in Italy. He will ensure they weed those temptations out of their game.

SAMOA

Elsewhere in the book I have made a plea for the islanders to be embraced in any future expansion of the Super 12 or Tri-Nations series. They are so important to the fabric of the game that we cannot let them wither in the professional age through lack of resources and games. It should be remembered they made the quarter-finals in their first two World Cup appearances in 1991 and 1995. Samoa was not invited to the 1987 tournament and missed the last eight in 1999.

They were most definitely a force a decade and more ago with their power running and ferocious defence. You knew you were going to be crunched when the Samoans launched themselves for a tackle. To me, they appear to lack technical support. They are still drafting players from club land in New Zealand, and the coaching staff need more time with them. A bit of cold hard cash from the International Rugby Board would not go astray in that area. They still play the game very physically and will be capable of causing upsets. But their depth is dwindling, especially when a lot of kids in New Zealand who could play with Samoa prefer to keep their options open so one day they might just be chosen to pull on the All Blacks jumper. It is a dilemma for the game in the islands that requires an urgent IRB investigation so hopefully something can be worked out to assist Samoa, Fiji and Tonga.

FIJI

This is one side I think is under-rated in world rugby and could surprise a few people. They have some of the most explosive backs in the game and their forwards seem to be improving in the ball-winning department. If they ever get their best team on the paddock, even the top sides will know they have to be wary. Like Samoa, their major concern is lack of funds. It is a credit to the Fijian Rugby Union and to their players that so many of them have decided to stay loyal and wear the white jumper when they could have turned down the opportunity and pursued a dream of future All Blacks representation.

Masters of Sevens rugby, they have managed to incorporate that flair into their 15-a-side game. The key to Fijian success, now and in the future, will hinge on their ability to develop a disciplined forward pack.

TONGA

It was back in 1973 that Tonga shocked the rugby world and beat Australia in Brisbane. They have been a nation gone missing ever since. Yet they have still managed to have a significant impact on the game in this country. Willie Ofahengaue, the great Wallabies flanker of the 1990's was of Tongan heritage, as is Australia's most capped No.8 Toutai Kefu and his younger brother, Steve, the Queensland and Test inside centre. The Kefus' father Fatai played in that Tongan side that beat Australia all those years ago at Ballymore.

Most of the players in the Tongan team play outside the country so they can make a living as a professional footballer. But the game is still followed like a religion on the island. They like a physical style of game. They like to belt you in tackles. It is all about a show of strength. Off the field they are gentle giants but if the Tongans get a chance to smash you during the game, they will. World rugby needs entertaining teams like the three island nations. More power to them.

USA

The Americans should be the next major force in the game. People have been saying it for the best part of 20 years and we're still waiting for the transformation. In a population of 290 million, there must be enough athletes prepared to work at the game to develop a strong playing core. What the Yanks need is technical knowledge. They have the potential to be anything. But rugby does not come naturally to them at a young age. Almost no-one under 16 years plays the game, so they can lack that bedrock of information locked into the mindsets of players who grew up with the game from their pre-teens.

It is a shame the game has not taken off there as much as we all would have liked. But it won't happen until a nursery is developed and young kids can take up the game, learn its nuances and most importantly its technical aspects, particularly in the forwards. We need a strong USA down the track because if rugby wants to run a World Cup where there are 10 or 12 genuine contenders rather than just a mere handful, then the Americans will have to be part of the mix. At the moment they just make up the numbers.

CANADA

Better placed than the Americans at present to roll out a competitive side. More than one third of their first-string team is now based in Europe, so they do receive top level competition. And the importance of those offshore stars was never more evident than when Canada toured Australia in June, 2002. The Australia A team put a century of points past them as the Maple Leafs struggled with the pace of the game and the finishing prowess of the homegrown talent.

That was a huge reality check for their Australian coach, David Clarke. He's been in the job for a long time now but the problems of depth are still painfully clear. Outside of their best XV, the Canadians struggle. Even new signings like former Randwick fullback James Pritchard are seen only as short-term band-aid solutions.

JAPAN

This country that gave Eddie Jones his coaching start has now drafted in the great Mark Ella to oversee the coaching of the national team for the World Cup in 2003. Ella runs the backline while former NSW hooker Mark Bell serves as the major advisor to the Japanese pack. Unfortunately, there is only so much a coach can do in six months, as Ella and Bell are finding out. The

Japanese team has unlimited pace. But they do not have a pack with the technical proficiency of the major nations. And they have the added disadvantage of producing fewer players of genuine size and strength. I have been to Japan several time over the years to assist with coaching and what struck me initially was their reluctance to think outside the square about their rugby. They will listen, there's no problem there, but then they tend to make their own decisions. They also struggle in defence out wide. Even their unyielding commitment to the game cannot overcome these deficiencies.

The remaining four teams — Uruguay, Namibia, Georgia and Romania — are off my World Cup radar. I know precious little about these minnows but, unless I miss my guess, any one of them will be fortunate to win a single game. If they do we should celebrate it in style. We need stronger teams to challenge the Big Five. There is more to this game than Australia, New Zealand, England, France and South Africa.

DAVID IAN CAMPESE – Playing career at a glance

Born: October 21, 1962

Height: 180cm

Weight: 82-92kg

Clubs: Queanbeyan Whites, Randwick, Petraca, Amatori Milano

Representative Honours: ACT Under 21s, Australian Under 21s, Australian Sevens, Barbarians, ACT, NSW, Australia

Major Achievements:

- Australia's most capped player with 101 Tests
- World record try-scorer with 64
- Test debut at age 19 against New Zealand in Christchurch in 1982
- Scored tries in first two Tests
- Equalled Australian try-scoring record for single Test with four against USA in 1983
- Member of 1984 Grand Slam winning Wallabies
- Member of 1986 Bledisloe Cup winning Wallabies
- Broke try-scoring world record in 1987 World Cup semi-final against France
- Named in Team of the Decade by Rothmans Rugby Union Yearbook in 1989

- Member of 1991 World Cup winning Wallabies
- Voted Player of Tournament at 1991 World Cup
- Leading try scorer at 1991 World Cup with six from six games
- Member of 1992 Bledisloe Cup winning Wallabies
- Scored 50th Test try against South Africa in Cape Town in 1992
- Member of 1994 Bledisloe Cup winning Wallabies
- Played in first three World Cups in 1987, 1991 and 1995
- Made 100th Test appearance against Italy in Padua in 1996
- Played last Test against Wales in Cardiff in 1996
- Captained Australian Sevens team to Commonwealth Games bronze medal in 1998
- Awarded AM in 2003

TEST CAREER BREAKDOWN

Versus	**Played**	**Won**	**Lost**	**Drawn**	**Tries**	**Conversions**	**Penalty Goals**	**Dropped Goals**	**Points**
Argentina	7	6	1	-	9	3	2	-	51
British Lions	3	1	2	-	-	-	-	-	-
Canada	3	3	-	-	4	-	-	-	20
England	8	6	2	-	5	-	-	-	20
Fiji	3	3	-	-	3	-	-	1	15
France	10	4	5	1	5	1	2	-	28
Ireland	6	6	-	-	4	-	-	-	18
Italy	6	6	-	-	6	3	1	-	34
Japan	1	1	-	-	1	-	-	-	4
New Zealand	29	11	17	1	8	-	2	-	39
Scotland	4	4	-	-	6	-	-	-	24
South Africa	7	4	3	-	1	-	-	-	5
Tonga	1	1	-	-	2	-	-	-	10
USA	3	3	-	-	6	1	-	1	29
Wales	8	7	1	-	3	-	-	-	13
Western Samoa	2	2	-	-	1	-	-	-	5
Total	**101**	**68**	**31**	**2**	**64**	**8**	**7**	**2**	**315**

CAMPO'S CUCINA

CAMPO'S HAM & PEA PASTA

This is one of those anytime, any weather dishes

2 tablespoons extra virgin oil

1 x chopped clove of garlic

Handful of fresh ham

Can of peas

Chilli (to your liking)

Salt and cracked pepper

Canned tomatoes

1 x teaspoon sugar

1 x diced onion

- Cook garlic and onion until brown in a pan
- Add chilli, salt and pepper
- Add ham, peas and canned tomatoes
- Simmer for a few minutes
- Add sugar
- Pasta — Penne. A lot has been said about boiling pasta with salt or oil — my preference is with salt because it enhances the flavour of the pasta
- Boil to required hardness
- Drain
- Throw pasta and sauce into a large pasta dish
- Glass of Shiraz would complement the meal

BAVETTI VONGOLE

This is a perfect Sunday afternoon lunch dish. Your guests will love it!

3 teaspoons of extra virgin oil

2 x garlic clove

1 x diced onion

1 kilo fresh vongole

Chilli (to your liking)

Salt and cracked pepper

2 x glasses champagne

- Cook garlic and onion until brown in a pan
- Add chilli, salt and pepper
- Add vongole and champagne
- Simmer for a few minutes
- Cook for approx 13 minutes. Some people like their pasta hard or soft — its your choice
- Drain pasta
- Throw pasta and sauce into a large pasta dish
- Glass of cold Chardonnay goes down well

RAGU (my favourite)

This is definitely a main meal enjoyed best on a cold winter's night!

2-3 tablespoons of extra virgin oil

2 x clove garlic

1 x onion diced

½ kilo lamb mince

Chilli (to your taste)

2 x cans whole tomatoes

2 x glass red wine

Can of peas

1 x carrot diced

1 x teaspoon sugar

- Cook garlic and onion until brown in a pot
- Add chilli salt and pepper
- Cook mince in separate saucepan
- Remove all oil and fat
- Add mince to sauce in pot
- Add peas and carrots
- Add canned tomatoes
- Add sugar and red wine
- Pasta — Penne. Boil in salted water for approx 13 minutes
- Drain water and add sauce
- Throw pasta and sauce into a large pasta dish
- A glass of Shiraz to complement meal

CHILLI PRAWN PASTA

This is a deliciously tasty dish and can be served as a lunch or dinner meal

2–3 tablespoons of extra virgin oil

2 x clove garlic

1 x onion diced

500g prawns

Chilli (to your taste)

Salt and cracked pepper

2 x glasses white wine

- Cook garlic and onion until brown in a pan
- Add chilli salt and pepper
- Add prawns and wine
- Simmer for 2–3 minutes
- Pasta — Bavette. Boil for approx 13 minutes
- Drain water and add sauce
- Throw pasta and sauce into a large pasta dish
- A glass of Semillon to finish off this deliciously light meal

SPAGHETTI WITH FRESH TOMATOES AND PARMAGIANO

This can be served as an entree

2–3 tablespoons of extra virgin oil

2 x clove garlic

1 x onion diced

Chilli (to your taste)

4 x fresh tomatoes quartered

Shaved Parmagiano

- Cook garlic and onion until brown in a pan
- Add chilli salt and pepper
- Add tomatoes
- Cook for 2-3 minutes
- Pasta — Bavetti. Boil for approx 12 minutes
- Drain water and add sauce
- Spread shaved Parmagiano on top of meal
- Add pasta and sauce to a large pasta dish
- Mix well and serve with a glass of Sauvignon Blanc

CHAMPAGNE RISOTTO

This is a great meal to serve to guests in winter

¼ block unsalted butter

1 x carton thickened cream

½ bottle champagne — room temperature

2 cups Arborio rice

1 x carton of liquid beef stock with 500ml of water

2 cups of grated Parmesan cheese

- Stir CONTINUOUSLY otherwise mixture can burn or stick
- In a deep pot, add 2 cups of rice and 1 cup champagne
- As liquid begins to boil add 1 cup of stock — continue adding 1 cup champagne and 1 cup stock until finished
- Stir for approx. 20 minutes whilst testing texture of rice. Must become soft
- Add unsalted butter and cream and stir
- Add cheese, simmer then serve
- Serve with a glass of Semillon

GNOCCHI WITH CANNED TOMATOES

This is a light, easy meal and should be served as an entrée

2-3 tablespoons of extra virgin oil

2 x clove garlic

1 x can tomatoes

Salt and cracked pepper

Fresh basil leaves

- Boil gnocchi in a pot until pieces begin to float
- In another pot, add oil, garlic and tomatoes
- Add salt and cracked pepper to your taste
- Remove from pot
- Add gnocchi to sauce
- Place fresh basil leaves on top of dish
- Throw gnocchi and sauce into a large pasta dish

GNOCCHI WITH 4 CHEESES

Extremely rich meal. A 'once in a blue moon' treat

1 tablespoon of extra virgin oil

Cheeses : 1 cup of each — parmagiano, ricotta, mozzarella, blue vein

Cracked pepper

- In a pan, add oil then all of the cheeses
- Add cracked pepper
- Simmer
- Boil gnocchi until pieces float to top of pot
- Strain gnocchi
- Add to cheese sauce in saucepan
- Throw pasta and sauce into a large pasta dish
- Mix well and serve

PUMPKIN AND PINENUT PASTA

This dish can be served as an entrée and complements a lamb main course

2-3 tablespoons of extra virgin oil
2 x clove garlic
1 x onion diced
Chilli (to your taste)
100g pinenuts
100g butternut pumpkin — diced

- Cook garlic and onion until brown in a pan
- Add chilli, salt and pepper
- Bake pumpkin in oven until soft
- In a separate pan, brown pinenuts
- Add pumpkin and pinenuts to garlic sauce
- Pasta – Linguine
- Cook for 12 minutes and drain
- Throw pasta and sauce into a large pasta dish.
- Mix well and serve
- Serve with Verdelho as a starter

GARLIC, CHILLI AND OIL PASTA

Simple yet so tasty! This dish helped me through few big nights out!

2–3 tablespoons of extra virgin oil

2 x clove garlic

Chilli (to your taste)

Salt and cracked pepper

- Cook garlic in a pan until brown
- Add chilli salt and pepper
- Pasta – Spaghetti. Boil for up to 10 mins and drain
- Add cooked spaghetti to saucepan and stir well
- Mix well and serve

MUSHROOM, OLIVE AND HAM PASTA

This is a 'winner' dish and one I cook all the time

2-3 tablespoons of extra virgin oil

2 x clove garlic

1 x onion diced

Chilli (to your taste)

1 x handful shaved ham

5 x big mushrooms sliced

2 x cups olives

2 x cans whole tomatoes

1 x teaspoon sugar

Salt and cracked pepper

- In a pan, cook garlic and onion until brown
- Add chilli salt and pepper
- Add mushrooms, then ham and olives
- Add canned tomatoes
- Simmer for approx 10–15 minutes
- Pasta — Tortiglioni. Cook for 12 minutes and drain
- Throw pasta and sauce into a large serving dish
- Mix well and serve

PASTA TONNO

Don' t mention the capers to your guests as people are often turned off by them however they won't even know they are in this dish!

2–3 tablespoons of extra virgin oil

2 x clove garlic

1 x onion diced

1 x can tuna (drained)

Chilli (to your taste)

2 x cans whole peeled tomatoes

Capers to taste

Salt and cracked pepper

- In a pan, cook garlic and onion until brown
- Add chilli, salt and pepper
- Add tuna
- Add canned tomatoes and capers
- Simmer for approx 10–15 minutes
- Pasta — Penne. Cook for 12 minutes and drain
- Throw pasta and sauce into a large serving dish
- Mix well and serve

CHERRY TOMATOES AND OLIVE PASTA SALAD

Great on a hot summer's day!

2–3 tablespoons of extra virgin oil

2 x clove garlic

1 x punnet cherry tomatoes – halved

2 x cup kalamata olives

Salt and cracked pepper

- In a pan, cook garlic until brown
- Add salt and pepper
- Add tomatoes and olives
- Pasta – Penne. Cook for 12 minutes and drain
- Allow to cool
- Toss pasta and sauce into a large salad dish
- Mix well and serve with a drizzle of olive oil

HEALTHY HOMEMADE PIZZA

Who said pizzas can't be healthy? Just check out this recipe and say goodbye to the unhealthy pizza stigma, minus the cheese!

1 x thin pizza base

1 x cup olives

1 x cup finely chopped ham

1 x cup sliced mushrooms

1 x cup sliced artichokes

1 x diced jalapeno pepper

- Smother base in tomato salsa mix
- Add olives, ham, artichokes, jalapenos, mushrooms
- Sprinkle with mixed herbs
- Bake in oven at 200 degrees Celsius until base is brown and crispy
- Serve with garden salad and a crisp Sauvignon Blanc

EGG AND ASPARAGUS ENTRÉE

An unusual dish, packed with loads of flavour

4 x eggs

1 x can white asparagus

2 x tablespoons extra virgin oil

Salt and cracked pepper

- Heat asparagus
- Boil eggs
- Place 4 pieces of asparagus onto each entrée dish
- Add one boiled egg on top of asparagus
- Drizzle with oil
- Finish off with cracked pepper

FRENCH STYLE BRAISED LAMB SHANKS

This is a delicious and extremely easy meal – it just takes a little time to put it all together

1 x tablespoon sea salt

4 x lamb shanks (ask your butcher to cut them 'French Style')

2 tablespoons extra virgin oil

1 x diced onion

1 x diced carrot

4 x garlic cloves, sliced

400g tinned tomatoes

200ml red wine

1 litre beef stock

4 tablespoons balsamic vinegar

2 teaspoons sugar

Green beans for serving

- Preheat oven to 140C
- Smother salt and pepper mixture over shanks
- In a deep ovenproof dish, heat oil and brown lamb shanks
- Remove meat and set aside
- Place onion and carrot in dish and saute over medium heat
- Pour in wine and vinegar and stir
- Add beef stock
- Bring to the boil then turn heat down
- Return lamb shanks to dish cover with lid or foil and leave in oven for approx 3 hrs
- Meat should be tender and falls off the bone
- Serve with crisp green beans and creamy mash potato
- A bottle of Cabernet finishes this meal off with style

OLD FAVOURITE CARBONARA

2–3 tablespoons extra virgin oil

Salt and cracked pepper

1x onion, diced

8–10 bacon strips (cut off excess fat)

2 fresh eggs

- Add oil and onion to fry pan
- Add diced bacon and salt, pepper
- When cooked add to pasta, then crack the eggs over the pasta and bacon and mix. The heat will cook the egg. Add cheese.
- Pasta – linguini
- Boil pasta to your preferred liking
- A cold glass of pinot noir. Enjoy

MY MUM'S PORKYPINES

750g ground beef

½ cup uncooked long grain rice

1 small onion, grated

1 carrot, grated

¼ cup Carnation evaporated milk

2 teaspoon salt

¼ teaspoon pepper

¼ teaspoon mixed herbs

284g can tomato soup

1 cup water

- Combine meat, rice, onion, carrot, Carnation milk and seasonings, and mix thoroughly
- Shape into small balls
- Heat tomato soup and water,drop meat balls into soup. Bring to boil then simmer gently for 30 minutes
- Garnish with chopped parsley. Serves 6 (makes 36 meatballs)
- Serve with mash, peas and pumpkin